NORTHERN CROWNS

THE KINGS OF MODERN

SCANDINAVIA

ALSO BY JOHN VAN DER KISTE

Frederick III: German Emperor 1888 (1981)

Queen Victoria's Family: a Select Bibliography (Clover, 1982)

Dearest Affie: Alfred, Duke of Edinburgh, Queen Victoria's Second Son, 1844–1900
[with Bee Jordaan] (1984, n.e. 1995)

Queen Victoria's Children (1986; large print edition, ISIS, 1987)

Windsor and Habsburg: the British and Austrian Reigning Houses 1848–1922
(1987)

Edward VII's Children (1989)

Princess Victoria Melita, Grand Duchess Cyril of Russia, 1876–1936 (1991, n.e.
1994)

George V's Children (1991)

George III's Children (1992)

Crowns in a Changing World: the British and European Monarchies 1901–36
(1993)

Kings of the Hellenes: the Greek Kings 1863–1974 (1994)

Childhood at Court 1819–1914 (1995)

King George II and Queen Caroline (1997)

all published by Sutton Publishing unless stated otherwise

NORTHERN CROWNS
THE KINGS OF MODERN
SCANDINAVIA

John Van der Kiste

SUTTON PUBLISHING

First published in the United Kingdom in 1996
Sutton Publishing Limited · Phoenix Mill · Thrupp · Stroud
Gloucestershire · GL5 2BU

Paperback edition first published in 1998

A catalogue record of this book is available from the British Library

ISBN 0-7509-1812-8

Cover illustration: detail from Tuxen's The family of King Christian IX and
Queen Louise of Denmark *(The Royal Collection © Her Majesty the Queen).*

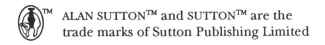 ALAN SUTTON™ and SUTTON™ are the
trade marks of Sutton Publishing Limited

Typeset in 10/13 pt New Baskerville
Typesetting and origination by
Sutton Publishing Limited
Printed in Great Britain by
Butler & Tanner, Frome, Somerset

Contents

List of Illustrations

Thanks are due to the following for kind permission to reproduce photographs; Hulton Deutsch Collection (43, 44); Robin Piguet (5, 8, 9, 12, 14–17, 19–21, 25–28, 31, 32, 36, 39–41); John Wimbles (11). The remainder are from private collections.

Preface

This book is a collective biography-cum-history of the modern Kings of the Scandinavian countries, their consorts, and to a lesser degree their families and dynasties. To cover such a wide canvas in detail, I have restricted the field to the Kings of Denmark from Christian IX (1863–1906) to his great-grandson Frederick IX (1947–72); the two twentieth-century Kings of Norway, Haakon VII (1905–57), and his son Olav V (1957–91); and the contemporary Kings of Sweden, namely Gustav V (1907–50) and his son Gustav VI Adolf (1950–73). Lest this dividing line should appear too arbitrary, I have also surveyed in passing the reign (1872–1907) of King Oscar II of Sweden, who also reigned over Norway for all but the last two years; and also, for the sake of completeness, republican Finland's short-lived experiment with the concept of monarchy at the close of the Great War in 1918.

By and large these monarchs kept within their constitutional limits. I therefore lay particular stress on the biographical, rather than historical, element. There is much to be said about them and their families, during a period of little more than a century which saw them marry more often than not within the Scandinavian circle, but also into other royal families, notably those of Great Britain and Belgium. There is also a considerable amount to be written about the countries which strove to maintain neutrality during both world wars, despite their proximity to the belligerent powers which meant that occupation or involvement in other ways was inevitable, and the divided loyalties of particular members of each dynasty. This is not the place for a full examination of political or governmental matters, apart from those rare occasions where the Kings were directly involved in the political process, such as King Gustav V of Sweden's address to the Peasants' Petition in 1914, and King Christian X of Denmark's role in the 'Easter crisis' six years later.

Outside their own countries, these Kings have received little attention from biographers. King Christian IX has been admirably served by an English translation of Hans Roger Madol's life, published in 1939, and his family more recently by Theo Aronson's exemplary *A Family of Kings*. The life and reign of his grandson King Haakon VII have been well documented by Maurice Michael and Tim Greve respectively. Otherwise, beyond a gossipy eightieth birthday tribute to King Gustav V by Basil Herbert and a life of his daughter-in-law, Queen Louise, by Margit Fjellman, the orchard is comparatively bare.

This is not surprising, given the extremely tight restrictions placed on access to the Royal Archives in these countries, and on private family papers of the Scandinavian royal families held in British archive collections. The present author is by no means the first to experience this.

It has been my privilege to be granted access for background reading and research purposes to previously unpublished material from collections, only to be refused permission to quote letters by the copyright holders. Some, who have expressly asked not to be identified, have been more accommodating than others in this respect. It goes without saying that the inclusion of such material, permission for which was withheld – which was of an uncontroversial nature and dated back to the first two decades of the twentieth century – would have enhanced the present work and helped to bring the major personalities to life in no small way. Later historians and biographers may be more fortunate. Until then, to those readers who might reasonably have hoped for and expected more generous use of primary sources, I can but apologize – or perhaps, to resort to an old cliché, 'Never apologize, merely explain.'

Notwithstanding the access to private papers which others have been kind enough to grant me (in some cases without any time restriction, in others nothing after 1920), there are obvious constraints in writing about monarchs who are comparatively recently deceased and their families. Readers will readily accept that the later stages of my narrative are of necessity somewhat brief and can be little more than an interim summary. Nevertheless I hope that this book will fill the gap in what I have found a fascinating and too often neglected field of modern European royalty.

It is not, I trust, being unreasonable or unfair to reiterate that writing about overseas royalty presents, for British authors (even those with a hardly British name), an ever-present minefield as regards the preferred form of Christian names. At the risk of lacking consistency, I have preferred Frederick where others might use Frederik (Denmark) and Friedrich (Germany); and Carl for Charles; while Gustav, William and Eric also seem to me to be more acceptable to the average British reader. Names quoted in correspondence or passages from previously published material are naturally left as in the original spelling.

I wish to acknowledge the gracious permission of Her Majesty Queen Elizabeth II to consult material from the Royal Archives, Windsor; the staff of the Public Record Office, London; the Astor family and Sir Edward Ford; and Viscount Montgomery of Alamein CBE and the Montgomery Collections Committee of the Trustees of The Imperial War Museum, for access to unpublished manuscripts. Robin Piguet, who originally suggested that I undertook this book, has encouraged me from the start, provided me with much valuable information, assisted with contacts at home and overseas, and kept me going 'when the going got tough'; while David Horbury's assistance in undertaking research at the Public Record Office on my behalf was likewise invaluable, as was Karen Roth's assistance with tracking down elusive material overseas. For various matters of advice, help and encouragement I am also indebted to His Excellency Lars-Ake Nilsson, Ambassador, the Swedish Embassy in London; Theo Aronson; Hamish and June Barclay; Steven Bunford; Knud J.V. Jespersen, De Kongelige Ordeners Historiograf, Copenhagen; Stanley Martin; Ricardo Mateos Sainz de Medrano; Jørgen Nein, Curator, De Danske Kongers Kronologiske Samling, Copenhagen; Henrik S. Nissen, Institut For Historie, Copenhagen Universitet; Ted Rosvall; Ian Shapiro; Arnout van Cruyningen; John Wimbles; and Charlotte Zeepvat. As ever, the staff at Kensington & Chelsea Public Libraries have been kind enough to let me loose in their invaluable biography reserve collection. Last but not least, my thanks to my parents, Wing Commander Guy and Nancy Van der Kiste, for reading through the manuscript and highlighting several infelicities of phrase which would otherwise have gone unnoticed until it was too late; and my editors Sarah Bragginton and Jaqueline Mitchell, for all their hard work in seeing the manuscript through to publication.

CHAPTER ONE

'A constitutional King'

Of the three Scandinavian kingdoms, Denmark was the most southerly, the smallest, and in the Middle Ages the most heavily populated. An alliance with France during the Napoleonic wars, and subsequent French defeat, left her virtually bankrupt, her fleet destroyed and her maritime trade in ruins. By the treaty of Kiel in 1814 she had to cede Norway to Sweden, thus dissolving a union which had lasted for over four centuries, and Heligoland to Britain. Apart from the Danish mainland, the duchies of Schleswig and Holstein, and a few overseas colonies, notably Greenland, were all that remained of the once extensive territories of the Danish Kings.

Such sadly reduced circumstances and loss of national prestige, however, made no difference to the admittedly modest style of King Frederick VI, who reigned from 1808 to 1839. Like his predecessors, he presided over his kingdom like an old-fashioned country squire. Each evening the keys of the gates of Copenhagen, his capital, were brought to him to be placed on his writing desk. Despite Denmark's autocratic constitution, the Danish way of life was essentially democratic. In theory the country was an autocratic monarchy, but any citizen, regardless of social status, could have direct personal contact with the sovereign.[1]

Almost three years after the final defeat of Napoleon, on 8 April 1818, a fourth son and sixth child was born to Duke William of Schleswig-Holstein-Sonderburg-Glucksburg at Gottorp Castle, in the capital of Schleswig. He was named after his godfather Prince Christian, heir to the throne of Denmark. His career seemed to be pre-ordained; as the family had little financial means, he would doubtless serve as an army officer under some royal relative and ultimately win honour on the field of battle. Nobody could have foreseen that he would one day wear a crown, let alone live to see his sons and daughters marry into royal and imperial courts throughout Europe.

The children had a stern upbringing. In later life, Christian would recall that although his father was severe, 'he would not tolerate our tutor's beating us. He told him that if anything was amiss he must report it, and father would punish us himself. The tutor understood this perfectly, but when we had done anything wrong he would first himself give us a good hiding till we were too sore to sit down, and then report us to father and let us in for a second thrashing.'[2]

In January 1831 Duke William's mother-in-law died, and at her funeral he caught a cold which he neglected to treat with care. By the end of the month two of Prince Christian's brothers had contracted scarlet fever, and though they recovered, the Duke's condition deteriorated and he died on 17 February. In accordance with his dying wish, King Frederick became the boys' legal guardian.

Prince Christian's first ambition was to enter the navy, but the King decided that he should come to Copenhagen and join the army instead. He attended the city military college, and in 1835 gained a commission in the Royal Horse Guards. Two years later, he was chosen to represent Denmark by going to the court of St James, London, to congratulate Queen Victoria on her accession. The Danish Ambassador in Britain assured the court that he would try to arrange an economical stay for the young Prince; 'there are sure to be marriage-rumours, and the shorter his stay the better'. Browne, the English Chargé d'Affaires in Copenhagen, noted that he 'cannot help surmising that his Highness, or rather his friends for him, anticipate the possibility of a further and far greater advantage for him'[3] beyond merely paying his respects to Queen Victoria. On his arrival in London, one of his first calls was on a tailor, as 'his Copenhagen outfit was at once condemned as poor and insufficient.'[4]

While in England Prince Christian was presented to the Queen, and her elderly aunts the Duchess of Gloucester, Princess Sophia and the Duchess of Inverness, all of whom gave him a friendly reception. The same could not be said for the Queen's mother, the Duchess of Kent, who was already determined that her daughter would marry her cousin, Prince Albert of Saxe-Coburg-Gotha. She naturally regarded his presence with some suspicion, and not without good reason. Prince Christian, it was believed, made an excellent impression on the Queen; 'He is invited out to every meal, and dances almost every evening till far into the night.'[5]

The following year he returned to London as Denmark's representative at the Queen's Coronation. Yet amid the vast congregation of foreign royalties and guests, and in the whirl of festivities, he apparently passed virtually unnoticed. No more was heard about his chances as a prospective bridegroom for the most eligible young spinster in the world.

In 1839 King Frederick VI died and was succeeded by his cousin, King Christian VIII. Three years later Prince Christian married the King's niece, Princess Louise of Hesse-Cassel. A more lively and forceful character than her mild-mannered, easy-going husband, she was thought by others to be domineering and self-opinionated, but the marriage proved happy and they always remained devoted to each other.

They settled in the Yellow Palace, adjacent to the King's official residence in Copenhagen, the Amalienborg Palace. A pleasant, unpretentious house in a side street, it was not the palatial dwelling its name suggested. The front door opened directly onto the pavement, and passers-by could glance in through the downstairs windows.

Prince and Princess Christian had six children. Frederick, known throughout childhood as 'Freddie with the pretty little face', was born in 1843, followed by Alexandra (1844), William (1845), Dagmar (1847), and after an interval Thyra (1853), and Waldemar (1858). The Yellow Palace was their official home, and summer was usually spent at Bernstorff, an eighteenth-century hunting lodge which King Christian VIII had put at the family's disposal. A small but elegant house, it was surrounded by a large, well-wooded park, an ideal playground for children. Every second summer, the family joined their relatives on Princess Louise's side at Schloss Rumpenheim near Frankfurt, the grand home which belonged to the Hesse-Cassel family.

By royal standards of the time, the family of eight lived modestly. As Prince Christian only received an army captain's pay, there was rarely any money to spare on luxuries, such as portraits of the youngsters in infancy. The parents assumed responsibility for their children's education, with Prince Christian taking charge of gymnastics himself. They were all healthy outdoor children, escaping severe illness in their formative years, and all six lived into their late sixties and beyond. None of them were particularly intellectual. Only Dagmar showed any inclination for books and literature. Nonetheless Princess Christian, who adored music, taught her daughters, all of whom shared her enthusiasm for playing the piano.

In 1848 King Christian VIII died and was succeeded by his son, who took the title of Frederick VII. Twice-married, twice-divorced and childless, he had set up house with his mistress, whom he created Countess Danner and later married morganatically. His private life had given some concern to his father and ministers, who had decreed that as heir he should remain in 'semi-imprisonment' while Prince Christian was given the honour of representing Denmark on the missions to England early in Queen Victoria's reign.

The question of who should be chosen to succeed King Frederick VII assumed some urgency. Nearest to the throne, should he die without leaving an heir – and it was believed that he was incapable of providing one – was Prince Frederick of Hesse-Cassel. However, when war broke out between Denmark and Holstein in 1848, the Prince had made his German sympathies self-evident by taking the side of Holstein. The fiercely patriotic Danes, determined to retain what was left of their territory in the aftermath of the Napoleonic wars, never forgave him.

That Prince Christian, who felt largely Danish through upbringing and through loyalty to the King who had done so much for him, was the only member of his family to stay loyal to the country, did not pass unnoticed. Princess Louise was closer to the throne than him, though she was debarred as the Salic Law applied to the duchies, though not in Denmark itself. On 8 May 1852 the London Protocol, a settlement guaranteed by Russia, France, England, Prussia, Austria and Sweden, affirmed the indivisibility of Danish territory and designated Prince Christian as heir to the Danish throne.

In 1853 the distinction of 'Royal Highnesses' was conferred upon all members of the family, and at last Prince Christian was granted a regular if still modest allowance. It made no change to their lifestyle, except in one relatively important matter – the provision for the appointment of tutors to their children. As the years passed, it became increasingly likely that Prince Christian would one day become King of Denmark, and his eldest son after him. Young Prince Frederick was taken out of his public school and his education henceforth became the responsibility of Professor Petersen, along with a group of masters specializing in particular subjects. In due course he was enrolled as an army cadet, and at the age of eighteen was commissioned as a second lieutenant in the Danish infantry.

Although the adolescent Prince Frederick, now second in line to the throne, was well aware of his eventual inheritance, nobody could have foreseen the dazzling destinies of two of his elder sisters and their elder brother. The former would become a Queen consort and Empress consort respectively, while the latter would wear a crown before their father.

In 1862 Princess Alexandra became betrothed to Albert Edward, Prince of Wales. It came as a considerable surprise to Queen Victoria's relations in Germany, who had taken it for granted that she would follow the family tradition of seeking a bride for her eldest son from the princely or ducal families who reigned or ruled within the German Confederation. Shortly after the wedding in March 1863, the new Princess of Wales's seventeen-year-old brother Prince William was offered the vacant throne of Greece in place of the well-meaning but inept King Otho, who had been deposed the previous autumn. To his parents' consternation he accepted, taking the title of King George. He left Copenhagen for his new capital, Athens, in October 1863.

Princess Louise, who was already recognized in royal circles as being a more forceful character and a more shrewd personality than her husband, insisted on the most favourable preconditions for her second son. Thanks to her, his annual income was almost doubled; he was guaranteed a pension if ever the Greeks should turn against him as they had his predecessor; and he was not required to change his religion.

By this time King Frederick VII was ailing. The question of a common constitution for Denmark and Schleswig, giving Holstein local government, had been the main issue of the day. The Danish parliament passed this on 13 November, but the King was lying ill, weakened by years of heavy drinking and suffering from erysipelas. Before he could add his signature to the document he died on 15 November, aged fifty-five.

Despite his personal shortcomings the impulsive, confident and thoroughly Danish King Frederick VII had been a popular monarch, and his death was sincerely mourned.

At the time of his accession, King Christian was still largely unknown to his people. Cautious, reserved, and with his confidence perhaps undermined by an appreciation of the political difficulties which surrounded him, King Christian was a thorough German. It was said that he spoke Danish like a German Schleswiger, and to the end of his long life he spoke Danish with a marked German accent.[6] With his ancestry, it was only to be expected, and his 'alien' origins aroused distrust in his subjects. His tone was military; he had the authority of an officer, and did not like to be contradicted. Brusque with those who sought audiences from him, he was not fond of pompous official ceremonies. However, his commonsense and instinctive powers of judgement would stand him in good stead during what gave every promise at first of being a troubled reign.

On his accession, the French Minister Dotezac telegraphed to Paris with unbridled enthusiasm that the new King, attired in military uniform and wearing the cordon of the Order of the Elephant, showed himself to the people on the palace balcony. 'Christian IX is tall, handsome and elegant and has an admirable presence. His Majesty was warmly applauded and had to show himself twice more.' Shortly afterwards, he sent a cipher telegram explaining that 'fearing a possible indiscretion of the post office, I intentionally exaggerated the warmth of the reception accorded to the new King. The truth is that his reception was no more than adequate, but rather better than might have been expected by a King called to succeed so popular a figure as Frederick VII, and one who has hitherto been so little known'.[7]

The most important issue facing the new King at his first Council was that of the Joint Constitution incorporating Schleswig into Denmark, contrary to the terms of the Treaty of London. Not to do so would bitterly offend the Danes; to do so would risk jeopardizing Denmark's standing among the other European nations. His hesitancy was well known, and when it was believed that he had decided not to sign, the municipal authorities of Copenhagen assembled and presented an address to him begging him to do so, as it would complete the work begun by King Frederick VII. When they handed him the address, he replied that he was a constitutional King, 'and it is my duty to rule as such. I must therefore reserve to myself time for reflection and you shall receive my answer through the Council of State.'[8]

At the Council meeting on 18 November, all the ministers spoke in favour of the Joint Constitution. The minister of the interior, Orla Lehmann, declared that 'King Christian must let us know at once whether he is a German or a Dane. The signature is his answer. If he hesitates overlong, 30,000 men will come and demand it.'[9] Even his confidantes whom he knew to be opposed to the Constitution recognized the impossibility of his refusing to sign, and prevailed upon him to bow to the mood of his subjects and government. Mindful of his obligations as a constitutional monarch he appended his signature. As he did so, he emphasized that he did so under pressure, believing that it would lead the country into misfortune, and that responsibility would thus rest on the ministry. It was, he felt, a legacy left him by his predecessor, and that he felt it his duty to carry out the dead King's wishes; the late King would have almost certainly have signed it if he had lived.

Dotezac thought that King Frederick VII had died either too soon or too late for King Christian's peace of mind. Had the new King ascended the throne two months earlier, the Joint Constitution would not have been ready for the monarch's signature, and might have been scrapped altogether; two months later, and the matter would have been settled without him. To have repudiated the Constitution would have permanently compromised him in Denmark, and perhaps provoked an uprising which would have driven him from his throne. Discontent in the duchies had been rekindled, but he had no choice.

The two main states of the German Confederation made their disapproval clear. In Vienna the government refused to receive the courier who had come to bring the news of King Christian's accession, and Otto von Bismarck, Minister-President of Prussia, advised that Berlin must also cordially decline to receive him.

King Christian was well aware that hostilities would soon break out. On 24 December he asked Sir Augustus Paget, the English Ambassador at Copenhagen, whether he could count on English support in the event of German aggression. At Westminster, Lord Palmerston had recently asserted that if any violent attempt was made to overthrow the rights of Denmark or to interfere with her independence and integrity, those who dared to make the attempt would find that 'it would not be Denmark alone with which they would have to contend.' All the same, his oratory seemed to count for nothing. Paget informed King Christian with regret that there was not the slightest hope. The King realized that he was on his own, and no help could be expected from any of the Great Powers who had signed the London Protocol.

Meanwhile, on the day after King Frederick VII's death, Prince Frederick of Augustenburg assumed the title of Frederick VIII of Schleswig-Holstein under the alleged rights conceded to him by his father, Duke Christian, and by virtue of the extinction of the royal agnatic line of King Frederick III of Denmark through the death of the last King. Throughout Germany his action was popular, as it was seen as severing ties with Denmark. Bismarck was opposed to the Augustenburg cause, a barrier to his intention of annexing Holstein and German Schleswig. A joint demand from the German Powers that the Joint Constitution should be rescinded was refused. An ultimatum from Germany and Austria, delivered on 16 January 1864, declared that if the Constitution was not withdrawn within three days, their Ministers would leave Copenhagen and their troops would then occupy Schleswig as a guarantee against its incorporation in the monarchy.

The Danish government replied that she was ready to summon without delay the Royal Council to submit a proposal for the abolition of the November Constitution, together with a plan for a new constitution based on the January declaration of 1852, the substance of which would be submitted in advance to a European conference.

Bismarck suggested the compromise of a 'Personal Union' between the kingdom of Denmark and the duchies under one sovereign similar to the union between Sweden and Norway. He realized that the Danish government would be unlikely to accept such a condition. Too late, the British government attempted to mediate with Prussia and Austria by suggesting a breathing space for Denmark to withdraw the Constitution in an orderly fashion. The result was a flat refusal, and France turned a deaf ear to a proposal by Britain for joint action against an attack on Denmark by the German Powers.

On 1 February 1864 Austrian and Prussian troops invaded the duchies. Acting on instructions from the government, the Danish troops evacuated Holstein and Lauenburg, which had already been occupied by Saxon and Hanoverian forces of the German federal government, without firing a shot. They withdrew to the Dannevirke, the frontier wall which been strongly fortified since 1850 for such an eventuality. After four days the army commanders thought their position untenable, and they retreated.

The news was greeted with dismay and anger in Copenhagen. Accusations of 'Traitor!' and 'The German' were openly flung at King Christian IX, together with shouts of 'Long live Frederick VIII!' (the Crown Prince), and 'Long live Carl XV!' (of Sweden). When he returned to Sonderburg, there was an effort by angry mobs to force the door of the castle where he was believed to be staying.

Displaying great calmness, Queen Louise sent for the Chief of Police and asked him what measures he had taken to ensure the peace of the city and the safety of the royal family. Trying to make light of the demonstrations, he gave her his personal assurances that the castle was safe. She was unconvinced, and told him that if he did not call the civic guard out himself, she would do so instead. Detachments from the guards patrolled the city until early the following morning and made several charges at the mob with drawn swords. Some demonstrators and members of the police force were wounded. While driving home from church with his sisters, Crown Prince Frederick was spat upon in the street 'and returned to the Castle in this state, for he was too proud to wipe off the marks of the people's ignoble fury.'[10]

These demonstrations put considerable strain on the royal family. At night King Christian would wander alone up and down the streets, 'sunk in melancholy thought'. He was particularly bitter that the Swedish government and forces had not lifted a finger to fight alongside Denmark; 'despite all their protestations, despite the "Unity of Scandinavia", they failed to come.'[11] The defeat was nothing short of a national catastrophe, and he was fortunate that no similar event would occur during the remainder of his long reign. Yet he never forgot the difficulties of his first few months as King. Although the war continued for a few more weeks, it was evident that without foreign assistance the Danes had no hope of victory.

A conference of the Powers which had signed the Treaty of 1852, which had been proposed by Lord Russell, the British Secretary of State for Foreign Affairs, only a few days after the outbreak of war, assembled in London on 25 April. An armistice was arranged, but the Prussians repudiated the twelve-year-old treaty and proposed the complete political independence of the duchies with common institutions. When the Danes refused to accept this, Lord Russell proposed that Schleswig might be partitioned according to nationalities, but the Prussians and Danes could not agree upon a strategy. A further proposal by Russell that the frontier line should be referred to a friendly Power was only conditionally accepted by the German Powers and firmly rejected by the Danes.

The armistice ended, the Conference broke down, and fighting resumed. On 29 June the Prussians landed in Alsen, drove the Danes out of the island, and occupied the remainder of Jutland. Defeat was inevitable, and the Danes had to accept the terms of the Allied Powers.

In England, Queen Victoria was painted a gloomy picture of the situation by Lord Clarendon, Chancellor of the Duchy of Lancaster and a senior British representative at the Conference. She noted in her journal (2 July) that Clarendon 'still much fears that there may be a revolution in Denmark, and that the poor King may be sent away, which would make a very bad impression here. Unfortunately he had shown no great moral courage or energy.'[12]

Peace was signed at Vienna in October, and King Christian was to cede to King William of Prussia and Emperor Francis Joseph of Austria all rights to the three duchies and pledge himself to whatever measures the two sovereigns should decide to impose upon them. The German duchies of Holstein and Lauenburg, and the whole of South Jutland, were ceded to Prussia and Austria.

The war had dismembered one of the oldest monarchies of Europe. Some doubted whether the country would emerge from such a disaster to her pride and integrity. Nonetheless, the phlegmatic Danish spirit had not been broken. King Christian never forgot this unhappy first year of his reign, but his solid commonsense helped him to ride the storm and reign for another four decades.

CHAPTER TWO

'He has distinctly gained ground'

Though the prestige of King Christian IX had suffered at the hands of Germany, his position of weakness proved to be to his advantage when it came to the next stage in the dynastic expansion of his family.

Matrimonial alliances between major powers, it had been realized – particularly by Queen Victoria, whose family reunions at Windsor led to brisk exchanges between her married children and their spouses in the wake of Bismarckian 'blood and iron' in Prussia – could lead to trouble. The Schleswig-Holstein question had been settled, albeit with the least favourable possible outcome as far as Denmark was concerned, and was no longer a bone of contention. The choice of a Danish bride for one of the heirs to another European throne could offend nobody.

Princess Dagmar, who celebrated her seventeenth birthday in November 1864, was regarded by other courts as a highly desirable bride. Though her good looks were less striking than those of her elder sister Alexandra, she was intelligent, well-read, and already showed promise of considerable personality. In the summer of 1864 Crown Prince Humbert of Italy had visited Copenhagen, and it was noticed that he seemed very much taken with her. Nothing came of this, but not long afterwards, King Christian was officially approached with a proposal that she should become engaged to Grand Duke Nicholas, heir apparent to the Russian imperial throne. The King had no intention of forcing her into a 'grand' marriage for reasons of prestige, and was prepared to let her make up her own mind. Fortunately for all concerned, she liked the Tsarevich and was prepared to cooperate with the suggestion. By the time he left Copenhagen in September 1864, the engagement had been agreed upon.

The Tsarevich and Princess Dagmar were due to marry in the spring of 1865. Unhappily those who feared or suspected that the intellectual, delicate-looking young man was not as strong as his towering, more well-built brothers, were about to be proved correct. That winter he suffered an attack of bronchitis. The doctors advised him to seek a warmer climate for the winter and he was sent to Nice, on the coast of France. He had promised that he would be back in Denmark the following spring to join in the celebrations for his future father-in-law's birthday, but when the time came he was in no fit state to travel north. When not praying fervently for his recovery, Princess Dagmar was learning Russian, but the Danes were 'wondering whether she will ever need it'. He was obviously dying and the Russian imperial family gathered sadly at Nice.

Accompanied by her mother and eldest brother, his fiancée hurried to join them. It was rumoured that she was going to marry him on his deathbed. They arrived in time to be with him shortly before he breathed his last that April. A story is told that the Tsarevich clasped his brother Alexander, who would become Tsarevich and heir on his death, to his breast and silently pointed to Princess Dagmar. A variation on the theme suggested that he put the hands of his betrothed into those of Alexander. Touching as they may sound, the tales are uncorroborated.

King Christian had been unable to leave his kingdom to be with the family, but as a mark of respect he wanted to order court mourning as if the Tsarevich had been his own son. The government prevented it, saying that mourning could only be observed as for a distant relative.

Plans for the marriage, however, had been well advanced. In addition to diligently learning Russian, the Princess had also worked hard at her religious studies so that she could be received into the Orthodox Church. It was apparently taken more or less for granted that she would conveniently transfer her affections to the new Tsarevich, who was quite unlike his late brother. He was a well-built if not bear-like, painstaking, conscientious young man with none of his brother's refinement or intellect. As for the Princess, she had the royal sense of dynastic obligation. If she was expected to marry the new Tsarevich she would do so. Although her father had acquired great prestige by virtue of his son becoming King of the Hellenes and his eldest daughter a future Queen of England, by royal standards he was still comparatively poor. She could hardly turn down the chance of becoming the future Tsarina.

When it was announced that Tsar Alexander II proposed to pay a visit of thanks to the court at Copenhagen for their sympathies after the death of his son in June, the inference was obvious.

The arrival of the Tsar and his sons at Fredensborg were more than fitting compensation for a rebuff which King Christian had just endured at the hands of Queen Victoria. Crown Prince Frederick, who had been studying at Oxford, had set his sights on her eldest unmarried daughter Princess Helena. Urged on, no doubt, by Queen Louise of Denmark, he considered himself an eligible suitor for her. However Queen Victoria had very different ideas. She had already lost her two eldest daughters to German princes, and the march of conquest of Prussia under Bismarck had strained family loyalties to a grave degree. The Schleswig-Holstein business had added to general unpleasantness and quarrels at family reunions within the walls of Windsor Castle. A second Danish alliance, she decided firmly, was out of the question.

It has been suggested that the Queen had also never forgiven Denmark for her treatment of her great-aunt Caroline Matilda, whose brief unhappy marriage to King Christian VII of Denmark in 1766 had ended in tears, imprisonment, and a mercifully early death from – officially – fever. However, for Queen Victoria to hold a grudge against the court on account of something which had happened almost a century earlier in less humane times is surely stretching credulity a little far.

Be that as it may, the chances of her third daughter becoming Crown Princess of Denmark were firmly ruled out. Queen Victoria suspected that the Prince's presence at Oxford was an underhand attempt by the Danish royal family to lay some kind of claim to Princess Helena. She asked General Grey to inform Sir Augustus Paget (18 September 1865), that 'Her Majesty can *never* entertain a question of marriage between the young Prince and any of her Daughters.'[1] To add insult to injury, in August Princess Helena became betrothed to the brother of King Christian's rival claimant to the duchies, the penniless Prince Christian, who consented to make his home in Britain close to the watchful eye of his mother-in-law.

King Christian felt the rejection bitterly. Speaking at a court dinner, he contrasted the early days of his daughter Alexandra's marriage, when the Danish court

> was overwhelmed with every possible token of affection and goodwill. Today, when the Queen's eldest son and heir is happily married, and my grandson is England's future Prince of Wales, everything is changed. They show us not the slightest consideration and wound our most sacred feelings. That is typically English. They think of nothing but their own advantage and never consult their heart.[2]

In June the engagement of Princess Dagmar to the Tsarevich was announced. Preparations for her to become a Romanov continued apace. She devoted herself with renewed zeal to learning Russian, taking instruction in the Orthodox faith, and assembling a wardrobe befitting a Grand Duchess in one of the most sumptuous courts in Europe. In the autumn she said goodbye to her family at Copenhagen and travelled to St Petersburg. On her way she visited the Cathedral of St Peter and St Paul, to lay a wreath on the white marble tomb of the late Tsarevich. When received into the Orthodox Church, she took the name Grand Duchess Marie Feodorovna.

The wedding took place on 9 November 1866. For reasons of economy, King Christian and Queen Louise did not attend. Their modest income would have been strained to the utmost by the expenses of travelling to St Petersburg, and the subsequent tipping which would have been expected of them; they were represented by the bachelor Crown Prince Frederick. At the time of Princess Alexandra's wedding, the Danish Riksdag had voted a sum to cover the expenses incurred by her family for the journey to England, but the financial consequences of war and defeat at the hands of Prussia made a similar grant enabling them to attend the ceremonies in Russia impossible.

In accordance with Romanov tradition, the wedding was a magnificent affair. The bride was formally dressed in the Malachite Room of the Winter Palace by the ladies of the imperial family. In a dress of silver tissue, a train of silver brocade lined with ermine, and sparkling with jewels, the new Grand Duchess had the special nuptial crown placed on her head by her future mother-in-law, the Tsarina. As a salute of twenty-one guns thundered out over St Petersburg, the giant Tsarevich, attired in the blue and silver uniform of his Cossack regiment, led her through a succession of crowded galleries to the Palace Church. At the long and elaborate ceremony four princes, including Crown Prince Frederick, took turns in holding the massive gold crowns above the heads of the bride and groom.

In April 1867 King Christian and Queen Louise went to visit the Princess of Wales, who had been seriously ill with rheumatic fever at her London home, Marlborough House, for several weeks. Queen Victoria met the King and noted that he 'seemed low and unhappy about his daughter'.[3] Queen Louise stayed on for several more weeks, though her husband was obliged to return to his kingdom once he was assured of the improvement in his eldest daughter's condition.

Before his departure he received a deputation representing the Danes living in England. When they spoke to him of Schleswig, he remarked with a heavy heart how strong pro-Danish feeling was in the duchy. Even in the extreme south, in the purely German districts, loyalty to Denmark was freely displayed. In South Schleswig, it was reported that they were saying, 'Better to die as a Dane than rot as a Prussian!' 'We can only hope for a speedy fulfilment of what has been held out or promised us,'[4] he remarked.

Such private remarks were reported in the British press and inevitably distorted. The subsequent attacks on him in the German press were ultimately to his benefit, as they helped to vindicate him in Denmark of the charge of being pro-German. For a King who had initially been considered too German by his people, this could only be to his advantage where his reputation with his subjects was concerned. They were united in their sadness at the loss of Schleswig and Holstein, yet steadfast in their hope that the territories would fly the Danish flag again one day.

In May 1867 King George of the Hellenes became betrothed to Grand Duchess Olga of Russia, and King Christian and Queen Louise celebrated their silver wedding. The anniversary saw a reunion of all six children in Copenhagen, and it was the first time that King George had returned to the country of his birth since being elected to the throne of the Hellenes.

Dotezac was impressed with the reception given to the family:

> This is the first time that the capital has abandoned the coldness of its
> attitude towards the King. Without attaining the great enthusiasm that
> was always shown to King Frederick VII, the cordiality and loyalty of the
> Copenhageners on this occasion exceeded all expectations. It is
> unquestionable that the number of houses decorated and illuminated
> and the cheers of the people, formed the greatest contrast to the usual icy
> behaviour of the inhabitants. It would be an exaggeration to say that King
> Christian has become popular, he has a good way to go yet; but he has
> distinctly gained ground, especially among the country folk.[5]

Despite the rebuff shown to the family by Queen Victoria over Princess
Helena's engagement, they did not altogether give up hope of making one
of the Queen's daughters a future Queen of Denmark. The Princess of
Wales had become particularly attached to her sister-in-law Louise, an
artistically-minded, attractive young woman who celebrated her twentieth
birthday in March 1868. Alix thought that Louise would be very much at
home in the informal family court life at Copenhagen, and at length make a
good Queen as well as a suitable wife for her brother. In May 1868 the
readers of *Dagestelegraphen* were informed that Crown Prince Frederick and
Princess Louise were engaged. A firm denial followed in *The Times* the next
day. This outcome was surely a fortunate one for both parties. Louise was
probably infertile. Unsubstantiated rumours persist that she had an
illegitimate child, but her marriage three years later to the Marquis of
Lorne was certainly childless, and it was unlikely that she would have given
Crown Prince Frederick an heir. Moreover she was temperamental, ever
chafing against the constraints (though not the privileges) of her royal
birth, and made it clear that she was more at home in the company of
painters and sculptors than her mother's courtiers.

In the following year the Crown Prince became betrothed to another
Princess Louise. Aged seventeen, she was the only surviving child of King
Carl XV and Queen Louise of Sweden.* Earlier, she had been considered as
a possible future wife for Alfred, Duke of Edinburgh, and a lady at the
English court informed Queen Victoria that she was 'not plain, promises to
be nice looking and is very well brought up'.[6]

Well brought up she may have been, but the rest of the statement was too
flattering. She was indeed a plain, shy girl with stiff manners, serious-
minded without being intellectual, and good-natured without being
animated. Even at the tender age of seventeen, she showed signs of the

---

* Their only son, Prince Carl Oscar, had died in infancy.

piety which would develop into positive bigotry. Beside her lively, pretty sisters-in-law, who found it difficult to accept her as one of the family, she cut an unimpressive figure. Nonetheless she was rich, and came with a good dowry from the fortune of her mother, born a Princess of the Netherlands.

The match was not without its political controversies. King Christian was still bitter about the Swedes' refusal to come to Denmark's aid in the war against Prussia, while Queen Louise of Sweden was thought to prefer a German son-in-law. However, the Danes looked on it approvingly as a guarantee of union between the two Scandinavian kingdoms. Those who optimistically forecast the dawn of a new era of Scandinavian solidarity were to be proved correct.

The nuptials took place at Stockholm on 28 July 1869. As this was one family wedding that they could afford to attend, King Christian and Queen Louise took as many members of their family with them as were available. Stockholm was at its best, with flags of Sweden and Denmark fluttering proudly in the summer breeze. The crowds were enthusiastic, and guns added to the general good-natured noise as they fired in salute from the ships of various nations.

After a short honeymoon at Haga Castle the young couple arrived in Copenhagen. They settled in their new quarters in the Amalienborg Palace, and in the summer they moved to Charlottenhund. Like the rest of his family, Frederick did not care for the excessive trappings of regal splendour, and Louise would have regarded anything too luxurious or ostentatious as simply sinful. They had a common interest in literature and the arts; Louise was a competent amateur artist, and in 1893 she was elected an extra-ordinary member of the Danish Royal Academy of Fine Arts. She built up a fine collection of silver and glass, including a unique collection of work by Emile Gallé, purchased at the Universal Exposition in Paris in 1900.

It was a happy marriage, though with the passing years Crown Prince Frederick was inclined to find his wife's priggishness tiresome, and it was said that he found some of his consolations elsewhere. Like his sister Alix's husband Bertie, he did not allow his marriage to come between himself and a pretty face. Court gossips would talk with a knowing smile of the two heirs discreetly comparing notes about a 'Miss Hannah', a 'Miss Ida', or 'that little very nice girl' in the perfume shop.[7]

Like the long-suffering Princess of Wales, who would declare many years later philosophically that 'after all he loved me the best', the Crown Princess of Denmark accepted her husband and his wayward ways with resignation. Both women appeared to acquiesce in the convention that there was one rule for men and another for women. Nevertheless, the fact that she bore him eight children was ample testimony to the fact that she was not neglected. Their eldest son and heir, Christian, was born on 26 September 1870, and baptized in the presence of King Carl and Queen

Louise of Sweden. With the succession thus assured for another generation, and with King Christian's grandsons also heirs to the thrones of Great Britain and Russia, his prestige increased.

Their second son was born on 3 August 1872. Within the family he was called Carl, in honour of his maternal grandfather and one of the eleven godparents, King Carl of Sweden. However, the family celebrations at Bernstorff Castle after his christening were relatively subdued. King Carl was gravely ill, and passed away eleven days later. Ironically the last years of his successor on the throne, Oscar II, would in due course be saddened by the dissolution of the union between Sweden and Norway, and it was this infant prince who would be called upon to wear the newly independent crown of Norway. Between 1875 and 1890 four daughters, Louise, Ingeborg, Thyra and Dagmar, and two more sons, Harald and Gustav, were born to the Crown Prince and Princess.

Prince Frederick was an affectionate, undemanding father. His children adored him but were always in awe of their pious, domineering mother. The Crown Princess's piety guided her upbringing of the children. She ensured that they had to learn a certain passage from the Bible every day, as well as memorizing hymns and attending church regularly. Like their father and his siblings, they were not spoilt with any material luxuries. They ate plain food and slept on hard beds; frugality was their watchword, children should be seen and not heard, they should be religious and dutiful, economical and helpful; the formation of character was more important than scholarship and learning from books. A daily round of duty, their mother steadfastly maintained, would surely contribute to their growing into useful members of society.

Such lofty ideals were faintly scorned by her in-laws, who could not but breathe a sigh of relief that Queen Louise had not been such a saintly mother. Equally relieved were her nieces and nephews, who nicknamed her 'the Despot'. The eldest daughter, another Louise, grew up into a shy, introspective young woman whose marriage to Prince Frederick of Schaumburg-Lippe ended, probably, in tragedy.* Apart from Ingeborg, who showed some strength of character from an early age, her brothers and sisters, it was said, 'formed a group of timorous, dispirited children who, under their mother's domestic tyranny, grew up to become quite anonymous characters'.[8]

The two elder sons had the strictest upbringing of all. They were educated together by a private tutor who visited the palace each day. The Crown Prince rose at 7 a.m. every morning for a morning walk, and the boys had to follow his example. A short session of gymnastics followed before

---

* See below, pp. 44–5.

breakfast. Their lessons lasted from 9 a.m. to 1 p.m., when they ate with the rest of the family. Lessons and preparation took up most of the afternoon, followed by another short walk before the evening meal at 7 p.m. Games were confined largely to weekends and holidays.

As eventual heir to the throne, Christian was to have an army officer's training, while Carl decided he would like to follow the example of his uncle Waldemar and join the navy, which he entered as a cadet at the age of fourteen, shortly after his confirmation. Before setting off on his first voyage he persuaded his mother to allow him to have an anchor tattooed on his arm. She consented with reluctance, as long as it was done properly at home by a naval captain, and not on one of the boats berthed in the old fish market where most of the other cadets went.

Political problems and international relations continued to concern King Christian IX. In 1870 when war appeared likely between Germany and France, public opinion in Denmark was overwhelmingly pro-French, as this seemed to offer the possibility of regaining Schleswig-Holstein. Napoleon, Emperor of the French, made overtures to King Christian to seek his co-operation, suggesting measures such as the landing of a French expeditionary force in Schleswig-Holstein. However the Tsar and the Prince of Wales strongly advised the King against an alliance with the Emperor, and suggested that Denmark should remain neutral. In view of France's swift defeat in the Franco-Prussian war, their judgment was vindicated. Yet King Christian looked with grave concern on the establishment of the new German Empire, and was one of the last sovereigns – only King Carl XV of Sweden had waited even longer – to offer his congratulations to Emperor William on assuming his imperial title.

With a daughter in Russia, a country which enjoyed good relations with Germany, he took steps to exploit the situation to Danish advantage, particularly with regard to the matter of Schleswig. In March 1871 he wrote to the Tsarevna:

One must admit that the Prussians and Germans have fought a glorious campaign in spite of a severe winter and difficult conditions; on the other hand the lack of organisation and of experience, and the wretched equipment of the French troops, contributed not a little to aggravate a desperate situation. One can only hope that this unfortunate war will be a lesson to them to be wiser and more efficient in the future, if so, within another twenty years they will again carry weight in the counsels of Europe. It is truly a blessing from God that we were able to keep out of it; and for this I must partly thank Tsar Alexander who worked so hard to induce all countries not directly involved to maintain their neutrality; this considerably lightened my efforts to keep Denmark neutral. If he would only strive with equal zeal to induce his uncle at last to give Danish Schleswig back to us. . . . I don't want to burden the Emperor by writing to him about all this, but I beg my dear Minny with her warm Danish heart to speak to him on the subject and try to induce him to influence his uncle in favour of this restitution, for which the present moment would seem to me propitious. Such a restoration of our territories would seem but a small reward for our having maintained strictly neutral and it would contribute to establishing friendly relations between Denmark and Germany.[9]

For the remaining three decades of King Christian's reign, relations between both countries were moderately friendly but always at some distance. The Schleswig dispute would continue to fester for nearly half a century. Meanwhile the bitter resentment which Queen Louise, more than her husband, bore towards Prussia, and the suspicion with which Otto von Bismarck, now Imperial Chancellor of the Second Reich, regarded Denmark would ensure that the distance remained.

CHAPTER THREE

'Wonderfully united – and never breathe one word against each other'

In 1873 Princess Thyra, youngest daughter of King Christian IX, was twenty years old. She was the gentlest and least attractive of the three, having neither Princess Alexandra's striking good looks nor Dagmar's vivacity. Queen Victoria, who could always be relied on for an honest – sometimes brutally honest – assessment, commented in a letter to the German Crown Princess (1 December 1875) that she had 'fine eyes, but I never saw so hideous a mouth with no chin and a flat nose. The eyebrows are too thick – and though she is straight and *élancée* the figure is angular and she moves ungracefully.'[1] However, good looks were not everything, and Queen Louise used to say that Thyra had the sweetest nature of all.

If rumour could be believed, she was also the only one with a past. In 1870, it was said, she had fallen in love with a Danish army officer and became pregnant by him. The following year she was hurried away to the seclusion of Rumpenheim, and a baby girl born to her was taken away immediately after birth and before the mother could see her. Two months later the father had an angry interview with King Christian and then shot himself.

Whatever the truth – or lack of it – in this story, there was no shortage of suitors for her hand. It was rumoured that she was to be betrothed to one of Queen Victoria's elder bachelor sons, either Alfred, Duke of Edinburgh, or Arthur, later Duke of Connaught. There was talk of a match with Louis, the exiled Prince Imperial of France; and of a purely political marriage with the widowed King William III of the Netherlands, whose three sons by his first wife had all predeceased him. However he was more than thirty-six years older than Thyra, and his prospects were never taken seriously.

The only rumour with any truth in it, apparently, was a proposal for Princess Thyra to marry Prince Arthur. Although the Danish royal family felt that Queen Victoria regarded them with coldness, for a time she was under the impression that Princess Thyra had been 'half-promised' as a bride of Prince Arthur. While the Princess of Wales might have thought that to have her sister as a bride for one of her brothers-in-law would be company for them both, her relations with Queen Victoria were none too easy at this time, mainly because she shared her parents' bitterness at what they saw as the political cold-shouldering of Denmark by Britain. Queen Louise insisted that she would not 'hand another daughter of mine to the maltreatment of Queen Victoria'. Alexandra also knew that Prince Alfred was more likely to marry the only surviving daughter of Tsar Alexander II of Russia, Grand Duchess Marie, which he did in 1874.

Thyra had already met Prince Ernest Augustus of Hanover in 1872, while she was in Rome after convalescing from a serious illness. The Prince was a kind-hearted bachelor of twenty-seven, but had little else to recommend him. Plain, long-necked, short-sighted and almost bald, in Princess Alexandra's blunt words, 'poor dear Ernest is the *ugliest* man there ever was made!!!'[2] Neither did he have any worldly inheritance to speak of. His father was King George V, the blind King of Hanover whose kingdom had been brutally absorbed by Bismarck's Prussia as the price of fighting on the side of Austria in the disastrous war of 1866. The King and Crown Prince had lost their titles, and their considerable personal fortune.

Princess Thyra became very fond of this young Prince on whom Providence had so far looked unkindly. King Christian was pleased that his daughter appeared to be like making a love-match, but almost at once he was warned of the political consequences.

Though the house of Hanover had been dispossessed by Prussia, it was still looked on as a formidable rival to the house of Hohenzollern. King Christian IX, four of whose children or children-in-law were sovereigns, heirs or consorts-in-waiting, had within a decade become dynastically the best-connected monarch in Europe after Queen Victoria. With his tendency to over-estimate, or over-emphasize, the dangers of royal influence and opposition, Bismarck trusted neither Prince Ernest nor his intentions. If he married into the Danish royal family, it would surely enhance his standing as a rallying point for anti-Prussian opinion. With the support of King Christian, he might become a force to be reckoned with. Most of the Danish ministers were united in advising their King of dire consequences to relations between Denmark and imperial Germany. Even the King's brother, Prince William of Glucksburg, and the Prince of Wales, were inclined to add their warning voices. Ever mindful of his limitations as a constitutional monarch, King Christian took their advice and asked the couple to wait.

In 1878 King George V of Hanover died in Paris. As the title 'King of Hanover' no longer existed, Prince Ernest assumed the title of Duke of Cumberland, last borne by his grandfather Prince Ernest Augustus, the fourth son of King George III. The Prince of Wales, who had initially had his doubts as to the political advisability of the marriage, readily came round to his wife's point of view, and gave the couple his ardent support. To demonstrate his solidarity with the Duke of Cumberland – or King of Hanover, as he privately maintained he was – the Prince walked beside him behind the coffin at the King's funeral in Paris. Both Bismarck and Queen Victoria were appalled at this display of partisanship.

Nobody had worked harder for the match than the Princess of Wales. Well aware of Thyra's feelings for Ernest, she organized a secret meeting between them at Frankfurt. Their determination and evident happiness together made political objections seem almost pointless. The storm of disapproval which they had expected on the announcement of their betrothal, made publicly in Fredensborg in the autumn of 1878, proved to be no more than a ripple, and they were married at Copenhagen two months later.

King Christian IX's growing prestige never altered the fact that he was first and foremost a family man, never happier than when his children and grandchildren were gathered around him. A few years after his accession, he had inaugurated what soon became a tradition of informal family gatherings in one of his palaces. As not all the relations could come every year, if it was a small group, the venue would be Bernstorff, near Copenhagen. As the family grew, they would assemble at the larger palace of Fredensborg, about twenty miles from Copenhagen. In addition to his six children and ever-increasing numbers of grandchildren, there were combined suites which would generally number over three hundred. Between them, the families spoke seven languages. It was fortunate that they were gifted with an ability to speak and learn several tongues other than their own.

Though these gatherings included several reigning Kings and royal and imperial heirs, informality was the keynote. King Christian IX had never aspired to be more than a country squire, and was happiest when ruling his family as a benevolent despot. King George I of the Hellenes, whose firmness as a father sometimes bordered on the tyrannical, had to listen humbly while his own father told him how to behave as King, or reproached him for ordering horses for a drive without first seeking his permission; while the Princess of Wales received many a lecture on how to manage her restless husband.

King Christian may have been a firm parent, but he was an indulgent grandfather. Even in his seventies he would challenge the youngsters to races along the palace paths. One morning the small Prince Christopher of Greece leapt up from the breakfast table to the mechanical piano and began to play, much to the annoyance of his father King George, who ordered him to stop. 'The child shall do as he likes,' King Christian insisted, and told the embarrassed Prince to go on playing to his heart's content.

According to King Christian IX's granddaughter, Grand Duchess Olga of Russia, it was 'such a cosmopolitan crowd', and she and her brother Grand Duke Michael learned to distinguish their cousins by smell. 'The English royalty smelled of fog and smoke, our Danish cousins reminded us of damp, newly washed linen, and we ourselves smelled of well-polished leather.'[3]

The younger generation usually did as they liked at Fredensborg, though the feeble-mindedness of Prince 'Eddy' of Wales gave his grandparents, if not his doting 'Motherdear', some cause for concern. While they were boating on the lake one day, without any warning he picked up his sisters' small dog and threw it into the water. 'Why did you do that?' asked King Christian in astonishment, pushing Eddy over the side himself. The young man seemed quite unconcerned as he scrambled back into the boat, announcing rather unnecessarily that he was very wet. 'Of course you're very wet,' his grandfather snapped, 'you've been in the lake.' 'Why did you do that to me?' 'Because you did it to the little dog.'[4]

One night at Fredensborg, Princess Marie of Greece and her cousins were sitting on a garden bench, when they saw something white coming through the trees. As it approached, they saw it getting taller and thinner. The castle was said to be haunted, and by the time the apparition was within twenty paces of them, they all got up and ran shrieking into the house – all except Grand Duke George of Russia. He waited until it was close to him, then leapt on it, hitting and pounding savagely until he heard muffled cries of, 'It's I, Apapa!' His Majesty the King of Denmark had draped himself in a sheet, which he held over his head with a broomstick, hence the appearance the 'ghost' had of getting taller and thinner. Grand Duke George was the hero of the hour, while his cousins were teased for their cowardice.

The Grand Duke's father had become Tsar Alexander III in March 1881, on the assassination of his father Alexander II, and the former Princess Dagmar of Denmark was now Her Imperial Majesty Empress Marie Feodorovna. At home in St Petersburg the giant autocrat and his consort lived in perpetual fear of suffering his father's fate. King Christian IX never ceased to brood on the possibility of his daughter's violent death at the hands of revolutionaries.

Almost a prisoner in his own empire, when he was on holiday with the family the Tsar's character changed completely. Once he confided to King Christian that he would much rather be King of Denmark than Tsar of All The Russias. In his wife's country, 'Uncle Sacha' stood revealed as an overgrown schoolboy, full of mischief. He could never resist wielding a hosepipe on the other grown-ups, and once directed a stream of water over the dignified, top-hatted and none too popular King Oscar of Sweden. Although he apologized, the humourless King never forgave him.

King Oscar was notoriously pedantic. One evening he hosted a hunt dinner at a forester's house on Hven Island, between Denmark and Sweden. Afterwards he made a seemingly interminable speech followed by long proposals of health of every royal guest in turn, shaking their hand continuously while doing so. If the Tsar was present at this repast, one can only assume that he was getting his own back as he boldly wielded the hosepipe.

To the children, Uncle Sacha was something of a magician. One of his favourite indoor activities was to demonstrate his extraordinary strength by tearing a pack of playing cards in half, or bending heavy gold and silver dishes in order to prove that they were genuine and not forgeries, while they looked on spellbound. Outside, if they went into muddy ponds to look for tadpoles and came back soaked through and filthy, or made their way into orchards to go helping themselves for apples, everybody knew who was responsible. Far too large to consider even attempting to ride a bicycle, the Tsar was nominated Honorary President by the youngsters when they founded a bicycle club. Taking the joke in good part, he pretended to be furious at this affront to his dignity, and chased them round the hall, for despite his physical bulk he was very light on his feet. When he could keep up the pretence of anger no longer, he burst into loud laughter. That evening he read aloud the patent of his new 'post' with all due solemnity to the ladies and gentlemen of his suite.

Some of the other adults took to bicycles, but with more courage than skill. Crown Prince Frederick had been on two wheels for only a week when he was riding along a road bordered on either side by a deep ditch. Two elderly ladies walking towards him recognized him and curtsied gracefully. He took one hand off the handlebar to raise his hat in gentlemanly greeting, lost control, and ended up in the ditch with his bicycle, the two astonished ladies temporarily trapped beneath their future sovereign and his machine.

It was as well that all the adults – King Oscar of Sweden excepted – were ready to laugh at themselves. One day a party went to the Copenhagen zoological gardens. The Tsarina was wearing a large hat, the brim trimmed with bright red cherries. Rather unwisely, she stopped to look at a chimpanzee – and stood rather too close to the cage. The chimp evidently decided that feeding time had come early that day, and he put his arms through the bars to help himself to the hat. Finding to his frustration that it was fastened to her head securely with elastic, he yelled and tugged more vigorously. The Princess of Wales seized her sister by the waist and pulled in the opposite direction, until the ape decided that this was one meal proving more trouble than it was worth. He let go of the hat so violently that the elastic snapped, the hat with accompanying fruit decoration flew off the Tsarina's head, and came to rest on the cap of a startled passer-by. The slightest mention of the episode kept everyone convulsed with mirth for the next few days. In Russia, the Grand Duchess Olga considered, her mother would have never contemplated going to a zoo, but if she had and anything of the sort had happened, there would have been a lengthy enquiry and the zoo keeper would have done well to seek alternative employment.

Queen Louise enjoyed playing her part in these family reunions as the country squire's wife. Every night at dinner, she would seat herself at the middle of the table and serve the food from dishes set before her, while the Princes acted as waiters. The children's favourite food was *øllebrød*, made from black bread boiled in beer, served steaming hot in a soup plate lined with brown sugar, all topped with cream. To the Greek princes, it never tasted the same outside Denmark.

After dinner, Queen Louise and her daughters would lead the children in simple parlour games until bedtime, or thump out eight-handed arrangements on two pianos. Although both Queen Louise and the Princess of Wales suffered from otosclerosis, the hereditary hearing defect which had made them profoundly deaf by middle age, music was still a source of abiding pleasure. Some years later, when the former Princess Dagmar (by then Dowager Tsarina) sent her father a phonograph for his eightieth birthday, Queen Louise – also aged eighty – sat down beside the horn and, according to an aide-de-camp, followed the music with a smile. One might well wonder whether the elderly deaf lady could really discern any music from the primitive invention which passed for state-of-the-art sound reproduction in April 1898.

The King and Queen presided over these gatherings with zest well into middle age and beyond. At an extra large party in September 1882 to mark the Queen's sixty-fifth birthday, it was noted that she was beginning to age a little, 'without, however, losing the grace and daintiness of her figure'. The King had 'kept himself light and slight by his regular gymnastics and riding, and remained a young man still though equal to his wife in years.'5

Not everybody enjoyed these country house parties. For all his love of practical jokes, the Prince of Wales found holidays in Denmark unbearably tedious. There was only one more boring place on earth than Fredensborg, he would tell his suite indignantly, and that was Bernstorff. During his increasingly infrequent visits, he did not sleep under the same roof, but retired to his yacht in Elsinore harbour.

Those who were not invited would call the reunions 'the whispering party' or 'Europe's whispering gallery'. Bismarck would angrily insist that pacts or political schemes against Germany, disdainfully called 'the robber' by the Princess of Wales, were always hatched at the castles. Queen Louise was rightly recognized as the driving force behind the family and the brilliant marriages made by her daughters, as well as the reunions at Fredensborg and Bernstorff. She was also regarded, with good reason, as the major influence on her family's anti-Prussianism. While her sons were more pragmatic, her daughters shared her loathing of the upstart German kingdom which now dominated the empire to the south of Denmark. That Britain and Russia were both allied against Germany at the outbreak of the Great War in 1914 can be ascribed, in part, to the hatred of Germany of Queen Alexandra, the Empress Marie Feodorovna, and the influence of both on their husbands.

Had he been a fly on the wall, Bismarck would have been agreeably surprised to learn that all political discussion was firmly forbidden. Any mention of the Dreyfus affair, the Balkans, Fashoda, or any other contentious issues of the day, would bring a frown to the face of King Christian and a tactful change of subject in the conversation. 'If anything, the Fredensborg reunions were a wedding market',[6] recalled Grand Duchess Olga.

Queen Victoria never came to any of these lively gatherings. It was unlikely that she would ever have accepted an invitation if one had been offered. In the personality of Denmark's great matriarch, whom she referred to scathingly as 'that odious, mischievous Queen Louise',[7] she recognized a formidable rival. Moreover, she remarked on more than one occasion that she would never have enjoyed 'such terrible noise', conveniently overlooking the fact that her ghillies' dances at Balmoral were scarcely models of decorum or tranquillity. On Deeside, naturally, Her Majesty Queen Victoria could have blown the whistle, metaphorically speaking; but at Fredensborg and Bernstorff, she would have been powerless.

Her eldest daughter was more tolerant. 'The noise they all made, and the wild romps they had were simply indescribable,' the widowed Empress Frederick wrote with some admiration after a visit in the summer of 1889, coinciding with the engagement of her daughter Sophie to Crown Prince Constantine of the Hellenes, grandson of King Christian IX. 'Once or twice I was obliged to laugh right out when they were all carrying each other. It was certainly a very novel and original sight, very absurd sometimes, and they seemed happier and to enjoy themselves more thoroughly than children of five or six. . . . The Queen of Denmark's furniture must be unusually strong – one sofa, I believe, had to have the springs renewed at different times.'[8]

Queen Louise may have been refreshingly carefree regarding the use of the house, but she was a skilled connoisseur of the fine arts. The Danish royal collections owed much to her knowledge and foresight. After the death of Countess Danner in 1872 her large collection of jewellery was sold at auction, and the Queen purchased three items. At another auction in 1881, after the death of King Christian VIII's widow Queen Caroline Amalie, she bought some of the furniture and family portraits, some of which still grace her drawing-room at the Amalienborg Palace to this day.

When Danish industry paid for the commissioning of the large group portrait of the royal family in the Garden Room at Fredensborg Palace, she personally chose the Danish painter Lauritz Tuxen to undertake the commission, and discussed the design of the painting with him. The picture, completed in 1883, was such a success that he was commissioned to paint Queen Victoria and her family in an even more ambitious group portrait marking her Golden Jubilee four years later. It set the seal on Tuxen's success, as forthcoming royal commissions included painting the weddings of the Duke and Duchess of York in 1893, and Prince and Princess Carl of Denmark in 1896.

Princess Thyra, now Duchess of Cumberland, was unable to come back to Denmark as often as she liked. Her husband proved to be something of a tyrant in domestic circles, and hated to be parted from his beloved house at Gmunden, the little Austrian town which had been home to the exiled house of Hanover for several years, where he could hunt and shoot to his heart's content. The main reason, others suspected, was because 'the ever-critical and laughter-loving Copenhageners' found his Tyrolese hunting costume with its lederhosen such an object of mirth.

The Duke and Duchess also had their political cross to bear. In 1884 the reigning Duke of Brunswick died, leaving Ernest as his lawful heir. Although the duchy of Brunswick would have been some recompense for the loss of Hanover, the Federal Council of the German Empire forbade his accession, and instead appointed Prince Albrecht of Prussia as regent. Angrily, Ernest refused to set foot on Prussian soil, or indeed remain in any place where the German Emperor was expected. As a loyal wife, Thyra suffered with him.

In 1885 King Christian IX's youngest child was married. Prince Waldemar, who was twenty-seven years old, had the temerity to fall in love with and marry a French princess, namely Marie d'Orléans, daughter of the Duc de Chartres and niece of the Comte de Paris, pretender to the French throne. Such a match was bad news for Bismarck, for she was an ardent French patriot, and as fiercely anti-German as the Danes. The civil marriage took place on 20 October in Paris, followed by a religious ceremony two days later at Château d'Eu, the seat of the Comte de Paris, in the presence of King Christian IX and Queen Louise, the Prince and Princess of Wales, and a number of Spanish and French members of the houses of Bourbon and Orléans. After a short honeymoon the couple settled at the Yellow Palace in Copenhagen, and within ten years Marie had presented her husband with four sons and a daughter.

King Christian's insistence on keeping politics firmly out of conversation was thoroughly vindicated the year after his youngest son's marriage. Prince Alexander of Battenberg had been forced at gunpoint to abdicate from the Principality of Bulgaria, largely as a result of his refusal to allow his state to become a satellite of Russia and thus incurring the anger of Tsar Alexander III. One morning, Prince Waldemar related, he received a telegram from Stamboulov, the prime minister of Bulgaria, informing him that he had been elected to the vacant throne. He had been warned to prepare himself for such a possibility and had recently discussed the situation with his brother King George of the Hellenes. Assured that Waldemar had no regal ambitions, King George approved, as there was 'sure to be war sooner or later between the two countries'. When Princess Marie was told of his telegram, she backed him up, declaring emphatically, 'Nothing would induce me to go down there – ever!'[9]

Although their marriage appeared satisfactory enough, it masked a rather less regular relationship. Prince Waldemar's affections were engaged elsewhere, with his 'dearest friend' and nephew Prince George of Greece, second son of King George of the Hellenes. Deprived of affection in such a bizarre manner, the very nature of which had to be treated with the utmost discretion, Princess Marie found her consolation in international politics, doing what she could to advance the cause of France. A vast tricolor adorned her drawing-room at Bernstorff. In common with her two elder sisters-in-law, she would take the greatest of pleasure in seeing Germany isolated, even if her influence was not so great.

In April 1888 King Christian celebrated his seventieth birthday. He had kept his physical powers, he informed others; it was for them to judge whether his intellectual abilities were also intact. 'They are only very mediocre,' he admitted, self-deprecatingly, 'but perhaps this is why they have kept all the better.'[10]

One of his favourite pastimes, particularly during the winter months, was a game of euchre. His equerry, Colonel C.H. Rørdam, left a charming description of the routine which took place in Queen Louise's library. Three large lamps were lit in the room renowned for its large collection of books in fine bindings, its old-fashioned, high-backed armchairs, thick portieres and Persian rugs, and on the table a gleaming brass tea set with an old-fashioned urn rumbling and hissing with bubbling water. Around it were cups, cream and a sugar bowl. The lamp was surrounded by plates with cut sandwiches, tea bread and Christmas cake, and an empty plate was set before each place, all laid out on a gleaming white cloth. The big red lampshade gave the room a subdued light, as a fire crackled brightly in the fireplace and shone through the glass screen. Either a lady-in-waiting, or Queen Louise herself, made tea. After they had refreshed themselves the King turned to Colonel Rørdam, asking, 'Would you be so kind as to ring?' The equerry pressed a little button and two lackeys in red entered, collecting the tea things on a tray. The lamp was lifted up, the cloth removed, and everything was ready for euchre. The King's brother, Prince

Hans, brought the Queen the box with the euchre markers, Rørdam took up paper and pencil to keep score, and the King would deal. The game lasted an hour at most, during which they chatted about the day's events. Then the King would call out '*Partagez!*', and the score was added up. Following further refreshments brought in by the servants, everyone bid each other goodnight and retired to bed.

On 26 May 1892 King Christian and Queen Louise celebrated their golden wedding. The reunion of so many members of the family in Denmark for the festivities undoubtedly helped to form a kind of healing process for those who had been recently bereaved. During the previous twelve months there had been two tragic losses among their grandchildren, that of Grand Duchess Paul of Russia, daughter of King George of the Hellenes, and that of the hapless Albert Victor, Duke of Clarence, eldest son of the Prince and Princess of Wales. In their grief, the prostrated parents turned to 'Apapa' and 'Amama' in Denmark.

Throughout Copenhagen the citizens spared no effort in celebrating the anniversary with their royal family. Grand displays of flags, garlands, flowers, triumphal arches and and performances of choral music combined to testify to the people's loyalty. The first greeting was a performance from a Copenhagen choir, numbering some seven hundred, in front of the open windows of the Amalienborg Palace. After they had finished, the King came out and thanked them for their 'unforgettable display of devotion'. The cheers grew even louder when he brought one of his infant great-grandchildren, Prince George of Greece (the future King George II of the Hellenes), not yet aged two, and held him in his arms.

The crowd were reluctant to let the King withdraw, but at length he and the Queen drove to the Chapel at Christiansborg Castle in a new gold state coach which the workers of Copenhagen had presented to them for the occasion. In the chapel of the Castle, Tsar Alexander had marshalled the numerous royal guests to form a guard of honour for the King and Queen as they entered. At dinner in the evening, the Crown Prince proposed the health of his parents and offered them the thanks of their children for the example they had given during their marriage. After dinner the royal party attended a special performance in the Royal Theatre, and afterwards drove round the city to see the illuminations.

Having never forgotten the inglorious first few months of his reign, King Christian found the reception heartwarming beyond measure. Denmark might have become sadly shrunken as a result of the war of 1864, but the brilliant marriages of the King's two elder daughters and the election of their second son as King of the Hellenes had conferred some measure of compensating glory. Moreover the happy royal family relationship of the sovereign and his consort reflected the nineteenth-century family ideal and helped to increase the King's popularity.

Even Queen Victoria, the self-proclaimed 'doyenne of sovereigns', had always envied her daughter-in-law's family. In 1872 she had written to her eldest daughter that they were 'wonderfully united – and never breathe one word against each other, and the daughters remain as unspoilt and as completely Children of the Home as when they were unmarried'.[11] The German Crown Princess Frederick William agreed, commenting in a letter to her mother (10 February 1874) that Queen Louise was 'a happy woman; there is not one of her children who is not universally liked and respected'.[12]

Yet even in this time of celebration the King could never forget the loss of Schleswig and Holstein. In a speech to the people of his capital, he announced with sadness, 'I am a Copenhagener myself, for it is more than three score years since I came as a boy to live here from that country which, alas, is ours no longer'.[13]

In 1890 the Reinsurance Treaty between Germany and Russia expired and Bismarck's successor as German Chancellor, Count von Caprivi, did not renew the arrangement. Tsar Alexander III looked towards France for an alliance. That his wife was actively pro-French, republic though it was, and furiously anti-German, played its part, as did the necessity for French loans. Much to the delight of Princess Marie, Prince Waldemar's wife, by 1893 a secret military convention had been negotiated between both countries, although Tsar Alexander was extraordinarily slow to sign. He and the Tsarina had been about to set out for their annual holiday in Denmark. His yacht had barely tied up in the harbour at Copenhagen before Marie strode briskly up the gangplank and asked him to his face why he did not hurry up and ratify the treaty.

The Tsar was astonished. He pacified her with a few non-committal remarks, and then asked King Christian IX to dissuade her from harassing him with political issues while he was on holiday. When the King sent a message to the government in Paris requesting them to approach the Tsar direct in future and not through Princess Marie, they were similarly amazed. She had been acting entirely on her own initiative. Despite this rather tactless intervention her dearest wish was granted, and shortly afterwards the treaty was signed.

Little did the family know that the Tsar's time was fast running out. During the summer of 1894 he suddenly fell ill. Nephritis was diagnosed, and by the autumn he was evidently dying. On 1 November he died at the early age of forty-nine. His eldest son, now Tsar Nicholas II, was the first grandson of King Christian to ascend a throne. Overawed by the responsibilities so suddenly thrust upon him, and with a wife who did not have the lively personality of his mother, he found it impossible to shake off affairs of state in Denmark as his father had done before him. After the death of 'Uncle Sasha', a considerable element of fun was missing from the annual reunions.

Nonetheless the 'marriage market' continued to provide matches among the younger generation. In October 1895 Crown Prince Frederick's second son, Prince Carl, became engaged to his cousin, Princess Maud of Wales. Carl had carved out for himself a career in the Danish navy, earning promotion by his own merits. In true democratic fashion the Crown Prince had requested the authorities that his son should not be shown preferential treatment. Carl became a first lieutenant in October 1894 at the age of twenty-two. When asked by his contemporaries why he had remained a second lieutenant so long, he answered good-humouredly, 'lack of strings and influence.'

Maud, the youngest child of the Prince and Princess of Wales, was the only one of the three daughters to inherit anything of their mother's good looks and high spirits. An unsophisticated young woman, she shared her Danish cousins' taste for outdoor life. The couple were married in the chapel at Buckingham Palace on 22 July 1896 and spent their honeymoon at Appleton House, on the Sandringham estate, which the Prince of Wales had given his daughter as a wedding present to use as a permanent holiday home throughout her married life. Her husband had been granted six weeks' leave of absence from the navy, and the intention was that after three weeks they would join the rest of the family for the annual summer gathering in Denmark. But the painfully shy Maud, desperately homesick, was loath to leave England until the very last moment. Not until the week before Christmas, as her husband's term of leave was about to expire, could she be persuaded to leave for Copenhagen.

At a banquet given by King Christian IX on the evening of their arrival at Amalienborg Palace, he proposed the health of Princess Maud, expressing the hope that as his daughter Alexandra had won all British hearts, so would his granddaughter win the hearts of the whole Danish nation. However she found it difficult to adjust to married life in a foreign land. Adding to her dissatisfaction with life in Denmark were her husband's frequent absences on naval service. Her complaints brought forth a swift rebuke from the Princess of Wales, who reminded her sharply that she must not forget that she had married a Danish prince and a naval man, 'and *he owes* his first duty both to *his country* and his profession'.[14]

One year later the heir presumptive of Denmark, Prince Christian, eldest son of Crown Prince Frederick, became engaged to Princess Alexandrine of Mecklenburg-Schwerin. Aged eighteen, she was the elder daughter of Grand Duke Frederick Francis III of Mecklenburg-Schwerin and the former Grand Duchess Anastasia. An attractive if diffident young woman, she was probably only too keen to find some kind of settled domestic life. Her mother had quickly tired of her role as Grand Duchess of the German state and made it obvious that she preferred living in Italy or France. Although an agreement was reached by which the grand ducal pair need only live in Schwerin for five months of the year and stay wherever they wanted for the remaining seven, she was bitterly reproached for demonstrating her lack of affection for her adopted land and for parading her pro-French sympathies so openly. After the birth of a third child they found a home in Cannes, the Villa Wenden – more of a palace than a villa. Ill-health compelled the Grand Duke to spend most of his life there instead of at Schwerin, while his wife spent most of her time and their money at the gambling tables in Monte Carlo. In 1897 the Grand Duke was found dead in the garden after a party given by his wife at which he had declined to appear because of ill-health. He had probably committed suicide, though the Grand Duchess's reputation was so unsavoury that her husband's subjects were convinced that she had killed him.*

According to precedent the wedding should have taken place in Schwerin, but the Grand Duchess intended to make her disdain for Mecklenburg evident by holding the nuptials at Cannes. Nevertheless she forced the grand duchy to pay for her daughter's trousseau, and as she did not consider some of the diamonds forming part of the bride's dowry 'handsome enough', she insisted on their being exchanged for jewels of considerably more value.

Despite these disagreeable overtones a splendid gathering of relations, including Crown Prince Frederick, and his wife and daughters, came to Cannes for the wedding on 26 April 1898 at the Villa Wenden. A civil marriage was conducted at 11.00 a.m., at which M. Hibert, the Mayor, read a formal declaration which was signed by witnesses, the Duke of Cumberland signing on behalf of the groom's family. The union was solemnized at a religious ceremony in the German church at Cannes at 2.30 p.m., at which emotions were freely displayed. The bride's sister, Princess Cecilie, noted that 'it was raining and my feelings were quite in keeping with the weather. I could not restrain my tears, and infected my sister with her sentimentality'.[15] Among the presents were a tortoiseshell fan with initials in diamonds from the Prince and Princess of Wales, and a necklace of diamonds and sapphires from the Tsar and Tsarina.

At their time of life, journeys to London and Cannes for their grandsons' marriages were too much for the elderly King Christian and Queen Louise.

---

* In 1902 she caused further scandal by giving birth to another son, fathered by a Russian member of her staff with whom she had been having an affair. Three years later her younger daughter, Princess Cecilie, married William, Crown Prince of Germany. Emperor William II loathed the Grand Duchess so much that he initially refused his consent to the marriage, and only agreed after insisting on several conditions, one of which was that she should never be allowed to come near her daughter except for the wedding and the christening of the Crown Prince's first son.

Yet their thoughts were with the young couple. On the evening of the ceremonies at Cannes he gave a gala dinner at the Amalienborg Palace, and the healths of the newly-weds were drunk by the guests. Meanwhile Copenhagen was decorated richly with flags to mark the occasion. At midday salutes were fired from the fort, and by Danish and foreign warships in harbour.

The bride and groom spent their honeymoon travelling to Genoa, Milan and Naples, arriving at Schwerin on 20 May for five days of festivities. Perhaps the citizens of the Grand Duchy fervently hoped that Princess Alexandrine would have more regard for her royal obligations and duties than her wayward mother. On their return to Copenhagen they settled in a suite prepared for them at Amalienborg Palace.

Like their parents the couple were content to lead a relatively modest, unassuming life. The Princess was keen on her privacy, and found public appearances an ordeal. However the marriage was a success, and over the next two years the couple had two sons, Prince Frederick, born in March 1899, and Knud, sixteen months later.

Queen Louise did not live to see the succession thus assured in the younger generation. By now she was stone deaf and confined to a wheelchair for most of the time. In the words of her grandson Prince Nicholas of Greece, she 'was just like a candle burning itself away'. That summer she fell ill, and King Christian sat by her bedside, clasping her hand as her strength ebbed. He was with her when she slipped away peacefully on 29 September, three weeks after her eighty-first birthday.

For many days afterwards the King seemed unable to grasp the truth. 'I need the Queen so much', he told the faithful Rørdam, with tears in his eyes, 'I simply cannot believe that she is dead'.[16]

CHAPTER FOUR

'A man in politics should sometimes be able to forget'

After the death of Queen Louise of Denmark, the daughters of King Christian IX made a special effort to stay with him regularly and assuage the loneliness of his old age. Above all, they made a point of being present as far as possible at the family reunion on his birthday each April. For the Dowager Empress Marie of Russia, and for King George of the Hellenes, it was not always easy to attend, but Crown Prince Frederick, Princess Alexandra, the Duchess of Cumberland, and Prince Waldemar were usually there. Although the family reunions were modest affairs without the Queen and without Tsar Alexander III, other relatives still gathered at Bernstorff or Fredensborg to try and keep alive what remained of the tribal spirit.

Some went more willingly than others. King Edward VII, who had succeeded Queen Victoria on the British throne in January 1901, now had the perfectly valid excuse that the cares of sovereignty left him less time than before. Others had to take his place, none more reluctantly than his methodical, serious-minded daughter-in-law, May, who became Princess of Wales that November. She resented the lack of intellectual stimulus in the Danish royal family gatherings, and like King Edward she was irked by their perpetual, easy-going dawdling. The King's spinster daughter Princess Victoria usually found herself obliged to accompany Queen Alexandra there. ''Toria has had to go to that vile D . . . k', the normally mild-mannered Princess of Wales noted in a letter in 1903.

Inevitably, as King Christian became older, so life at the court of Denmark became ever more dull for most of the dutiful souls compelled to attend him. His daughters did not see it that way, especially Queen Alexandra who was 'in the seventh heaven and delighted to be in her old home surrounded by friends of her youth'.[1] For everybody else, Copenhagen court life at the turn of the twentieth century was sheer boredom personified. Sir Frederick Ponsonby, King Edward VII's private secretary, found life in the Amalienborg Palace particularly tedious with its heavy, indifferent food and uncomfortable rooms.

Most excruciating of all was the stultifying routine, Evenings were the worst part, with dinner served at 6.30 p.m., the Households drawn up round a large room when the royal family came in. King Christian, his sprightliness belying his octogenarian years, went solemnly round the room with a word for everyone present. Dinner, consisting of several courses and many wines, lasted about one and a half hours. Afterwards everybody filed out arm in arm to the drawing room, where King Christian and the family circled the room again. They then retired to their rooms to smoke, but as the Danish suite accompanied them, the conversation was limited to such bland subjects as polite enquiries into the customs of both countries. At 9.00 p.m. they returned to the drawing room for card games, generally whist or loo, without stakes. At 10.00 p.m. the company were 'mercifully released'. King Christian retired to bed, the signal for King Edward, Ponsonby, and one or two selected guests to play bridge for high stakes until the early hours.

The Danish suite agreed that these evenings were a nightmare, as they ruefully told Ponsonby and others. However, His Majesty had gone through this routine for so many years that it was quite impossible to change anything.

Appreciating that people in their mid-eighties found it impossible to remember what had happened the previous day, but generally had a marvellous memory for events from their early life, Ponsonby had the bright idea of trying to get King Christian to talk about the things which interested him. He borrowed a biography of the King up to the age of fifty, written in German, which was so dull as to be almost unreadable, but nevertheless proved ideal for skimming through and giving him a certain amount of raw material for conversation.

One evening when the King approached him after dinner, Ponsonby decided to put his homework to good use and plunged boldly into the earlier part of the nineteenth century. He asked the King if there was any truth in the report that at one time he was going to marry Queen Victoria, and whether he had attended her Coronation. At once he became quite amused, telling Ponsonby that there was no truth in the report and that he did not attend the Coronation (which does indeed suggest a lapse of memory), but he had paid her a visit about ten years later. Afterwards he went through his usual routine of perfunctory questions to the rest of the company, before returning to Ponsonby with evident enthusiasm, chatting about old times as if they were contemporaries, though the latter was forty-nine years younger. One evening the King began his conversation with, 'You will remember General Stewart'. Ponsonby did not like to be entirely truthful and point out that he did not remember the gentleman, so he nodded sagely and the King rambled cheerfully on. Later he found out that the General had died at a ripe old age some thirty years before he himself was born. King Edward was astonished at the equerry's success with his father-in-law, and quite puzzled to be told later that they were talking about his early life.

With his regular routine of riding and taking long walks, the elderly King astonished those who saw him from a distance. Maurice Baring, third secretary at the British Legation in Copenhagen, frequently saw him on horseback, and thought he looked like a young man of thirty. Jean Jules Jusserand, Minister of France to Denmark, found him extraordinarily lively when he went to present his credentials on taking up office.

With the dawn of the twentieth century came the birth of parliamentary democracy in Denmark and the appointment by King Christian IX of his first liberal cabinet, although not without some reservations on his part.

For most of his reign Denmark had been governed by a Conservative cabinet, backed by the Landsting, the upper house of the Riksdag. The Folketing, or lower house, became more liberal with each election, with inevitable friction between right and left. Elections in 1901 left the Conservatives with only eight seats in the Folketing out of 114, and the prime minister, Hannibal Sehested, resigned. Princess Marie, the King's daughter-in-law, who was known to have some influence with him, was asked to suggest as tactfully as possible that it would be for the good of all if he could choose his cabinet from the majority party in the lower house. A professor of jurisprudence, Dr Johan Henrik Deuntzer, was invited to form a new administration of the left. Although he had never played an active part in Danish politics, he was widely known and respected as one of the leading figures in public life as well as a man of the moderate left, and in sympathy with the *Venstrereformparti* (the Left Reform Party).

Unaware of what was afoot, he was invited to the Palace by Princess Marie, with the King's consent. During dinner the King raised his glass and proposed Dr Deuntzer's health. When Deuntzer rose, bowing deeply, his glass in his hand, the King turned to him, saying, 'It's true, isn't it, Professor, that you are a Left man?' Completely taken aback, he answered hesitantly, 'Yes – yes – to be sure I am, Your Majesty – up to a certain point.'[2]

A few days later the Professor was summoned to an audience at Amalienborg and entrusted with the duty of forming a ministry comprising the leaders of the Left. Reluctant to relinquish conservative rule, the King was determined to use his prerogative by choosing a man whom he liked and respected rather than Jens Christian Christensen, leader of the *Venstrereformparti*.* Honoured to be chosen, and agreeably surprised by his sovereign's modest demeanour and friendly manner, Deuntzer forgot himself so far as to slap the King cheerfully on the back, a gesture which brought forth a look of royal amazement.

---

* Christensen became Minister of Education, and was generally recognized as 'the strong man of the new cabinet'. He remained a leader-in-waiting, and was appointed Prime Minister on the fall of the government in January 1905.

The *systemkiftet* (new system) was commemorated in a national fête, held in Copenhagen on 1 September, with a torchlight procession to Amalienborg Palace to present the King with an address of loyal gratitude. Later the King opened the Riksdag in person, for the first time in many years. In his speech he said that he looked forward confidently to fruitful cooperation between the government and Riksdag as a means of preserving the country's independence in friendly relations with foreign powers, serving to advance personal and political freedom and to elevate the mental and moral life of the nation.

The new government indeed marked a fresh start in Denmark. Instead of aristocrats and academics turned professional politicians, there was now a healthy infusion of farmers, schoolteachers and others from civilian life. Military and naval matters henceforth became the concern of men from the services with professional knowledge. There was a genuine effort to bring in politicians and non-politicians alike whose views could be broadly classed as left, and who could be regarded as specialists in their field. At the same time new finance policies were introduced, with the reduction of land taxes in the countryside, a corresponding increase in property taxes, and direct income tax for the first time.

If the twentieth century had begun in Denmark on a note of triumph for the people and for parliamentary democracy, the next four years were to see another astonishing personal family success for King Christian IX.

Sweden, in earlier ages a dominant power in the Baltic, had entered the nineteenth century with less influence than before. With Napoleon Bonaparte at the height of his power, King Gustav IV Adolf, who had reigned since 1792, saw himself as a rival to the French leader. However, his military campaigns resulted in defeat and the subsequent loss of Finland to Russia in 1809, whereupon he abdicated in favour of his childless uncle, who reigned as King Carl XIII. In 1810 the Swedish Estates elected the French Marshal Jean Baptiste Bernadotte heir to the throne, and he succeeded as Carl XIV in 1818. An enlightened King, he granted concessions to the Norwegians, as Norway had been united with Sweden in the peace settlement of 1814, handed over control of Swedish revenues to parliament, and encouraged education. On his death in his eightieth year in 1844, he was succeeded by his son as Oscar I. He became seriously ill in 1857 and his son Carl assumed the Regency. Two years later, the Regent became King Carl XV, and on his death he was succeeded by his brother as King Oscar II.

Sensitive, authoritarian and intellectual, King Oscar had written and published several volumes of history and poetry before his accession to the throne in 1872. A staunch defender of the royal prerogative, his political initiatives – chiefly connected with taxation and defence – and contacts with leading politicians were a constant source of parliamentary resentment.

Nonetheless, the greatest cross he had to bear throughout his thirty-five-year reign was the issue of deteriorating relations with his country's neighbour. During the twilight years of the nineteenth century the union between Sweden and Norway had become increasingly strained, although he appreciated the problem less than his son and heir, Crown Prince Gustav. While visiting Christiania in March 1905, the latter realized that strength of feeling had reached such a pitch that the union was beyond salvation. Once back in Stockholm, he proposed to the Riksdag privy council that the Swedish government should propose an amicable solution, 'rather than so to speak be kicked out of the union.'

Before his wise words could be acted upon, matters came to a head when King Oscar refused the royal assent to a bill affirming independent Norwegian consular representation. A period of constitutional wrangling followed, and in June 1905 the Storting in Norway declared that the union with Sweden under one King was dissolved, 'as a consequence of the King having ceased to fulfil his functions as King of Norway.'[3]

As a gesture of goodwill, the president of the Storting invited King Oscar to allow a prince from his family to become the independent sovereign of Norway. Declining to recognize Norwegian independence, the King refused the offer. Yet in order to legitimize this peaceful revolution, the Norwegians knew that other European countries would look more kindly on her if her head of state was a monarch. A King of Norway would bring them international recognition and strengthen their hand in negotiations with Sweden for an amicable dissolution of the Act of Union.

Political considerations ruled out the appointment of a Prince from one of the Great Powers. Anglo-German relations were tense, and if a British or German Prince was selected, the other country would be offended. Rumours that Emperor William II was proposing to nominate one of his sons as a suitable candidate had already provoked alarm at the Foreign Office in London. Princes from Greece and Spain were suggested, but at length the Storting agreed that only somebody from the reigning houses of Sweden or Denmark would be acceptable. King Oscar's attitude made the former impracticable, so that left only the family of King Christian IX.

At first glance there were four obvious candidates, namely a son and three grandsons of the King. The first was Prince Waldemar; the second was his eldest son, eighteen-year-old Prince Aage; the third was Prince Nicholas, third son of King George of the Hellenes; and finally there was Prince Carl, second son of Crown Prince Frederick. Waldemar, who had rejected an invitation to become sovereign Prince of Bulgaria in 1886, still harboured no regal ambitions. He was favoured by Tsar Nicholas of Russia and Emperor William, on the grounds that 'he has experience of life, a charming wife and strapping, healthy children.'[4] Yet he, Princess Marie and their children had no enthusiasm for the idea. Nicholas, in his early thirties, would have been an ideal choice but for his religion and other family connections. Being Greek Orthodox, with a Russian mother and a Russian wife, he was thus regarded by the other European powers as a potential pawn of St Petersburg.

Only Carl, aged thirty-two, appeared really eligible. The same age as his cousin Nicholas, he was married to King Edward VII's daughter Maud, with a two-year-old son Alexander. Moreover he had Bernadotte blood in his veins; his mother was the former Princess Louise of Sweden, a niece of King Oscar. His claim could scarcely be bettered. The only dissenting voice was raised by Emperor William, who was suspicious of his 'uncle Bertie', King Edward VII, and had no wish to see him advance his family's prestige in this way.

Having made their choice, the Norwegian government asked their envoys, the explorer Fridtjof Nansen and the Norwegian Minister at Copenhagen, Baron Fritz Wedel Jarlsberg, to negotiate with the Danish and British authorities and royal families in order to secure official recognition for the independence of Norway and later to secure the election of Prince Carl as King. When Jarlsberg arrived at Copenhagen King Christian IX was away, and he presented himself to Crown Prince Frederick, whose overriding consideration was that King Oscar should not be upset by the negotiations. Only if his approval was obtained would he himself, acting on behalf of his father King Christian, be prepared to consider the matter.

Content with his career in the Danish navy, Prince Carl had no enthusiasm for this unexpected new dignity. His shy retiring wife, Maud, fully supported him. She was content with her quiet life divided between Copenhagen and Appleton, in the grounds of her childhood home at Sandringham in Norfolk, well away from the public gaze. Yet they could hardly refuse the call of duty. As that indefatigable gossip from Berlin, Prince Bernhard von Bülow, later noted in his memoirs (albeit doubtless with some exaggeration), the Princess 'told her father she would rather live on the smallest English, or even Irish farm, rather than sit on the Norwegian throne. King Edward, who with all his good-nature tolerated no contradiction from his family, replied to his daughter's prayers and lamentations: "Princesses have duties and not hobbies".'[5] Bülow was notorious for twisting the words of others, although in this case at least there was perhaps more than a grain of truth.

All Carl could do was stipulate that he would accept the crown if he could be of real service to Norway; if Sweden, Denmark and Great Britain fully endorsed his accession; and if the Norwegian people gave their wholehearted consent in a plebiscite.

Alarmed by the apparent strength of Norwegian republicanism, the German Emperor begged King Oscar to recognize the country's independence and accept the crown for a member of the Bernadotte dynasty. The summer of 1905 saw one delay after another. Carl refused to behave like an adventurer going to stake a claim to the crown as if he were some medieval baron. He would not go to Norway without permission from his grandfather, King Christian IX, who withheld his permission until King Oscar had formally renounced the crown. This he would not do until negotiations on the dissolution of the union had been amicably concluded. It was a vicious circle.

In Britain King Edward was in an awkward position. Desperate as he was to further the candidature of his son-in-law, he was equally anxious to maintain good relations with the Swedish royal family. The issue came at a crucial time, particularly in view of the impending marriage of his niece. Princess Margaret, daughter of his only surviving brother Arthur, Duke of Connaught, was betrothed to the Swedish heir apparent, Prince Gustav Adolf, King Oscar's grandson. More than ever, it was vital for Britain to preserve friendly relations with the court of Sweden. As a gesture of friendship and goodwill, King Edward announced that he would make King Oscar an Honorary Admiral of the British Fleet, in addition to conferring the Order of the Garter on Prince Gustav Adolf. On 15 June, the day on which the latter married the Princess at St James's Chapel, the King of Sweden made King Edward an Admiral of the Swedish navy.

With this exchange of courtesies, King Edward felt himself at liberty to encourage Prince Carl before Norway had time to consider too closely the possibility of becoming an independent republic. 'I strongly urge that you should go to Norway as soon as possible to prevent some one else taking your place,'[6] he telegraphed him on 30 July. The following month he voiced his opinion to Alan Johnstone, the British Minister at Copenhagen, suggesting that if a formal offer of the crown was made direct to Prince Carl, Sweden could be induced to give way and King Christian IX of Denmark and Crown Prince Frederick might allow him to accept even if Sweden did not yield, 'the only alternative apparently being a Republic. It seems absurd to King that affair should fall through owing to punctiliousness of Sweden.'[7]

Crown Prince Frederick of Denmark was unwilling to incur the displeasure of King Oscar by pressing his son's candidature till the latter had made an official proclamation of farewell. King Edward was anxious that Norway might declare herself a republic simply through a delay in which each of the parties concerned was waiting for the other to make the next move. Johnstone feared that, even after the union had been legally dissolved, King Oscar might still nominate a Bernadotte prince to succeed him, and Baron Jarlsberg thought that Norway would fight rather than have another Swedish King thrust on them without their consent.

Matters had reached deadlock between Norway and Sweden. Neither could agree on the precise terms by which separation should take place, and until such terms were settled, Sweden thought it premature for Norway's provisional government to choose a new ruler. Yet leading members of the government still thought it best to have a head of state who could take part in the final settlement with Sweden.

'The time has now come for you to act or lose the Crown of Norway,' King Edward VII bluntly informed his son-in-law on 11 August. 'On good authority I am informed your sister in Sweden* is intriguing against you. I urge you to go at once to Norway, with or without the consent of the Danish government, and help in the negotiations between the two countries.'[8]

Yet Prince Carl declined to do anything which might hurt the feelings of his grandfather, King Christian IX. He had been led to understand that Sweden would give a firm answer within a week, and was prepared to wait until then. This was not enough for King Edward, who had heard that the German Emperor was actively intriguing for the vacant throne to be filled by one of his sons. The King therefore wrote to Crown Prince Gustav of Sweden, impressing on him the view that Prince Carl's presence would hasten a final settlement. Reiterating the Swedish government's attitude, the Crown Prince replied that the candidature could not be discussed until the union of both countries had been formally dissolved. Having done all he could, King Edward was now prepared to let matters take their own course.

The only solution, both countries agreed, lay in a conference. Agreement was reached within a few days and ratified by the Storting on 9 October 1905. Formalities for the dissolution of the union were completed shortly afterwards, with the Riksdag in Sweden passing an act acknowledging separation of the union and King Oscar's recognition of independence.

Prince Carl had only one further stipulation to make. Aware of the growing tide of Norwegian republicanism, he insisted that his acceptance of the throne should be supported by a plebiscite. The Norwegian government agreed to hold one, not so much because of his demands, but more in order to silence criticism from the republican opposition in the Storting. 260,000 votes were cast in favour of a monarchy and only 70,000 against. The Storting endorsed this verdict by meeting to elect Prince Carl as their King.

On 20 November 1905 he formally accepted the crown at a ceremony held in the throne room of the Amalienborg Palace, Copenhagen, with Maud beside him. He declared that he would choose the regnal name of Haakon VII, and on his son Prince Alexander he conferred the name Crown Prince Olav. Four days later, the family sailed into Christiania.

---

* Princess Ingeborg of Denmark, daughter of Crown Prince Frederick, who was married to King Oscar's third son Carl, Duke of Västergötland. Any evidence of intrigue by the Princess against her brother remains unproven.

The new King and Queen, King Edward VII noted approvingly a few days later, had both 'won golden opinions and Charles's speeches are *very* good.'[9] The octogenarian British-born Dowager Duchess of Mecklenburg-Strelitz was less impressed. She was affronted at the thought of an English princess sitting on 'a Revolutionary Throne', while her husband went around making speeches thanking the revolutionary Norwegians for having elected him. Besides, 'they have but that one *peaky* boy'.[10]

A less jaundiced verdict came from Sir Arthur Herbert, the British Minister in Christiania, writing to Lord Knollys, King Edward VII's private secretary (1 December 1905):

> I am happy to say that everything seems to go on well here, and that the King seems quite to have ingratiated himself with the Norwegians, and has already announced that in the course of the summer he intends to visit as much of his country as he can. This will be most popular as King Oscar never found time during his 33 years reign to do this, or even send some one to represent him. . . . A Norwegian said to me the other day – we cannot really believe that we have a King of our own as we always think that after a fortnight he will go away like King Oscar.[11]

Despite the caution he had shown when the offer was originally made, King Christian IX was delighted to see this new honour conferred on his family. At eighty-seven, Europe's oldest monarch was aware that he had not long to live. When he was brought the telegram from Christian Michelsen, prime minister of Norway, announcing the decision of the Storting, he exclaimed, 'If you had known King Frederick VI to whom I owe so much, and the grief he always felt over the loss of Norway, you would better understand how rejoiced I am today!'[12] King Frederick VI had been almost like a father to the young Prince Christian, and he had felt deeply the loss of Norway in 1814. Now, some ninety years later, Norway once again had a 'Danish' King. Three European dynasties – those of Denmark, Greece and Norway – now bore the same family name: Schleswig-Holstein-Sonderburg-Glucksburg.

Although their reigns had lasted – or would last – longer than his, by 1905 King Christian IX had lived long enough to be regarded as a national institution by his people much as Queen Victoria had in Britain in her last years, or as Emperor Francis Joseph would in Austria in the next decade. Born in the second decade of the nineteenth century while King George III, a deranged object of pity at Windsor, still survived, and Napoleon Bonaparte eked out his last years as an exile on St Helena, he had been brought up in the twilight of absolute monarchy under King Frederick VI. Democracy had been an almost revolutionary concept to the young Prince Christian; now, in his ninth decade, the constitutional issues had been resolved and Denmark was indeed a parliamentary democracy.

By this time King Christian was living increasingly in the past. He had left the rooms occupied by the Queen untouched since her death, but 'he visited them now and then as if to hold council with the dear departed one'.[13] To friends he remarked that when he could not sleep at night, he would press a button by his headboard and turn the light on, so he could gaze at the pictures that hung in his bedroom: 'mostly those of my dear ones, whom the Lord has called home. Then it is like being with them once more, and it cannot be long, either, before I shall see them again.'[14]

Nevertheless he still took an interest in the present, especially where members of his family were involved. His last years were darkened by anxiety over the state of Russia, the empire's defeat in the war with Japan, and the apparent obstinacy of his grandson Tsar Nicholas II. More liberty had to be granted to the people of Russia, he insisted. 'My Liberal Ministry is moderate and gives me every satisfaction. My daughter did everything to enlighten her son, but in vain.'[15] He might have added that the fault lay not so much with the young Tsar, so much as with the reactionary father whose example he tried to follow.

Guests to Amalienborg Palace were fascinated to see the virtual museum in his living rooms on the ground floor. They contained his old furniture, portraits of ancestors, and several large silver mugs. There was also a vast accumulation of scrapbooks, notes and newspaper cuttings on Danish politics, each one marked and annotated in his own hand. He would show these proudly, talking all the time about the dim and distant past. 'An implacable memory, still further fortified by these aids,' observed Jusserand, 'prevented his forgetting anything, either services rendered or wrongs inflicted, whereas a man in politics should sometimes be able to forget.'[16]

Towards the end of 1905 King Christian was a martyr to lumbago, and suffered from a heavy cold and cough, but early in the new year he seemed to be much fitter. On 29 January 1906 he received several people in audience at the Amalienborg, and then sat down to lunch with the family as usual.

When the Dowager Tsarina asked with concern if he was tired, he shook his head genially. As if to prove his point, he placed his arm round her shoulder and danced a couple of steps with her. He then went into a nearby room to fetch a cigar, but when he returned he was pale, admitted that he was not feeling very well, and said he would rest on the sofa. When the Dowager Tsarina suggested cancelling dinner that evening, he insisted he would feel better after a rest. After making sure he was comfortable in bed, she went into the next room to write a note to the Crown Prince. Shortly afterwards she heard a deep sigh and returned immediately. She raised his head gently, but he had passed away.

When the news reached the citizens outside, they gathered quietly in the Amalienborg Square and gazed up in forlorn silence at the palace windows.

As darkness fell, church bells throughout the city tolled to announce the death of their sovereign; by evening, all the belfries in the country rang out their mournful refrain. His reign had begun in inauspicious circumstances, and before the first anniversary of his accession he had all but feared for his throne. Some four decades later, the ignominious defeat was forgotten. Like Queen Victoria in England, he had come to personify Denmark and stamp his own modest personality on the kingdom.

The English Minister in Copenhagen, Alan Johnstone, forecast that deep grief would be felt by all classes at the passing of a sovereign so universally beloved. During nearly six years of office, he wrote later that day, 'I have never heard a harsh word or criticism directed against His Majesty, and even the bitterest opponents of the various Governments have never, during late years, expressed anything but approval and love of King Christian IX'.[17]

One of the most graceful tributes came from the head of state which Denmark had had little reason to love, the German Emperor William. 'It seemed, though he was so aged, as if he could never be ill or be taken from us', he wrote to his uncle, King Edward VII (1 February 1906). 'One was so accustomed to count on his fine constitution! And yet what a lovely and peaceful end! It was that of a patriarch!'[18] He was laid to rest beside his predecessors in the Cathedral at Roskilde.

CHAPTER FIVE

'He seemed anxious for popularity'

King Frederick VIII of Denmark, who was aged sixty-two at the time of his accession, was an astute character though he lacked his father's charm of manner. Sir Frederick Ponsonby, King Edward VII's equerry, thought him 'a nonentity, having none of the ability of his brother, King George of Greece. He seemed anxious for popularity and to gain this he was quite willing to don the cap of liberty and promise anything to the people'.[1]*

His wife, the pious, humourless and increasingly eccentric Queen Louise, certainly had none of the charm, or ease of personality, of her predecessor. Her in-laws referred to her behind her back as 'the Swan' or 'Aunt Swan', because of her long neck and swaying body. With her austere if not forbidding presence, over the years she had become such a religious bigot that she would have nothing to do with Copenhagen society. With her husband's 'frivolous' relations she was equally ill at ease. 'She is a good soul,' the Duchess of York (now Princess of Wales) had commented some ten years earlier, 'but a little queer in the head & very difficult to get on with as she is so stiff.'[2] Jusserand declared bluntly that '*Ce n'est pas permis d'être si laide*'. Ponsonby likewise thought Queen Louise was one of the ugliest women he had ever seen, but he added with faint praise that she was 'reputed to be charming'.

She claimed that she was psychic, always seeing accidents before they happened or knowing about deaths just before they occurred. Did she foresee the untimely passing of her unhappy eldest daughter? The shy, reserved Princess Louise, who so resembled a darker, prettier version of her mother, had married Prince Frederick of Schaumburg-Lippe in 1896, but the match was not a success. She died at the age of thirty-one on 4 April 1906 at her marital home, Nachod Castle, in Bohemia, a mere five hours after her elderly father-in-law Prince William of Schaumburg-Lippe had succumbed to a fit of apoplexy. A few discreet paragraphs in the press at home and abroad informed their readership that she had been in failing health for some time, and the official cause of death was attributed to 'cerebral inflammation', or 'inflammation of the heart membrane'.

---

* According to Colin Welch, who edited Ponsonby's memoirs for posthumous publication, such comments were 'hardly fair to such a liberal and well-liked man' as King Frederick VIII.

There was probably more truth in persistent rumours that she had been so depressed and miserable in her married life, and so homesick for Denmark, that she had drowned herself in the palace lake. News of royal suicides in Europe was to be concealed wherever possible. The most notorious of the era, and the one which nobody – least of all bungling court officials at Vienna – could keep secret, that of Crown Prince Rudolf of Austria-Hungary in January 1889, had been explained to some extent by his mental derangement. On the other hand, the cause of death ten years later of Prince Alfred, heir to the duchy of Saxe-Coburg-Gotha, was officially given as consumption. His self-inflicted gunshot wound, like Princess Louise's apparent desire to end it all in the water, remained a secret for some years. In fact, the Princess's name and memory were to all intents and purposes virtually erased from public memory. Some seventy years later a respected Danish royal biographer could write that very few people in Denmark were aware that this Princess Louise had ever existed.

Queen Alexandra of Great Britain and the Dowager Tsarina were ill at ease in the company of their sister-in-law Queen Louise. Knowing that the palaces of their childhood would never be the same as they had been in their father's day, they decided that the solution would be a *pied à terre* of their own in Denmark. By coincidence, exactly a week after their father's death, Queen Alexandra saw a newspaper advertisement offering a suitable residence for sale. Hvidøre (literally 'White Gravel') was a white Italianate villa at Strandvejen, north of Copenhagen, near the beach at Klampenburg where they had bathed as children. It had just been offered for sale by a councillor at the Danish Embassy. She asked Rørdam to make enquiries, and within a month he had purchased it on their behalf for Kr28,000 (about £1,500 at 1906 figures).

Soon they were busy with decorations and furnishings for this holiday home, the first property which they could truly call their own. Here they could while away the time watching ships passing in the harbour, picking fruit in the orchard or wandering along the shore of the private beach from which it took its name, collecting pieces of amber washed up by the tide. Now, as old age approached, they could come close to recreating and re-experiencing the delights of childhood and an age long since vanished. Most visitors agreed that it was a charming place, although Lord Hardinge of the Foreign Office remarked that he had 'never seen a more ghastly property', lacking privacy as the road was so close to the house, 'so that those on the road could look straight into the windows, whilst access to the sea could be obtained only by crossing the road.'[3] To the Queen and Dowager Empress, brought up in an unpretentious palace in Copenhagen, the lack of privacy – if Hardinge's scathing description can be taken at face value – evidently mattered little.

Like his brother-in-law in England, King Frederick VIII had the misfortune to succeed a venerable, much-loved parent who had virtually become a national living legend. Nonetheless he was cautious and intelligent, appreciating the necessity for letting the crown be identified with progressive movements. Despite his ingrained conservatism he was a man of his time. During his long apprenticeship as Crown Prince he had followed political, cultural and social issues of the day with keen interest, from reforms of the prison system to Denmark's participation in world exhibitions, and from meetings of the Royal Danish Academy of Sciences and Letters to attendance at sessions of Parliament. From time to time he had aired his opinions in pseudonymously-written letters to editors of the daily press. He had spoken in favour of parliamentary rule at the time of his silver wedding anniversary in 1894, and unlike his father never had any reservations about the *systemkiftet* in 1901, feeling that it brought Denmark into the twentieth century. By the standards of the time, there was enough of the democrat in King Frederick VIII to welcome moves such as the extension of the franchise and the additional taxation of the rich.

On his proclamation by the prime minister, Jens Christian Christensen, from the balcony of Amalienborg Palace on 30 January, he spoke to the assembled crowds of his hopes and prayers 'that the Almighty may grant me the strength and the happiness to carry on the government in the spirit of my dearly-beloved father, and the good fortune to arrive at an understanding with the people and their chosen representatives on all that tends to the good of the people and to the happiness and well-being of the beloved Fatherland.'[1] Such words were not mere pious rhetoric, but those of a man who recognized that monarchs had to move with the times. During his short reign he made it his objective to fight for the rights of Danes living in German-ruled Schleswig, make regular tours of his kingdom, and espouse charitable causes. It was said that he had the royal gift of never forgetting a face.

One of his first acts as King was to address himself to the problem of Iceland. With her demands for full self-government, the northerly island was described by *The Times* as 'the Ireland of Denmark'. King Frederick was determined to show concern for Icelandic aspirations, and invited all members of the island parliament to Copenhagen. Thirty-eight of them, leaving only two absentees who sent apologies for their absence, arrived at the Danish capital to a warm welcome in July 1906. A dinner at Fredensborg Palace, attended by all members of the Danish and Icelandic parliaments, was the first time that a Danish King had had the opportunity of seeing together both the legislative bodies of his peoples together. In his address he promised to pay a visit to Iceland the following summer, and announced that henceforth he would change his title from 'King of Denmark' to 'King of Denmark and Iceland'.

Throughout his reign, King Frederick paid frequent visits to the other capitals of Europe. The first, in September 1906, was to Stockholm, out of respect to his wife's country. It also gave him the opportunity to help smooth the feelings of his wife's family, still ruffled after the affair of the Norwegian crown. According to *The Times* correspondent, his sojourn at the court of the elderly King Oscar II so soon after the dissolution of the Swedish-Norwegian union was 'calculated to pacify these feelings and to facilitate a return to the former sentiments of friendship, solidarity, and mutual confidence which served the interests of both and which time will undoubtedly restore'.[5]

With the death of Queen Louise, consort of King Christian IX, in September 1898, the bitterest foe of Prussia had gone from Copenhagen, and as Crown Prince, Frederick had been anxious to extend the hand of friendship to his mighty neighbour. The attendance of Emperor William II at the funeral of King Christian IX some seven years later opened the way for a *rapprochement* between both countries and sovereigns. Germany was just as anxious to gain Danish support as Denmark was to keep German friendship. It was a hearty Berlin welcome which greeted King Frederick and Queen Louise on their arrival on 19 November, with the usual exchanges and pronouncements that the German Empire and Denmark 'might remain upon terms of good and cordial understanding.' While in Berlin, Emperor William conferred the Order of the Black Eagle on his guest, and the King received a deputation representative of all classes of the Danish colony in Berlin.

The Germans were just as anxious to woo their Danish neighbours, although the Emperor and his associates differed in their assessments of the likelihood of being able to do so. Early in 1907 Bülow concluded a treaty with Denmark by which the children of the disputed territory of Optants, until then without any recognized nationality of their own, could now either be nationalized as Danes or Germans as they wished. The treaty was favourably received by the Danes. Official newspapers called it the most significant event since 1864 in the history of Danish-German relations, and expressed their hopes that the treaty would mark the beginning of a new era. Emperor William was optimistic in bringing about a closer union with Denmark, and in the interests of German naval policy, Admiral von Tirpitz was in full agreement. Bülow, on the other hand, felt that 'correct relations, without any *arrière pensée*, were as much as we could ever hope [for] from the Danes. These could be obtained by the reasonable and tactful handling of the Danish inhabitants of North-Schleswig'.[6]

Throughout the first few months of 1907, there was persistent speculation in the press of the countries concerned as to Denmark's position in the event on Anglo-German conflict. At length Christensen was obliged to declare unequivocally that 'the simple and undeniable truth is that the

Government has not concluded any secret treaty with Germany and is not working for any. The policy of the Government is neutrality and not alliances of any kind'.[7]

The next state visit of King Frederick and Queen Louise was to England, in June 1907. Their programme included a banquet at Buckingham Palace, dinner at Marlborough House with the Prince and Princess of Wales, a review at Aldershot and a gala performance at the Royal Opera, Covent Garden, to hear Enrico Caruso and Dame Nellie Melba sing. After luncheon at the Guildhall, King Frederick declared in his speech that it would 'be my endeavour, as that of my people, to preserve and increase the bonds of sincere friendship which unite the two peoples together today'.[8] The ominous rumblings of the German press gave added weight to what might in less uneasy times have sounded like mere platitudes.

One member of the House of Commons at Westminster had his own novel if hardly serious idea for strengthening the bonds of Anglo-Danish friendship. The Lord Chamberlain, with the full approval of King Edward VII, had temporarily banned public performances of Gilbert & Sullivan's opera *The Mikado*, on the grounds that it might offend the susceptibilities of a Japanese prince who was about to visit England. An Irish Nationalist member, Vincent Kennedy, promptly announced his intention of asking the prime minister whether his attention had been called to the fact that in Shakespeare's *Hamlet* the King of Denmark was portrayed as a murderer; and whether, in view of the fact that Denmark was a friendly power, this reference to the King was liable to cause offence in that country; and, if so, should the play not be subject to a similar ban. Needless to say, no such action was taken.

Early in July King Frederick and Queen Louise welcomed the German Emperor William on a state visit to Copenhagen. Public opinion in Denmark was satisfied after the Berlin government's surprising concession of certain Danish claims in Schleswig and a more lenient attitude towards the nationalistic sensibilities of the Danes in both duchies, but it was generally agreed that Denmark, for reasons of principle, could never agree to any kind of alliance with Germany. After a dinner at Fredensborg Castle in honour of the Emperor and Empress, King Frederick thanked his guest for his friendly reception in Berlin the previous autumn. The Emperor alluded graciously to days passed as a guest of King Christian IX, and thanked him for the kind welcome, 'which I trust is a token of hearty friendship between our two Houses'.[9]

With this establishment of good relations, the German press were quick to interpret the Emperor's cordial reception by the King and people of Denmark as a timely symptom of the decline of Danish suspicion, and as spontaneous acknowledgement that German policy had no intention of impairing the independent existence of her smaller neighbours or obstructing their own individual development.

Less than a month later, King Frederick fulfilled his promise to go to Iceland. Shortly after the deputation in Copenhagen the previous year he had appointed a commission to undertake preliminary arrangements for fresh legislation regarding the constitutional status of Iceland in the Danish dominions. There was therefore considerable warmth in the welcome given him as he arrived on board the steamship *Birma* at Reykjavik on 30 July, accompanied by his son Prince Harald and M. Christensen, as well as several Danish ministers and members of the Riksdag. At a banquet in the King's honour the following evening, he spoke of his desire that the Icelanders should

> have every facility for the development of their national characteristics and their country, so far as is consistent with the unity of the kingdom. I have inherited the kingdom as a unit, and as such it shall remain from generation to generation. But I have also inherited from my father the tradition that the Icelanders are to be a free people, cooperating with the King in framing the laws under which they are to live, and it is my will to continue building on the foundation of this inheritance.[10]

King Frederick's evident personal interest in Iceland was much appreciated by the people, while at Copenhagen there was relief that the island's radicals did not spoil the King's visit by any demonstrations or hoisting of unlawful Icelandic flags.

While his foreign diplomacy had helped to establish his reputation abroad, King Frederick VIII's dealings with his ministers at home led him into a *faux pas* which, while it stopped short of bringing the throne into temporary disrepute, threatened to besmirch the reputation of a crown that strove to remain above politics.

For many years he had been on friendly terms with Christensen, who had become prime minister in 1905. In this capacity he arranged a trip for the King and Queen to Jutland in 1908, during which the King visited Christensen's home to symbolize the good relationship between King and head of government.

Although leader of the political left in Denmark, Christensen agreed with the King that national defences should be strong enough to act as a deterrent to any neighbouring or foreign power who might desire to carry out a bloodless invasion. Much had been spent on fortifications in the Copenhagen area and to arsenals which improved the mobilization arrangements of the army, giving priority to defence by land, much to the indignation of the navy and its officers. During his last years King Christian IX, as well as Crown Prince Frederick, had been gravely concerned over disagreements between the services. With Germany's ambitious naval expansion under Emperor William II, and international tension in the wake of the Russo-Japanese war of 1904–5, settling the matter became an increasing priority. A defence commission produced a report which failed to draw any clear conclusions as its members could not agree among themselves as to the extent of Danish land and sea defences, or the proportion of expenditure to be involved in each. Christensen was about to take action on the problem himself when he was distracted by the Alberti scandal.

In May 1908 the minister of justice, Peter Adler Alberti, had asked Christensen for a loan from state funds to save the Zealand Farmers' Savings Bank, of which he was a director, from liquidation. Under a secret arrangement Christensen granted his request, and was entrusted with the bank's mortgage deeds as security. Two months later rumours began to circulate about the matter, and Alberti was forced to resign pending an investigation.

Nevertheless the King had never been in any doubt concerning the integrity of Alberti, although this may have been no more than an honest belief in the innocence of an esteemed servant of the crown until or unless proved guilty. Irritated by the constant accusations against the former minister, he unhesitatingly followed Christensen's recommendation that Alberti should be granted the title of Privy Councillor on his resignation, as a reward for years of public service. Shortly afterwards Alberti admitted to embezzling a sum of around nine million Kroner. The government committee investigating the affair discovered that the amount was nearer fifteen million Kroner. Under pressure Christensen was forced to admit that the cabinet had no prior knowledge of Alberti's misdemeanours. However, lest the good name of Denmark might be damaged abroad, the Prime Minister resigned, and in due course Alberti was sentenced to eight years' imprisonment.

Although no lasting damage was done to the King's reputation, it was felt that he had been unwise to honour a former minister while under suspicion of major financial irregularities. For his part, he was angry at having been let down by a politician in whom he had placed such great faith, and like Christensen he was concerned at the stain that could be left on his country's honour.

By 1907 King Oscar II of Sweden was in failing health. From the time of his accession, his motto had been 'the two peoples' fraternal welfare', and he had set much store on trying to keep Norway and Sweden together. The dissolution of the union was a bitter blow which, although regarded by most politicians in both countries as inevitable for a long time, hit him hard. To Sir Rennell Rodd, British minister at Stockholm, he said ruefully that 'they might have waited a little till I had been carried out to the church at Riddarholm.' He died on 8 December 1907, aged seventy-eight.

His eldest son ascended the throne as King Gustav V. In his first proclamation, he declared that he would dispense with a coronation. Such ceremonies and festivities, he said, would be a waste of money; 'an elaborate Coronation will not make my people love, respect or trust me any more than if I am merely declared King by a public crier!'[11] Perhaps he was wise not to add that the money would probably have been his own. Ministers had refused to defray the expenses for a similar ceremony for his father in 1872, thus forcing King Oscar to pay all the costs from his own pocket.

In all fairness to the shy, retiring new King, he had a pronounced distaste for the regal displays of pomp and circumstance so beloved by his father. When he contented himself with taking the royal oath at a simple ceremony at the palace in the presence of members of the Riksdag, his subjects thought that this would indicate his intention of being a more democratic King. Yet in time he would show himself just as determined to retain the royal prerogative as King Oscar II.

Of the late King's talent for public speaking and intellectual pursuits, his son and successor had but little. Although extremely short-sighted he was devoted to sport, particularly tennis (the popularity of which owed much to his encouragement), hunting, and shooting. In the evenings he relaxed by playing bridge and later canasta.

He was also a keen collector of Swedish silver and Sèvres porcelain. Paying a visit incognito to the Sèvres factory, he was shown some prize pieces by the manager. 'Is this all you have?' the King asked. The manager said it was; 'there is only one man who has more!' When King Gustav said he had some three hundred pieces himself, he was told that he was surely exaggerating. 'But, sir, only the King of Sweden can say that!' 'Exactly', the King retorted. 'And I am saying it, am I not?'[12]

One thing which he had in common with his father was a keen desire to put behind him the bitterness left by Denmark's sympathies for Norway during the struggle for independence. In the first week of June 1908 he paid a state visit to Copenhagen. At a speech after dinner at Amalienborg Palace, he declared that the 'gloomy clouds had now dispersed', and the way was open for a closely united Scandinavia.

The King's marriage had been no love match. On 20 September 1881, the same day as Grand Duke Frederick of Baden celebrated his silver wedding with Louise, daughter of the German Emperor William I at Carlsruhe, Crown Prince Gustav of Sweden married their daughter Princess Victoria. Guests and observers at the wedding thought that 'the Prince seemed sullen and angry; the Princess cold and almost antagonistic!'[13]

There were three sons of the marriage. Prince Gustav Adolf, born in 1882 and married to Princess Margaret of Connaught, became Crown Prince on his father's accession. Prince William, born in 1884, was later created Duke of Södermanland. His marriage to Grand Duchess Marie of Russia produced one son but ended in divorce after six years; thereafter he devoted himself to a literary career, publishing several volumes of travel recollections, plays and poetry. Eric, born in 1889 and created Duke of Västmanland, was epileptic from birth and slightly mentally retarded. He lived away from the family – who came to visit him regularly – and was looked after by a nanny, Louise Rinman. Dogs and a parrot kept him company, and he was passionately interested in history, geography and music. At the age of twenty-nine he succumbed to the epidemic of Spanish influenza which ravaged Europe in 1918.

Crown Princess Victoria, never strong herself, was a perpetual martyr to weak lungs and pulmonary trouble. Very German in her outlook, characteristics and general behaviour, she was keen to bring Berlin etiquette into the Swedish court. A first cousin of Emperor William II, she was said to possess exaggerated 'Germanic ideas of the Divine Right of Kings', and to have a baleful influence on her mild-mannered husband. Yet she did at least introduce him to the art of embroidery, allegedly in an effort to help him cut down on his smoking, and under her guidance he produced several altar cloths.

Throughout her married life she spent much of her time in Germany, partly for health reasons, partly out of homesickness. Neither she nor her husband strove to maintain any public semblance of marital happiness. From 1890 onwards, on medical advice, she went to North Africa during the winter, allowing her ample time to indulge her artistic interests. From adolescence she had been a skilled sculptor and painter in watercolours, and in Egypt she developed her passion for photography. Several bearers and donkeys were needed to carry her equipment into the desert; the results were highly praised, and in 1894 she had a major exhibition of photographs at Stockholm. The following year, she was made an honorary member of the National Photographic Society.

During her absences from Sweden, her place was generally filled by the King's sister-in-law Ingeborg, Duchess of Västergötland. The daughter of King Frederick VIII of Denmark, she had married the then Crown Prince Gustav's younger brother Prince Carl in 1897. At the time of her brother-in-law's accession they had three daughters, all of whom made good inter-royal marriages. The eldest, Margaretha, became the wife of Prince Axel of Denmark, son of King Christian IX's youngest child Prince Waldemar; while Princesses Märtha and Astrid would in time marry the future Kings of Norway and Belgium respectively.

Although profoundly deaf, Prince Carl, Duke of Västergötland, was President of the Swedish Red Cross and an indefatigable worker for humanitarian causes. Princess Ingeborg was likewise a tireless patron of charities, supporting her husband in his Red Cross work, as well as being

Chairman of *Sällskapet barnavaard*, the Swedish Child Care Society. Described by the contemporary press as 'amusing and accessible', she would often be seen with her husband or the children on Saturday afternoons enjoying a snack at the Grand Hotel in Stockholm, in order to give herself a rest from housekeeping and to allow their servants some time off. She schooled her daughters well in undertaking medical and nursing work at home. Before marrying Crown Prince Olav of Norway, Princess Märtha took courses in child care; while during the economic depression of the 1930s Queen Astrid in Belgium helped to arrange national collections in aid of the unemployed, and took a personal role in the distribution of funds afterwards.

King Gustav bore his loneliness stoically. To the rest of his family he was a kindly, considerate figure, and for all his regal dignity had a keen sense of humour. His daughter-in-law, born Grand Duchess Marie of Russia, married the Duke of Södermanland in 1908. Thoroughly homesick on her arrival in Stockholm, she was deeply touched when her brother Grand Duke Dmitri appeared as part of the royal party to greet her when her carriage drew up at the palace. The King had brought him secretly to Sweden to surprise her and help make her feel more at home during her first days in a strange land. A high-spirited young woman, her love of receptions, entertainments and parties at court were said to make him 'wag his head in disapproval', but although he might comment sharply on her conduct to his son, he never scolded her. On the contrary he was thoroughly charmed by her, played tennis with her every day on the indoor courts at Stockholm in winter, and sometimes took her on elk hunts at which she was the only woman present.

He spoilt her so much that she could not resist playing jokes on him sometimes, but he always took them in good part. Once as they were on their way to a skiing expedition, she decided to dress up as an old lady and present flowers to the King, who was playing bridge in the carriage ahead. She used a burnt cork to produce wrinkles on her face, rubbed slices of beetroot on her cheeks, hid her eyes behind dark glasses, covered her head with a woollen shawl, and borrowed a fur-lined cloak from one of the maids. The conductor stopped the train at the first station and she alighted, carrying three fading tulips wrapped in a piece of newspaper. One of the aides-de-camp sportingly obliged by telling the King that an aged woman wished to come and pay her respects.

Entering his carriage she presented him with the meagre bouquet, but at the sight of his serious face and the equally dignified aides, she could no longer keep a straight face. She collapsed on the floor, laughing hysterically, hoping her mirth would be taken for tears. Turning to his Chamberlain, the alarmed King asked him, *'Enlevez-la, elle est folle!'* Two aides gently took hold of her, and she had visions of being left on the platform while the train sped on without her. 'It is I, Papa!' she cried out, still laughing. The King bent close to her, recognized her and laughed heartily himself.[14]

Another time a young cavalry officer also had good reason to be grateful for his sovereign's tact and sense of humour. King Gustav V was presenting him with a cavalry prize. In his excitement the officer had the misfortune to break wind at the crucial moment. Overcome with embarrassment and blushing deeply, he begged for forgiveness. 'Really?' the King replied phlegmatically. 'I thought it was your horse.'[15]

In the spring of 1907, King Haakon and Queen Maud paid a three-day state visit to Paris. Neither of them had looked forward to it. Maud confessed in a spirit of apprehension mingled with mischief that 'everything is so stiff, and I am certain I will never be able to be on my best behaviour for long!'[16] She dreaded not only a prolonged separation from her young son, but also the inevitable public appearances, which made her nervous.

However their Parisian sojourn was a great success, not least because of their self-control when the carriage horses fell off a low bridge during a drive in the park at Versailles. Queen Maud's presence of mind and prompt concern for the slightly injured coachman and his team made a favourable contrast to the hysterics of Madame Fallières, wife of the French President, seated beside her.

In July and August they undertook a nineteen-day tour of remote settlements in North Norway, with the purpose of seeing something of their kingdom. They were accompanied by Fridtjof Nansen, Norwegian Ambassador to London, who had become a close personal friend. The Queen and the Crown Prince were frequently seasick as the weather was unseasonably windy and cold, even by the standards of the average Arctic summer; nevertheless they followed quite a demanding schedule, visiting small communities at the end of the long fiords, medieval fortresses and army training centres.

At times they were astonished by the primitive way of life, quite beyond anything in their previous experience. King Haakon wrote to his father about the poverty which they had seen on their travels: 'one really wonders how people manage to live at all in such places, for it does not look as though anything could grow there to feed these folk. Many of their houses are nothing but earth huts.'[17] With some concern he noted the potential problems created for North Norway by the immigration of Finns, would-be revolutionaries intent on escaping from what was then the Russian Grand Duchy of Finland. For them Norway was safer territory than Tsarist Russia and her dominions, and the King was aware that they might help any revolution in Russia to spread west into Scandinavia. He also realized, perhaps thanks to the plain-speaking Nansen – who knew that it was in his sovereign's best interests to be advised of any unpalatable matters of importance – that the absence of anti-monarchical demonstrations was only 'as the police did not think they ought to be at large that day'.

Nonetheless this northern tour had its lighter moments. A reception given by the dignitaries of Vadsø allowed the royal sense of humour to come to the surface. After luncheon, the party rose from their table to go upstairs to the next floor for the reception. Only then did the King and Queen find that the stairs were almost blocked with empty and half-empty beer bottles left by the band, who were in a hurry to go. Servants set about clearing them as quickly as possible, but in their confusion and haste several bottles were knocked over and the stairs were awash with beer. The Queen was in agonies of suppressed laughter.

Eventually they reached the landing, where the King turned and whispered gravely to Nansen that there was a seat for him. On the landing was an old-fashioned commode, past which the King, Queen and entire company had to file to reach the room where the local ladies were to be presented to them. With his naval training King Haakon managed to keep a straight face, but Queen Maud was choking with laughter by the time they reached the room, while Nansen could not restrain his mirth, for which he received an indignant rebuke from a lady-in-waiting.[18]

Despite such moments of unplanned informality, Queen Maud never ceased to count the days until she could go and stay again at her beloved Appleton. For her it was an opportunity to revisit childhood haunts; while as an only child Crown Prince Olav needed the companionship of his contemporaries, particularly his cousins in England. As he was close in age to the younger sons of the Prince of Wales, who succeeded his father as King George V in May 1910, he spent many happy hours playing with them and their model soldiers. King George looked indulgently on the children's war games, but not without insisting on one condition: their opposing armies should not represent different nations, but rather planets, such as Earth and Mars. An attendant policeman on the estate later recalled that when the young Princes were discussing their ambitions, Prince Olav announced that when he was grown up he intended to abolish the collar.

In April and May 1908 King Edward VII and Queen Alexandra paid official visits to each of the Scandinavian capitals in turn. For family reasons they had visited Denmark almost every year, but this time they included Norway and Sweden on the itinerary as well. At Copenhagen they stayed with King Frederick VIII at the Amalienborg Palace, and were treated to the customary round of banquets and receptions. Because of the poor weather King Edward declined to attend an open-air procession of the members of a number of Danish institutions and societies, but instead received a deputation representing agriculture, commerce, science and art. In his reply to the address, he congratulated Denmark on the country's recent development in such fields: 'nor can it be said that science and art in

Denmark are eclipsed by the successful extension of commerce and agriculture, since some of the most remarkable of recent discoveries in science are due to Danish invention, and Denmark more than holds her own in the field of culture and the arts of peace.'[19]

Their appearance in Stockholm later that week was the first occasion that a reigning British monarch had ever visited Sweden. A banquet was held at the royal palace for the guests, and during his stay King Edward, accompanied by King Gustav, went to Riddarholm Church and laid a wreath of flowers on the tomb of King Oscar II. Afterwards he received a deputation from the Swedish navy, of which he was an honorary Admiral, and after dining with the Crown Prince and Princess, attended a gala performance at the opera.

On arriving in Christiania the King's equerry, Sir Frederick Ponsonby, was interested to see how King Haakon and Queen Maud were faring. Had the Left been in power instead of the Right in 1905, he felt, the Norwegians would certainly have had a republic; they found Christiania 'so socialistic that a King and Queen seemed out of place.' King Haakon, he considered, was 'playing his part very well and had secured the love and respect of the majority of the people.'

Queen Maud had responded quickly to welfare initiatives. Shortly after her husband's accession she had taken a leading role in subscribing to a home for unmarried mothers and attending a public meeting on its behalf, a bold stand that flew in the face of 'respectable' opinion among those who considered such good works to be beneath them.

King and equerry had somewhat differing views. King Haakon confided his difficulties to Ponsonby, saying that in view of the opposition's republican leanings he had to be extremely careful as to what he said and did. He intended 'to go as much as possible among the people and thought it would be popular if, instead of going in a motor car, he and Queen Maud were to use the tramways.' Ponsonby tried to dissuade him, on the grounds that familiarity bred contempt: 'he must get up on a pedestal and remain there.' People in Norway would be disappointed 'if they saw him going about like an ordinary man in the street.'[20] As far as Ponsonby could recall, the advice fell on fertile soil, as he could never recollect King Haakon using a tram.

Nonetheless the British visitors found Kongens Slot, the royal palace, far from comfortable. The massive, barrack-like building had been designed for ceremonial purposes, as during the nineteenth century the King of Sweden and Norway never resided in what he regarded as the lesser of his kingdoms. King Haakon and Queen Maud were faced with the daunting task of making a proper home out of the magnificent-looking but cheerless edifice which, at the time of their arrival, had one bath but no lavatories. All water had to be brought up from a kitchen in the basement. Most of the furniture had been taken back to Stockholm, as the personal property of the Swedish crown. Such goods and chattels as there were at the time of King Edward's visit consisted mostly of what his son-in-law and daughter had been able to bring with them from Copenhagen, supplemented by what a reluctant Norwegian government had been able to obtain for them in sales. Although modest improvements had been made by then, the general standard of comfort and hygiene still fell a long way short of those of Buckingham Palace and Windsor Castle.

From the start King Haakon VII devoted himself conscientiously to his responsibilities. Every day he studied the newspapers carefully, cutting out comments about the royal family, political debates and major questions of foreign policy, and pasting them systematically into albums. People regularly came to be received in audience with him for a variety of reasons, perhaps to thank him for a long service medal, or to invite him to attend art exhibitions, sports meetings, farm fairs, or cultural evenings. He enjoyed meeting people face to face, as they gave him an insight – however brief – into matters or conditions with which he would otherwise have had no contact at all.

He made a habit of attending lecture meetings of bodies including the Polytechnic Society, the Oslo Military Club, the Norwegian Society of Engineers and the Academy of Sciences. In the first year of his reign he began a tradition by which all members of the Storting and government should come to dinner at the palace early in the year, and a few weeks later he would host a similar function for the foreign diplomats and representatives of the foreign ministry.

The Norwegians, the American President Theodore Roosevelt wrote to the historian George Otto Trevelyan (1 October 1911), had the most genuinely democratic society to be found in Europe, not excepting Switzerland: 'They have no nobles, hardly even gentry; they are peasants and small townspeople – farmers, sailors, fisherfolk, mechanics, small traders. On this community a royal family is suddenly plumped down. It is as much as if Vermont should offhand try the experiment of having a King.' King Haakon, he observed, 'took a keen and intelligent interest in every question affecting his people, treated them and was treated by them, with a curiously simple democracy of attitude which was free from make-believe on either side, and while he unhesitatingly and openly discussed questions with his ministers, never in the slightest way sought to interfere with or hamper their free action.'[21]

King Frederick VIII had long appreciated the value of friendly relations with Germany. Even so, he had inherited his mother's deep distrust of the Emperor, though he was more careful to disguise his feelings than his sister in England and his sister-in-law Marie, wife of Prince Waldemar, at home.

Despite his overwhelming affection for his nephew Prince George of Greece, who had remained his 'dearest friend' in the discreet parlance of the day, Waldemar and Marie had settled into a tolerant brother-sister relationship. He was modest, unassuming, and content with his career in the Danish navy. By contrast she was a veritable dynamo who threw herself heart and soul into all her interests, perhaps to compensate for the failure to gain her husband's abiding affection. Passionately devoted to French interests and eager to further the cause of any alliances against Germany, she was in regular correspondence with Tsar Nicholas II and his foreign ministers, as well as with successive French presidents, sometimes working at her desk till 4 a.m. She busied herself with painting, sculpture, horse riding, and also membership of the Copenhagen fire brigade. Entertaining guests one day (in more sense than one, perhaps), she heard an alarm bell, ran from the room and returned with a fireman's helmet on her head. Shouting her apologies, she dashed off to help fight a fire which had broken out aboard one of the ships in the harbour.

According to Princess George of Greece, their niece by marriage, Bernstorff was 'lit up by that vibrant and enlightened woman'. It made such a refreshing contrast with the 'slow and dreary evenings after dinner at Uncle Freddy's [Frederick VIII] in . . . the Palace of Desolation',[22] as she christened Amalienborg.

Family and friends warned her that she was tiring herself out, but she retorted that she had no intention of spending her old age in a wheelchair. As if to prove her point, she collapsed and died after a short illness in December 1909 at the early age of forty-four. Her heartbroken husband initially had her coffin kept in the Sailors' Church at Copenhagen, so that he could visit it more easily. Not for some time did he allow her to be buried with the rest of the family at Roskilde Cathedral.

On the day after King Edward VII's death (7 May 1910), King Frederick VIII wrote to the new King, now George V, that 'thanks to [King Edward] I believe peace was kept here in Europe, and I had that particular feeling that no harm would happen to us and that is the reason, why I only beg you not to forget our Country, and I believe you understand what I mean.'[23]

King Edward VII had died after a reign of nine years. That of his brother-in-law, who had likewise served a long apprenticeship as Crown Prince during the long reign of an octogenarian parent, was to be even shorter. In the spring of 1912, after a winter of ill-health, he was recommended by his doctor to go south for a few weeks. Accompanied by Queen Louise and the younger children, Princesses Thyra and Dagmar, and Prince Gustav, he went to stay in the south of France. The warmer weather seemed to do him good. and they set out for the return to Denmark in the second week of May. At Hamburg they broke their journey for a few days, arriving in the city on 13 May.

On the following afternoon, the King visited the Hagenbeck Zoological Gardens. After dining at the Hamburger Hof that evening he went for a walk. It was typical of his informality that he should go into the streets alone, unaccompanied even by a detective or an aide. After strolling for about forty-five minutes he was seen to stagger, and collapsed on the steps of a butcher's shop. By pure good fortune a passing surgeon, Dr Seeligmann, came to his assistance. Without revealing his identity, the King assured him that he was staying at the hotel, he felt perfectly well and intended to continue his walk. After taking a few more paces he collapsed again, and Dr Seeligmann ran after him. Checking his pulse, he found that it had already stopped. He summoned a policeman, between them they helped him into a taxi, and told the driver to take him to the nearest hospital.

By the time they arrived, King Frederick was dead, and his body was put in the mortuary. As he was carrying no identification, nobody had any idea who he was.

Meanwhile back at the Hamburger Hof Queen Louise, the family and their Court Marshal, Count Brockenhuus-Schack, were becoming increasingly concerned. They searched the streets themselves, and then contacted the police, who confirmed that an unidentified gentleman had been found dying in the street. Not until 4.00 the following morning did the full truth dawn on everyone.

In Copenhagen the people had looked forward to welcoming their sovereign home that evening. Instead, dawn was breaking as the sad news reached the city. Flags were lowered to half-mast, and church bells tolled. 'I need not dwell on the tragedy of the event', Conyngham Greene reported from the British legation (15 May), 'nor the irony of fate which snatched King Frederick from His people, on the threshold of His own country, and just at the moment when He was looking forward to His homecoming. His Majesty has passed from His people, but His handsome presence, His gracious courtesy, and His unaffected simplicity will not lightly be forgotten by those who were privileged to meet Him'.[24]

The King's body was brought back to the hotel, and on the following day it was taken to Travemünde, put aboard the royal yacht, *Dannebrog*, accompanied by a convoy of Danish and German warships, and carried to Copenhagen. On arrival the bier was taken to the Chapel of Christiansborg Castle until the funeral on 24 May.

Throughout the royal courts of Europe, everyone was shocked. 'It is all very sad', Queen Mary wrote to her aunt Augusta, Dowager Duchess of Mecklenburg-Strelitz (18 May 1912), 'and his dying in the street quite alone makes it worse'.[25]

King Frederick VIII was succeeded by his eldest son, who took the title of King Christian X. The new King was stunned at how suddenly everything had happened, as he recounted in a letter to King George V later that month. Despite the King's recent ill health, the news had been so unexpected that the family had been looking forward to dinner together the day of his return home. Everything, he admitted, was 'so changed', yet his mother, now Queen Dowager, had 'showed a remarkable force' in the face of such sorrow.[26]

In a short address from the palace balcony after being proclaimed King by the prime minister, Klaus Berntsen on 15 May, the King spoke gravely of the heavy responsibility 'now laid on my shoulders, but I hope that the same confidence will be extended to me as was extended to my beloved father. Denmark's happiness, freedom, and independence will be my own, and may all Danes who wish for the same join hands to this end.'[27]

CHAPTER SIX

'These sad times'

At the time of his accession King Christian X was forty-one years of age. He had made the army his career, and risen to the rank of Major-General. To at least one observer, he was a great improvement on King Frederick VIII. Even during the last years of King Christian IX, Sir Frederick Ponsonby had considered him to be 'much cleverer and a stronger character'[1] than his father.

He shared the family's love of sport, being an excellent shot and an enthusiastic huntsman. Equally fond of yachting, he held a master's certificate, was honorary Chairman of the Royal Danish Yacht Club, and took part successfully in regattas at home and at Cannes, where he and his wife still usually took their holidays in the spring and could often be seen on their bicycles. He regularly attended football matches in Copenhagen, and several challenge cups and prizes for athletics were associated with his name. Keenly interested in flying, he took lessons himself while aviation was still in its infancy.

At six foot four inches, he was slightly taller than King Haakon, if not as handsome. Once at a reception he overheard two ladies talking about him. 'Well, he's not very good looking', one commented. 'No, but his hearing's good!' he exclaimed loudly.

His consort, now Queen Alexandrine, was ever a dutiful figure by his side in public, though like her mother-in-law she was a reserved figure who liked her own privacy. She generally spent summer at Skagen, North Jutland, where she mixed freely with the local people. Her abiding passion was music, an interest which her elder son was to inherit. She was often seen at important concerts in Copenhagen, and as a devotee of Wagner she frequently attended the Wagner festival at Bayreuth.

The Queen was devoted to her sons, who in turn adored her but were frightened of their tyrannical father. King Christian X had evidently suffered throughout childhood at the hands of his strict, domineering mother. Incapable of showing warmth in relationships with most of his family, he kept his boys at arm's length. Had Queen Alexandrine been a stronger personality in her own right, perhaps she would have taken their side more readily against him; but, one has to surmise, maybe she shared the dictum of a contemporary queen consort in Britain that 'I have to remember that their father is also their King'.

With the accession of King Christian X, the Scandinavian monarchies were very much a family. The Kings of Denmark and Norway were brothers, only two years apart in age, while the King of Sweden was their second cousin.

The two brothers, who had shared a difficult childhood, were always close. They maintained regular contact by letter and telephone, and King Christian paid a state visit to Christiania in February 1913. However, there was always a distance between them and the royal family of Sweden. The Kings of Denmark and Norway had close ties with Britain, while King Gustav V and Queen Louise were naturally more in sympathy with the increasingly bellicose Germany and the sabre-rattling Emperor William II. There was an element of irony in the fact that the ruling dynasties of Denmark and Norway, like those of several other nations then at war with the Second Reich and her allies, bore a German name, while the Bernadottes of Sweden were one of the few royal houses not of German origin. Although both the brother Kings were always civil to Emperor William, they could not but regard him at best with suspicion, at worst a dangerous intriguer.

On 9 May 1914 King Christian X paid a state visit to England. He was entertained at Buckingham Palace with a banquet in the ballroom followed by a gala performance at the opera, and a film of Scott's expedition to the Antarctic was shown to the guests. Perhaps it was just coincidence that on the previous day King George V had breakfasted with his Hohenzollern cousin Prince Henry of Prussia, only surviving brother of the German Emperor, who was noted by his cousins in England for his affability. The spring and early summer of 1914 saw a whirl of royal visits throughout the courts of Europe, yet few if any of those at the centre of events had more than a vague suspicion that within weeks the gathering storm would break.

These were to be uncertain days in domestic affairs as well as in the rest of Europe. In Sweden, King Gustav V was ready for a battle to assert the royal prerogative. A new Liberal government under Carl Staaff had been elected to power in 1911 partly on a manifesto to disarm, and refused to present a bill to increase the defence budget and prolong the period of military service. They also annulled a plan by the previous government to build a new battleship, a decision which brought a formal protest from the King. As a result money was collected by public subscription, and such was the strength of feeling that the sum was raised within a few months.

The King demanded an immediate commitment to strengthen the country's defences. Throughout Sweden, public opinion was on the side of opposition politicians who felt that national defences were inadequate to guarantee foreign respect for neutrality in the event of an European war. The government and its allies, denouncing the concept of 'a fortified poorhouse', held fast to their principles of reducing defence expenditure, particularly on the navy. Defence, the public maintained, was of more than party political interest. The Peasants' Party, which had hitherto been inclined to discourage undue expenditure on what they saw as unproductive armaments, were supposed to have supported the Staaff ministry with the express intention of curtailing outlay on the navy in the Riksdag.

Nonetheless they took the opposite view. On 6 February 1914 a well-organized demonstration of more than 30,000 Peasants and their supporters from all parts of the country assembled in churches and marched to the palace at Stockholm, forming up in a prescribed order on the esplanade inside the palace quadrangle. At the upper end King Gustav V stood awaiting them on a dais. The deputation of 200 Peasants, ten from each Province, surrounded the dais, and one speaker, addressing the King, stated that they were approaching His Majesty in order to affirm their willingness to accept the burden of increased armaments necessary for the country's defence, and that the matter should be resolved without delay. Another speaker added that other classes of the population shared this feeling, as the Peasant Committee had received telegrams expressing solidarity with the object of the demonstration, and a petition with over 60,000 signatures. They declared themselves ready to make whatever sacrifices might be required in the way of prolonged military service and higher taxes.

In his reply the King thanked the Peasants for their patriotism and devotion to the public weal. He did not share the prime minister's attitude to defence, he told them, but thought it should 'be treated as a whole and decided now, forthwith, and in a single context'; and that an absolute condition for this should be 'a longer period of military service for conscripts, among other things because of the need for winter training'. He shared their opinion that national defences must be completed without delay, and the size of the army and navy increased. On this point he would accept no compromise, and their attitude helped to strengthen his resolve that the recommendations of the competent authorities as to the needs of the army and navy must be carried out. 'Let us work together', he said to them, 'and this important matter will find its solution. The generations that are past and the generations that are to come will hold us responsible for this our decision. May God help us not to fail in it'.[2]

Thunderous applause greeted his speech. Though the guards had been doubled at the palace that afternoon, there was no disturbance, apart from a few dissenting shouts of 'Long live the republic!' and 'Long live President Staaff!' The band struck up the National Anthem, sung in unison by the whole assembly, after which the King retired amid vociferous cheering. The procession then reformed and marched through the palace, passing before the King, Queen and royal family who were seated in state at the upper end of the reception rooms surrounded by the whole court. The procession broke up after leaving the palace, and a deputation of 200 presented a petition to Herr Staaff. In the evening, 2,000 of the Peasants were invited to supper at the palace.

On 8 February the Swedish Labour Party staged its own counter-demonstration. Several thousand workmen, flying banners representing different trade unions, marched to the Home Office and presented an address to Herr Staaff declaring their opposition to any increase in the army or navy, and demanding the adoption of a system of gradual disarmament. The foreign minister, Count Ehrensvärd, declared that Swedish foreign policy remained one of 'absolutely free and independent neutrality'. Staaff told the workmen that increased armaments were an absolute necessity for the safety and independence of Sweden.

The King discussed his address to the Peasants in private with Staaff, who appeared satisfied by the meeting; but that weekend the left wing of the governing party brought pressure to bear on the prime minister. He demanded that the King should publicly declare that his speech, not having been approved in advance by government, had been no action of state, thus enabling if not calling upon him to retract his promises, and requested a binding assurance from the King regarding advance agreement on any such future speeches. King Gustav refused to assent to such conditions. Accordingly Staaff resigned on 10 February, complaining that he and his ministry had not been made aware of the tenor of the King's speech to the Peasants before it was delivered, and that certain assurances conveyed therein had not been constitutionally considered in council. The King maintained that no decision had been conveyed in his speech; matters had been left in the hands of his constitutional advisers, who would submit to him their advice in council. He added that the constitution did not deprive him of the right to speak his mind freely to the Swedish people; he would not countenance any move 'to deprive myself of the right to speak freely to the Swedish nation'.

In view of the popular demonstrations of loyalty from cheering crowds before the palace, and a procession of over 2,000 university students who marched from the Stockholm railway station to the palace singing patriotic songs and cheering when the King came out to thank them, it was evident with whom the sympathies of the country lay.

To succeed Staaff the King appointed Baron Louis de Geer, governor of Christianstad and a moderate Liberal senator, to form a new cabinet. He failed, and after lengthy negotiations King Gustav entrusted Hjalmar Hammarskjöld with the seals of office. The new government thus formed, lacking sufficient parliamentary support to justify its existence, stood for the King's personal power. Its first act was to dissolve the second chamber and call for new elections, as a result of which Hammarskjöld remained in power for three years.

By testing his prerogative as a constitutional monarch to its limits, King Gustav V had trod a delicate line. He had attempted by extra-parliamentary means to force through the royal will in the defence question, without respect to the country's legitimate government or the majority in the lower chamber. This went beyond the defence question, and raised the issue of whether the country should be governed by the King, personally, or by government, led by the prime minister.

Hjalmar Branting, the leader of the Social Democrats, declared that the King's manner of formulating his speech was an unmistakeable declaration of war: 'His Majesty, by grace of the peasants' petition, can be sure the gauntlet will be taken up by the real people.' In this critical state of affairs, the Bernadotte dynasty's future seemed less assured than ever before.

The future of the monarchy itself was on the point of being questioned. By his courtyard speech, the King had unequivocally taken sides in the most important issue of the day. The speech had been formulated after discussions with private advisers, and without reference to his cabinet. Officially the King had exceeded his authority; nonetheless, he was within the bounds of the constitution as it existed in 1914. All legal and political authorities agreed that the King had every right to promote a policy of his own, providing he could get a government willing to assume constitutional responsibility for its implementation.

King Gustav V had spoken up on behalf of the monarch's personal power. His speech had been drafted by the explorer Sven Hedin, but the King himself had added the crucial turns of phrase, and thus assumed responsibility for it. His intervention could easily have ended in catastrophe for himself and the Bernadotte dynasty. Demands for his abdication and the declaration of a Swedish republic were heard from some of the socialists.

Nevertheless the mood of the time, as well as that of his people, was on his side. More than the main party leaders, like other crowned heads throughout the continent he had understood the true state of European affairs. He knew he was right to insist on a strong defence policy for the country. European eyes turned on Sweden with interest. In Berlin, the demonstration by King Gustav with the Peasants against his ministry was the subject of much comment. German ministers, disregarding Scandinavian cohesion and Swedish neutrality, saw Sweden as 'a weight in the German scale against Russia'. The right-wing Berlin journal *Kreuzzeitung* called on Sweden to repair her 'neglected Navy' and build Dreadnoughts.

Though King Gustav V had no intention of dancing to Berlin's tune, whatever the extent of his privately pro-German sympathies, the uneasy peace of the continent was about to explode into armed conflict. Some four and a half months later, on 28 June, several hundred miles away, in Sarajevo, the shots rang out that claimed the lives of Archduke Francis Ferdinand and his wife Sophie. The heir to the throne of Austria-Hungary and his wife were not merely the victims of yet another royal assassination; they were the first casualties of the war which was shortly to convulse most of Europe.

Meanwhile, in Norway King Haakon VII and his kingdom were celebrating the century of the free Norwegian constitution. The highlight of the programme was a national exhibition in Christiania which he opened on 15 May, when he and Queen Maud were shown over sections devoted to Norwegian industry, handicrafts, fisheries and agriculture. Various other commemorative events followed, including a special celebration service at Trondheim Cathedral. A large international regatta was held at Horten in the third week of July 1914, and it finished with many of the competitors sailing behind the King's ship to Christiania for a gala distribution of prizes on 22 July.

Emperor William had been following his customary summer routine of cruising at Balholm in the Sognefiord. Distressed by the assassination of Archduke Francis Ferdinand and his wife, with whom he had personally been on the best of terms, his initial reaction was to try and cancel his holiday. His ministers at Berlin had persuaded him that the situation in the Balkans gave no real cause for alarm, and it was important to preserve an air of imperturbability.

Gradually it became apparent that international tension was accelerating. On 25 July Prince Henry of the Netherlands arrived in Norway. King Haakon showed him around the national exhibition and entertained him at dinner at Bygdöy, with the president of the Storting and foreign ministers among the guests. President Poincaré of France, at that time visiting Russia, was expected in Christiania at the end of the month. However, that same day the German Emperor left Balholm in great haste for Berlin, and Poincaré likewise returned to his capital.

On Monday, 27 July, the Norwegian newspapers remarked that war between Austria-Hungary and Serbia was inevitable. At a Cabinet council on 31 July, King Haakon raised the issue of precautionary measures. He felt that the Norwegian navy should be fully mobilized, and coastal defences adequately manned. He also thought that the government should ensure there was sufficient grain in the country, but the prime minister, Gunnar Knudsen, believed this to be unnecessary. Knudsen was confident that tension would soon subside; and that if war was to break out, it would be over within a few months if not weeks. King Haakon was less optimistic, and suspected that any conflict would be prolonged. With his naval experience, he appreciated and recognized the strategic value of naval bases along the Norwegian coast, and feared that either Britain or Germany would exert pressure to acquire these bases. More energetic emergency preparations, he believed, would reduce the risk of Norway being pressurized to join one side or the other.

Shortly after the outbreak of war in August 1914, the Norwegian government reaffirmed its neutrality. A declaration was made jointly with Sweden, announcing a firm intention 'to maintain the neutrality of the respective kingdoms as against all the belligerent powers'. In December all three Scandinavian Kings met at Malmö to proclaim solidarity and joint neutrality. It was the first time since the separation of Norway from Sweden that their heads of state had met in friendly conference. No practical results were achieved, beyond the dubious reckoning that it had been a good public relations exercise.

Certainly it did nothing to lessen the fears of King Haakon and King Christian that Sweden might enter the war on the German side. The pro-German feelings of King Gustav V and his German-born consort were well known, as was the Swedish economy's dependence on exports to Germany. The Swedish government did not entirely share this bias. The Crown Princess of Sweden told Queen Mary in a letter (24 January 1915) that she had recently met the minister for foreign affairs: 'he happened to sit next to me at dinner & he was about as much against Germany & the Germans as any neutral could be'.[3]

The outbreak of war saw intense efforts on the part of Queen Victoria of Sweden and the Crown Princess in humanitarian causes. The Queen's initiative resulted in the formation of the Queen's Central Committee, the task of which was to organize individual aid programmes and their mutual coordination, and with what was being done by the state and local authorities. She presided over the working committee, which gave financial assistance to families to which mobilization had brought economic distress; provided kitchen equipment to municipalities which could not afford it, but undertook to feed children free; presented carbide lamps to poor homes and allocated considerable sums to those suffering from Spanish influenza and polio. Infant care equipment was distributed to the poorest municipalities in the extreme north. Altogether the Central Committee provided several million kroner to needy persons throughout Sweden during and immediately after the war years.

Because of her ill health, the Queen's role was limited. Crown Princess Margaret took on a more active role, starting a sewing society which knitted socks and rolled bandages for the troops. Before long she had over a hundred active helpers, and by late autumn 1914 they had about 2,000 garments ready for despatch to the Swedish Hospital in London, to the Red Cross and to poor people in Stockholm and elsewhere. In addition she helped to trace missing British soldiers and prisoners of war in Germany, a task which as Crown Princess of a neutral country she was well placed to perform.

As the country which shared a border with Germany, Denmark was the most vulnerable of the Scandinavian nations. Virtually defenceless and with no hope of outside assistance if Germany crossed her frontier, Denmark was determined to remain neutral as far as possible. On the night of 4 August, when England declared war on Germany, the Germans began to lay mines in the southern side of the Langeland Belt. Next day, the Danish government was asked by the German minister in Copenhagen whether they wished to close the Great Belt to both parties at war. The Danish cabinet hesitated between mobilization and the laying of mines in the Great Belt and the Little Belt. In the end they decided that the two should be mined, that auxiliary forces should be called up to fill the divisions of the line, and that the possibility of forming a Coalition government should be carefully examined.

Aware that England would surely disapprove of the laying of mines in the Belts, King Christian addressed a telegram to King George V, who replied that he well understood Denmark's delicate position. King Christian was grateful for British sympathy in the face of German aggression and curiosity, holding out against demands from his powerful southern neighbour to send to Kiel the news from Danish coastguards, or maps of Danish mines. Such questions, he informed Germany coldly, were an affair of honour and Denmark could not do more for them than she had already done.[4]

That autumn the British threatened to stop the sale of fuel oil and coal to Norway, and Norwegian authorities began to intervene against the buying-up of fish by the Germans. King Haakon repeatedly advised his government not to get itself into such a position that Norway was brought into conflict with Britain. He understood that pressure on the Scandinavian countries was likely to increase; the Germans would try to extend their influence in Sweden, and the Norwegian government ought not to be too sure that Sweden would manage to withstand the German pressure.

In the spring of 1915, King Christian X suggested to King George V that Copenhagen would be the ideal venue for a peace conference. It was a suggestion which had the support of the German Emperor William and Tsar Nicholas II of Russia, who were on opposite sides. King George was tempted, but knew that he was unlikely to be able to persuade his government to agree:

> . . . the end of this appalling war still seems a long way off. We cannot be satisfied with anything but an honourable and lasting peace. The world will not stand a repetition of such an outrage to humanity and civilization. The allies are every week in a better position to carry on the war than they were at its beginning, while it is fair to assume that our enemies are weakening.[5]

During the war years Queen Alexandrine helped to forward letters between royal relations on opposing sides, copying them out and re-addressing them

Crown Princess Louise of Denmark and her elder children, 1875. Left to right: Prince Carl, later King Haakon VII of Norway; Princess Louise; Prince Christian

The Danish royal family at the time of the engagement of Princess Alexandra (seated right), early 1863. Others, left to right: Princess Dagmar; Prince Frederick; Prince Waldemar (front); Princess Christian; her husband Prince Christian, soon to become King Christian IX; Princess Thyra; Prince William, soon to become King George I of the Hellenes

København. Amalienborg.

Amalienborg, Copenhagen, c. 1900 with Crown Princess Louise and Crown Prince Frederick (later King Frederick VIII) of Denmark, inset. The equestrian statue is of King Frederick V

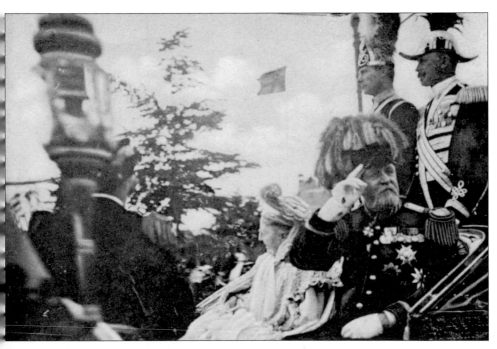

King Oscar II and Queen Sophia of Sweden, 1905

Family group at Fredensborg, Denmark, September 1900. Standing, left to right: Princess Frederick of Schaumburg-Lippe; her mother Louise, Crown Princess of Denmark; Prince Gustav of Denmark; Prince Julius of Denmark; Thyra, Duchess of Cumberland; Ernest, Duke of Cumberland; Prince Carl of Denmark; Prince Christian of Denmark; Princess Alexandrine of Denmark; George Mikhailovitch, Grand Duke of Russia, and his fiancée, Princess Marie of Greece; King George I of the Hellenes; Princess Thyra of Denmark. Seated centre, left to right: Frederick, Crown Prince of Denmark; Marie, Dowager Tsarina of Russia; King Christian IX; Alexandra, Princess of Wales; Princess Carl of Denmark. Seated front: Princess Dagmar of Denmark; Princess Alexandra of Hanover; Grand Duchess Olga of Russia; Prince Christian of Schaumburg-Lippe; Prince Christian of Hanover

*King Haakon VII and Queen Maud
of Norway*

*King Haakon VII, Queen Maud and Prince
Alexander*

Crown Prince Gustav Adolf of Sweden and Princess Margaret of Connaught at the time of their engagement, 1905

726

King Frederick VIII of Denmark

Queen Louise of Denmark

Princess Frederick of Schaumburg-Lippe

The Swedish royal family at the christening of Prince Sigvard, second son of Prince Gustav Adolf, 1907. Standing, left to right: Prince Eugen, Duke of Närke; Prince William, Duke of Södermanland; Crown Prince Gustav; Prince Gustav Adolf, holding his eldest son and namesake; Carl, Duke of Västergötland. Seated, left to right: Thérèse, Duchess of Dalecarlia (widow of the King's brother, Prince August); King Oscar II; Crown Princess Margaret, holding Prince Sigvard; Princess Ingeborg, Duchess of Västergötland, holding Princess Astrid. Seated at front: Princess Margaret, holding Prince Sigvard; Queen Sophia; Princess Ingeborg, Duchess of Västergötland, holding Princess Astrid.

herself for security reasons. It was thanks to her efforts that the Russian-born Dowager Duchess of Saxe-Coburg, widow of Queen Victoria's second son Alfred, was able to keep in touch with her sister-in-law Grand Duchess Vladimir and her two elder daughters, Queen Marie of Roumania and Grand Duchess Cyril. At the same time King Christian's uncle Prince Waldemar was president of the Danish Red Cross. When prisoners passed through Denmark from belligerent countries to be exchanged, his numerous connections in foreign states proved invaluable.

The war was indirectly responsible for Denmark's loss of one of her last remaining overseas possessions, the West Indian islands. They had acquired particular strategic importance with the opening of the Panama Canal in 1914, and two years later the United States opened negotiations to purchase them. The cabinet in Copenhagen asked the Riksdag to approve the sale, on the grounds that the islands' population was declining, and they were a financial drain on the national economy. The parties were far from united on the issue, some maintaining that it would be an abrogation of the country's responsibilities, and others wishing the matter to be placed in abeyance until after the war. A plebiscite produced a large majority vote in favour of the sale, much to King Christian's regret. It was a wrench to relinquish territory which had belonged to Denmark for two hundred years. He had appreciated that America was afraid Germany would force Denmark to give her the islands for a war harbour, and that the last thing America wanted was a German submarine station just outside the Channel of Panama.[6] Nevertheless the Danish treasury benefited by $25,000,000, and the territory reverted to its original name, the Virgin Islands.

King Haakon feared that Sweden would enter the war on the side of Germany, chiefly because of the importance of the Swedish economy and its exports. To his relief the government in Stockholm remained prudently neutral, while asserting its right to trade with belligerent countries. This arrangement favoured Germany in particular; the blockade was an important weapon in Britain's fight against that country, and the Allies stopped a large percentage of Scandinavian trade, which affected exports to Germany and also caused an acute food shortage in Sweden by the summer of 1916. King Gustav V was moved to complain to King George V of Great Britain (16 July 1916) of the fact that 'certain measures taken by the British authorities regarding our trade seems – according to our views – not to be consistent with our rights and interests.'[7] King George V regretted the inconvenience, suggesting that the matter could be solved by a general agreement which would secure for Sweden and her people the free importation of sufficient goods for domestic needs, while assuring that none of these would go to 'my enemies'.

In the autumn of 1916, an expansion of German submarine warfare

NORTHERN CROWNS: *The Kings of Modern Scandinavia*

against Norwegian shipping aroused strong feelings throughout Norway; the territorial waters were subsequently closed to all foreign submarines, a move which primarily affected German vessels. A strong reply from Germany increased fears in Norway of war; a Norwegian rejoinder on 8 November was cautiously expressed, maintaining that the submarine decree placed all belligerent powers on an equal footing and repudiating the German suggestion that the ban had been introduced under British pressure. King Haakon was annoyed as he had not been a party to the formulation of the reply, of which he did not receive the text before the German minister had been given the note.

Throughout the conflict, King Haakon was able to form an independent opinion on current problems by supplementing the reports of the Foreign Ministry and the newspapers with correspondence from his relations in Copenhagen and London. The British minister provided courier facilities, and the King was also kept informed with news from abroad when he received Norwegian diplomatic representatives who were called home. He repeatedly impressed on the foreign minister the importance of maintaining Norwegian neutrality, and appropriate balance between both sides so that they incurred nobody's ill will.

With several close relations on active service in the British army or navy, Queen Maud was particularly distressed at having to go so long without news from her family. Visits to Appleton House were out of question while hostilities lasted. At Christmas 1916, she wrote to Queen Mary that they had taken Prince Olav to the Opera for the first time: 'It is also the first time I go to the theatre since months as I don't care going about in these *sad times*.'[8]

Particularly distressing to the King and Queen was the sinking of many Norwegian ships with great loss of life. They had a great admiration for the merchant navy, and were deeply affected by the revelations of German espionage and sabotage of ships in Norwegian harbours in the summer of 1917. Yet King Haakon's sense of correctness made him extremely careful not to say anything unfavourable to Germany in public.

1917 brought greater worries than enemy action at sea. In March, revolution swept Russia and toppled Tsar Nicholas II. The overthrow of Tsarism had repercussions for monarchs across most of Europe, whether of belligerent powers or not. The Crown Princess of Sweden wrote to Queen Mary on 22 May 1917 of

a good deal of unrest in the country, partly owing to the shortage of food & partly owing to the Russian revolution. The Socialist party mean to have several more or less fundamental laws changed & I fear my father in law will have anything but a pleasant time! My mother in law too has contrived to make herself more & more unpopular & that falls back on him, people even go as far as comparing her to poor Alicky & say she is just as reactionary! I'm awfully sorry about it yet at the same time, I can't help agreeing with a lot of what these same people say.[9]

The anxiety of King Haakon and Queen Maud over the eventual fate of their Romanov cousins was coupled with disquiet lest the seeds of revolution should bear fruit in neutral countries. Many feared that the Russians would now negotiate separately for peace, thus strengthening the chances of German victory. Demonstrations against the high cost of living in Norway took place in several towns during the spring and summer. The royal family set an example by spending little on themselves; entertainment and visits to the theatre and concerts were reduced to a minimum, and the King impressed on his ministers that economies must be made wherever possible. It was his own idea to plough up some of the palace park for potatoes and give the surplus to the poor of the city. Several rooms in the palace were used for government offices on his recommendation.

Even so, King Haakon was not optimistic about the international situation, as the conflict dragged on into a fourth winter. 'One can not but wonder how it will all end and if it will not end by all the lower classes refusing to continue the war,' he wrote to Queen Mary in England (25 December 1917). 'The Germans and now also the Russian Socialists are hard at work even here in the neutral countries and as we are in for very hard and strong restrictions I suppose even we may have interior troubles as I fear people will not understand that we who are neutral have to put up with that sort of thing as well as everybody else.'[10]

During the previous month, all three Scandinavian monarchs had held a second meeting. King Haakon had had grave misgivings about the necessity of holding a conference at all. He was unhappy that King Gustav had taken the initiative and held it in Christiania; he felt that it would make a bad impression at home and abroad to hold large dinner parties at the palace in such hard economic times; it would damage the case for monarchy and be misunderstood in Washington, where Norway was negotiating for essential supplies on the basis of its grave difficulties. Moreover he felt that Scandinavian solidarity did not need emphasizing. In Sweden, a general election had resulted in defeat for the Conservatives and a coalition government comprising Liberals and Social Democrats, resulting in an apparent reduction in the role of the King. The Swedish government desired closer inter-Scandinavian cooperation, but King Haakon was equivocal. Sweden was regarded with suspicion in American political circles as her neutrality policy leant towards Germany.

King Haakon comforted himself with the knowledge that his brother Christian would be there as well. The two visiting monarchs arrived in Christiania on 28 November, for a meeting which was also attended by senior Norwegian ministers. After a gala dinner at the palace, King Gustav spoke of his feelings on returning to the country which four of his predecessors, and himself briefly as regent, had ruled for more than ninety years. Referring to the 'deep wound upon the thought of unity in our Scandinavian peninsula' caused by the dissolution of the union in 1905, he said he hoped to contribute to the healing of the wound by assisting in the creation of a new union of hearts and minds. Such well-intentioned words did not win over any hearts in Norway, and suggested that King Gustav was brooding on past history. Scandinavian solidarity was one thing, but the Norwegians had no desire for any further unity, let alone utterances on the subject from the King of Sweden.

King Haakon's lack of enthusiasm for this second conference was fully justified. It achieved nothing, and there was no attempt to harmonize relations between the belligerent powers. The Kings had no penetrating exchange of opinions about future prospects, and King Gustav wisely refrained from disclosing a recent offer from the German Emperor of support for an eventual Swedish occupation of the Aland Islands, if Sweden in return would show goodwill to Germany over iron exports.

By 1918 King Haakon was worried that his government's policy appeared to be damaging goodwill for Norway among the western powers. He thought he saw indications that the British did not rely upon Norway in the same way as before, as they were suspicious about the level of Norway's exports to Germany and the Central Powers. Nevertheless, personal appeals by King Haakon to King George V played a part in efforts to delay fulfilment of the British demand on 7 August for the mining of Norwegian territorial waters, in order to close the allegedly important gap in the new Anglo-American North Sea anti-submarine barrage.

To Queen Maud it often seemed, as she wrote to Queen Mary (21 May) as if the war 'would *never* end – and I feel as if I can never come home, it *is* so hard not seeing any of you for nearly five years now! But still one must always hope for the best!'[11]

The closing months of the conflict saw a brief monarchical experiment on the part of Scandinavia's remaining state, Finland. Formerly an autonomous Grand Duchy under the Tsar of Russia, Finland became theoretically independent after the Russian revolution and collapse of Tsarist rule, and declared independence formally on 6 December 1917. Although this was recognized by her Scandinavian neighbours and Russia, civil war still broke out in Finland in January 1918 between the Finnish Socialists and Communists, supported by Soviet Russia, and the White nationalist government. The prime minister, Dr Pehr Svinhufvud, appealed to Sweden for armed assistance, but Sweden was determined not to become officially involved, although Swedish volunteers joined the Finnish army. Turning to Germany for help, in April 40,000 German troops arrived in the country, and within a few weeks had helped the government to military victory.

To most of the Finns – as it had to the Norwegians in 1905 – it appeared that the best guarantee for the country's future lay in the monarchical form of government. There was sufficient respect in Finland for monarchical tradition to make the election of a King a natural move after the severing of ties with Russia. The general prestige that Germany had gained among the people made the choice of a German prince almost inevitable, and in August 1918 the government voted in favour of establishing a Finnish monarchy. At first it was proposed to invite either Grand Duke Frederick Francis IV of Mecklenburg-Schwerin, or the German Emperor's fifth son Prince Oscar, to become King. The latter seemed more favourable, as the election of the Emperor's son alone could, it was presumed, give Finland some guarantee of Germany's military support against Russia. However Germany was not attracted by the prospect of having Finland so firmly bound to her own destiny, for the preservation of Finnish independence in 1918 was apparently far from certain.

The decisive defeat of German forces in France later in August 1918 made it apparent to most observers that the end of the war was in sight. Nevertheless on 9 October the legislature elected Prince Frederick Charles of Hesse, brother-in-law of the German Emperor William, King of Finland. The Emperor looked approvingly on the choice of such a close relative. Ironically he had initially looked down on his brother-in-law and had been reluctant to give his assent to the marriage between him and his sister Margaret in 1893, only agreeing to what he disparagingly called a 'poor match' because she was his youngest sister and therefore unimportant from a dynastic point of view. However the French consul in Helsinki had warned the Finnish government that, by choosing a German prince, Finland was effectively siding with the Central Powers. Prudently, Prince Frederick Charles declared that he could not give an answer for two months, as he did not wish to place any obstacles in the way of peace.

The abdication of Emperor William on 9 November effectively sealed the fate of the embryonic Finnish monarchy. Allied heads of state made it clear that to have a German King would compromise Finnish independence, and when Prince Frederick Charles informed the government the following month that he could not accept the throne, the monarchist movement in Finland collapsed.*

---

* After a general election in March 1919 and a change of government, a bill to establish a republican form of government in Finland was passed by 163 votes to 33.

The Armistice which formally marked the cessation of hostilities in Europe was signed by Germany on 11 November. Throughout Scandinavia the news was just as welcome as it was to the heads of state of the allied powers. In particular Queen Maud of Norway, cut off from her relations in England and her beloved Appleton, wrote to Queen Mary (30 November) that she was 'wild with excitement. . . . It seems all like a *dream* to me, everything has changed so quickly from the *awful* war into peace'.[12] For King Christian X, the prospect of peace meant even more – the chance of reunion with Schleswig.

CHAPTER SEVEN

'Be ready for a popular rising'

The end of hostilities brought military peace to a war-weary Europe, but everywhere the economic scars remained – scars which the surviving monarchs realized could so easily crystallize into unrest and revolutionary activity. The idyllic summers of some thirty years before, when so many crowned heads had gathered with their wives and children at Fredensborg and Bernstorff under the watchful yet kindly eye of 'Apapa' and 'Amama', seemed but faint memories of a distant, long-vanished world. The fate of the Romanovs never ceased to cast a dark shadow. King George of the Hellenes, 'Uncle Willy', had fallen victim to the revolver of an assassin in 1913, and his son and successor, King Constantine, had been forced to abdicate four years later because he forbore to abandon his convictions that neutrality was the only sensible option for his kingdom, virtually impoverished by the Balkan wars.

In Denmark, where a quarter of the labour force had been unemployed at the beginning of 1918 as a consequence of the shortage of raw materials and factory closures, foodstuffs were rationed and wages failed to keep pace with inflation. Some industrialists were making healthy profits, as were speculators in shipping shares, and the 'goulash barons' who were making fortunes out of tinned meat exports to Germany. The Danish labour movement responded accordingly with lightning strikes and street demonstrations, actively encouraged by those who were inspired by Russian Bolshevism and aimed at the total overthrow of the existing social and economic system.

King Christian X was fearful of what he called 'the propaganda by discontent' in Danish industry, while in Norway King Haakon VII looked with unease at the activities of the country's Labour party and its national congress in March 1918 which passed a resolution demanding to reserve the right to resort to 'revolutionary mass action in the struggle for economic liberation of the working class.'

Scarcely less unsettling was the state of chaos in neighbouring Finland, which both Kings feared could move westwards if not checked. After a visit from General Mannerheim, a former officer in the Russian imperial army and standard-bearer of the 'white Russian' cause against the Bolsheviks, King Christian was thoroughly alarmed by what he heard of the state of matters in Russia. There seemed to be no limit to the cruelty and plundering, the destruction of the countryside and the general atmosphere of terror. While Finland had not been dragged down to the same depths, the Finns had no effective watch on their common frontier with Russia, and the Russians with their propaganda were difficult to keep out.[1]

At the end of the Great War, there was perhaps no more ideal, charming couple in the younger royal generations of Europe than the Crown Prince and Princess of Sweden. Crown Prince Gustav Adolf was a tall, handsome figure, gentle by nature with a kindly studious air. Having done his obligatory service in the army as a young man, he gave military matters very little thought thereafter. A student of politics and a progressive thinker, he was an ardent democrat. To some, not least to both the princesses he married, he seemed more like a professor than a future King. He never lost his interest in history, art, music or gardening. Archaeology was his abiding lifelong passion, and he was one of Sweden's foremost authorities on Chinese antiquities.

The family always knew what presents to give him at birthdays and Christmas. He thanked the Duke and Duchess of Connaught for a Christmas gift (31 December 1908) of 'splendid Chinese bowls. I think the little yellow one is nearly the best we have got at this moment. We are now going to order a special cupboard to be made for all the china and I think we shall have it fitted with electric light inside so as to be able to show it off also in the evening!'[2]

The transformation of their living quarters progressed steadily into a museum, as exactly a year later he was thanking his parents-in-law again for some more: 'I have now put it with the rest of our collection in the china-cupboard, where it looks extremely well. As we got other china as well, the whole cupboard is quite filled now and our sitting room will soon be simply creeping with chinese porcelain!'[3]

The former Princess Margaret of Connaught was a vivacious, outgoing personality who easily endeared herself far more to the Swedish nation than had her frequently absent mother-in-law. Keen to explore her new country, she often travelled incognito, under suitable escort. Sometimes she met people who were unaware of her identity, with suitably amusing results. One day she was chatting to an elderly woman, and asked her if she had seen the Crown Princess. No, was the reply, 'but my daughter has, and she says she does not think she can be English, for she smiles much, and often she kisses the babies!'[4]

The breath of fresh air which she brought to the house of Bernadotte was evident to that indefatigable royal observer, the Infanta Eulalia of Spain: 'The Queen of Sweden's health is too bad to allow her to appear in public. Hence the principal figure at Court, apart from the King, is the Crown

Princess – before her marriage Princess Margaret of Connaught – and she has contrived to give it just a touch of the elegance of the Court of St James's. I lunched with her when I was at Stockholm, and she told me how much she loves her Swedish life.'[5] The Infanta was notorious for her outspoken attacks on most royalty (not least her own relations in Spain), her ardent belief in socialism and a more equitable redistribution of wealth, but she was gracious enough to praise the Scandinavian democracies while defending the concept of republicanism elsewhere.

The Crown Prince and Princess had five children. The eldest, Prince Gustav, was born on 22 April 1906. Three more sons followed, Sigvard (1907), Bertil (1912), and Carl Johan (1916), and a daughter, Ingrid, born in 1910. A devoted mother, the Crown Princess was anxious to spend a good deal of time with her children. She had no intention of handing them over to nursery staff so much that they would grow up hardly knowing her.

Crown Princess Margaret was a talented artist. Whereas most other English princesses had been taught to paint in watercolour and content themselves with conventional academic styles, she had been instructed by the French Impressionist Madeleine Fleury and learnt to handle oils, and on a visit to Paris a couple of years before her marriage she had seen and admired the work of Claude Monet, still regarded as quite revolutionary. When not busy bringing up her five children, or working in philanthropic schemes for infant welfare and orphanages in Sweden, she found painting an ideal outlet for her energies and her artistic talents.

Her son Sigvard described her methods; 'The canvas set up on the easel, the landscape extremely schematically sketched in, trees and buildings she'd decided to paint, the paints were squeezed out of the tubes onto her palette, always in a definite order, and away she went. She was concentrated and energetic, one brushstroke quickly following another.'[6] At the Baltic Exhibition in Malmö in 1914 she exhibited ten works. Over 250 of her oils, watercolours and drawings are in the Swedish royal collection. Some fifty years after her death, the art historian Professor Oscar Reutersvärd said that certain members of court did their utmost to make sure that she was regarded as an amateur despite the fact that her work was much better than that of most contemporary Swedish landscape painters: 'like the princess in the fairy story, Margaret was doomed to lifetime imprisonment in the palace tower'.[7] The court at Stockholm was evidently just as reactionary as many of its European contemporaries in frowning on Princesses who were too talented to confine themselves to *Kinder, Kirche und Küche.*

Even artistic princes fared little better. King Gustav V's youngest brother, Prince Eugen, Duke of Närke, a talented landscape painter who supported and encouraged many similarly gifted artists in Sweden – not least his niece by marriage – was regarded disparagingly by some as a mere royal dilettante. Thankfully, art historians recognized that his work as an

77

unofficial but influential patron of the arts was achieved in spite of, rather than thanks to, his royal birth. Through his purchase of paintings at the first exhibitions of young artists of the day he assembled a magnificent collection which he donated to the nation shortly before his death in 1947, and his home, Valdemarsudde, became a leading centre for the arts in Stockholm and later an art gallery and museum.

The Crown Princess was an enthusiastic gardener and imaginative garden designer as well. One of their wedding gifts was the residence of Sofiero (literally 'Sophia's Rest', named thus by the consort of King Oscar, for whom it had been built), which she transformed after years of neglect. She also wrote and published a book, *The Garden that we made*, describing each area of the garden and many of the flowers in detail, illustrated with four of her sketches in oils, as well as several photographs by her and her husband.

Tragically the Crown Princess's life was destined to be cut short. Her charity and nursing work during the war, and the burden of constant anxiety over the fate of some of her relatives, had taxed her strength more than she was prepared to admit. Early in the new year of 1920, shortly after her thirty-eighth birthday, she learnt that she was expecting a sixth child in June. In February she suffered from ear trouble, and a few weeks later she fell ill with chickenpox. Trouble with her cheekbone aggravated the problem, and on medical advice she was sent north for a change of air. By the end of April she appeared to be making a good recovery, but she had a sudden relapse and passed away on 1 May.

It was a cruel and unexpected blow for her husband, her children, and in England for her widowed father, who was celebrating his seventieth birthday the same day. 'Such a friend!' her friend Princess Henry of Pless wrote. 'Time, trouble, risk: at need all these were as nothing.'[8]

Perhaps the most surprising tribute came from the socialist leader Hjalmar Branting, who was addressing a mass meeting when he was given news of her death. Interrupting his speech, he said, 'The sun has just set over the palace.' Afterwards he went to convey his condolences to Crown Prince Gustav in person.

Socialism and republicanism did not go hand in hand in Sweden. On the contrary, the King and Crown Prince liked and respected the socialist leaders. A future socialist prime minister of Sweden, Per Albin Hansson, was a close personal friend of the King, both in council and at the bridge table.

The widower and his five children were not deprived of a wife or stepmother for long. In June 1923 the Crown Prince and his two eldest sons came to England for a brief holiday. Within a few days of their arrival in London, it was noticed by newspaper columnists that he had appeared at Ascot with Lady Louise Mountbatten, and was also a regular guest at weekend parties at a country house in Southsea belonging to Louise's eldest brother, George, Marquess of Milford Haven. As the Mountbattens were closely related to the royal family, and as he had frequently met the Battenbergs (as they were then) before the Great War it was hardly surprising, but the fact that the Crown Prince was frequently in Louise's company was noticed.

Lady Louise, who was thirty-four in July 1923, had already passed up on one chance of becoming Queen in a foreign country. At the age of twenty she had turned down a proposal from King Manuel of Portugal. In view of the revolution which proclaimed a Portuguese republic and sent him into exile (in England) a year later, her move had been fortuitous. She confided to a friend at the time that she would never marry a King or a widower.

That she might marry the widower who would ascend the throne of Sweden one day had not escaped the family's notice. Shortly before his death in September 1921 her father Louis, Marquis of Milford Haven, had remarked prophetically that there was only one person who would suit his spinster daughter, and that was Prince Gustav; and that the only person who would suit him was Louise. They had known each other for some years, but when Prince Gustav Adolf began paying close attention to her, she tried to avoid being left alone with him. Panic-stricken, she begged her nieces Margarita and Theodora or 'Dolla', daughters of Prince and Princess Andrew of Greece and elder sisters of Prince Philip, later Duke of Edinburgh, not to leave her alone. 'Naturally we did exactly the opposite', Princess Theodora, by then Margravine of Baden, later recalled. 'Uncle Gustav' was extremely grateful to them, telling them, 'You are bricks!'[9]

What helped the Princess to make up her mind, however, was her mother's persuasion. She had always been fond of Prince Gustav Adolf, and she knew he would offer her a home and ready-made family life in a safe and pleasant country. Moreover, at her age, Louise must have realized that she would be unlikely to receive many more proposals.

There was nothing about the blushing bride, the Margravine noted, when she told them of her impending marriage. 'She seemed embarrassed, almost annoyed with herself, and with her typical inclination to understatement, especially on her own account, she explained that she thought she was much too old and thin to be a bride. And what was her bridal gown going to be like? She was certainly not going to wear white!'[10]

Despite her reservations, not the least of which were connected with leaving England for a strange country, Prince Gustav Adolf proposed and she accepted. Reactions in Sweden were guarded, chiefly as the government was uncertain as to whether the Mountbattens were of royal blood or not; the heir to the Swedish throne would be debarred from the succession if he married a commoner. To allay anxieties Stanley Baldwin, the British prime minister, produced a copy of the official printed list of precedence at Court of the members of the royal family. It confirmed that, by special direction of

King George V, their names had remained on the list when they received their new names and title.

After their initial shyness, the young motherless children soon took to their stepmother. The couple were married in the Chapel Royal at St James's Palace on 3 November at a ceremony arranged mainly by King George V, the groom looking uncharacteristically military in the uniform of a Swedish general, while the bride wore a dress of silvery white silk (notwithstanding her pre-wedding protest), made from material sent to her from Darmstadt by her uncle Ernest, former Grand Duke of Hesse and the Rhine.

Lady Astor, Conservative Member of Parliament for the Sutton division of Plymouth, who numbered several members of British and European royalty among her friends, lent them her house at Sandwich, Kent, for their honeymoon. During the years ahead the outspoken American-born politician would form a close relationship with the Crown Prince and Princess. She was regarded as something of a radical by the Conservative standards of the day, and it was remarked on by mutual friends that the couple's outlook on life and views of the role of monarchy in the twentieth century were as advanced as her own.

King Gustav V and Queen Victoria warmly welcomed their new daughter-in-law into the family when she and Crown Prince Gustav Adolf returned to Sweden in December after the honeymoon. Elsewhere in Scandinavia, the same hospitality was not always extended so readily.

After escaping from Bolshevik Russia in 1919, the Dowager Tsarina had settled briefly in England with her elder sister Alexandra, now the Queen Mother. It proved an unsatisfactory arrangement. 'Alix' and 'Minnie', once so close, now found in their querulous old age that they merely got on each others' nerves. The Empress Marie returned to her native Denmark, and was installed in a wing of the Amalienborg Palace, close to her nephew, King Christian X. The Grand Duchess Olga, her daughter, and husband, joined her in 1920. The King disliked having his impoverished relations so close, and made no effort to hide his feelings.

One evening Grand Duchess Olga and her mother were sitting quietly knitting in the living room of the palace when the door opened and a footman walked in. Rather nervously, he said in a whisper that His Majesty had sent him over to ask them to switch off their lights, as the last electricity bill he had had to pay was excessive. In her anger, all colour drained from the Empress's face. She rang for one of her servants, and in front of the footman, she ordered him to turn on all the lights in her part of the palace from cellar to attic.

Sometimes King Christian would come and stroll around the rooms, making it obvious that every piece of furniture and all the ornaments belonged to him. If he suspected that anything was missing, he would ask her sharply whether she had pawned it. Surely she could sell her jewellery, he would insist coldly, if she was in financial difficulties. Relations became so strained that eventually her other nephew, King George V of Great Britain, settled an annual pension on her and helped her to move from the Amalienborg to Hvidøre. Although the villa was owned jointly by all three daughters of King Christian IX, Queen Alexandra – now too infirm to travel outside England – and the Duchess of Cumberland made it over to their less fortunate sister. While King Christian X was grateful that his kinsman in England should come to the rescue in this way, he was reluctant to show it. In 1925 the Soviet government, badly in need of foreign currency, despatched a large quantity of confiscated Romanov jewellery and treasures for sale in England, and Queen Mary purchased some, including a collection of Fabergé eggs. That King George V and Queen Mary should apparently have first refusal on material to which he felt he had an equal, if not prior, claim, rankled deeply with King Christian.

The Dowager Empress's humiliations continued after her move. When King Victor Emmanuel III and Queen Elena of Italy paid a state visit to Denmark, she and her daughters longed to meet the Russian-educated Queen, but King Christian made it clear that he had no intention of inviting them to the official banquet at the Amalienborg, or any of the other festivities. He merely sent a telephone message to say that he and his guests would call at Hvidøre one afternoon. She said nothing, but waited until the royal party arrived. They were met by a humble footman, who informed them that Her Imperial Majesty was indisposed and would not receive anyone that day. The King was furious, but could not bring himself to say anything as he realized he had brought the snub on himself.

His attitude towards the Romanov relations now fallen on hard times was not shared by the rest of the Danish royal family. In particular Queen Alexandrine was so ashamed of his behaviour towards the aunt and cousins who had endured such tragedy that on more than one occasion she burst into tears.

The Dowager Empress had not, however, been singled out on her own for such treatment. As his granddaughter, later Queen Margrethe, readily admitted, King Christian X had a reputation for being harsh towards the entire family. The Dowager Empress was unused to taking care of her money, while the King was inclined to be parsimonious as well as domineering. But, Queen Margrethe continued, she very much doubted whether the Empress of Russia 'allowed herself to be dictated to by her far younger nephew. She was a very determined lady.'[11] Having once defiantly stood her ground against a mob of Bolshevik soldiers who had ransacked her room and possessions during the Russian revolution, she was unlikely to let one of her nephews – even if he was her King – get off lightly.

In her old age the Dowager Empress had grown apart from her elder sister Queen Alexandra; there was an even deeper gulf between them and their younger sister Thyra, Duchess of Cumberland. They had never been close, and divided loyalties during the war drove them still further apart. Although the Duke and Duchess of Cumberland had long harboured a perfectly understandable grudge against Prussia, the hatchet with Emperor William had been buried with the engagement and marriage of their son, Prince Ernest Augustus to the Emperor's only daughter, Princess Victoria Louise, in May 1913. For 'Alix' and 'Minnie', such a match must have seemed like betrayal of almost everything they and their mother had stood for. The collapse of Germany in 1918 might have been seen as divine retribution for Bismarck's spiritual heirs by the elder sisters, but certainly not by the more Germanized Thyra.*

A few years later, the appearance of a woman claiming to be Tsar Nicholas's daughter, Grand Duchess Anastasia, provided another bone of contention between the Dowager Empress and the Duchess of Cumberland. The former was convinced that her claims were fraudulent and that she was nothing but an impostor. Nonetheless Thyra and their surviving brother Prince Waldemar showed what she saw as an unseemly interest in the matter. Largely out of kindness Waldemar sent the impoverished woman some money, while Thyra begged her sister to investigate the affair, if only to clear up the case once and for all. The Dowager Empress refused to have anything to do with it, but much against her wishes, her daughter Grand Duchess Olga decided to go and see for herself. In 1925 she spent four days by the bedside of the sick woman, and as a result had to agree that her mother was right. 'Anastasia', she concluded, was undoubtedly a fraud.

With the defeat of Germany in 1918, many throughout Europe looked forward to a permanent peace settlement based on President Wilson's Fourteen Points. The Austro-Prussian peace treaty in 1866 had made provision for the duchy of Schleswig to be returned to Denmark if a majority vote by the inhabitants in a referendum should demand thus. No referendum was held, and to great Danish fury Germany and Austria called for abrogation of the clause in 1878. After the armistice the leaders of the Danish-speaking population of Schleswig appealed to the government in Copenhagen to request the Allies to permit them the principle of self-determination, in other words the redrawing of national frontiers in accordance with the wishes of those who lived within them. To every Dane this meant the return of Schleswig. Some in Denmark thought that the

* Thyra, Duchess of Cumberland, outlived her husband by ten years. She died, aged seventy-nine, in March 1933, the month after Adolf Hitler came to power as Chancellor of Germany.

duchy should be returned complete as it had been seized by force, but all political parties backed the cabinet's decision to ask the victorious powers to arrange referenda in northern and mid-Schleswig.

A clause in the treaty of Versailles, signed in June 1919, called for the Dano-German border to be fixed in accordance with the results of plebiscites to be held early the following year. The electorate of North Schleswig returned a three-quarters majority for reunion with Denmark, but national euphoria was cut short by the second set of results in the thoroughly Germanized south, which showed an even more overwhelming majority the other way.

Despite the southern pro-German vote, at the opening of the state council in February, the prime minister Theodore Carl Zahle announced triumphantly that telegraphic reports proclaimed to the world what the people of North Schleswig had been repeating for the last fifty-six years, namely that they were Danish and intended to remain Danish. In his address to the council, King Christian said:

> When my dear grandfather fifty-six years ago took farewell of the population whose descendants will now soon return to Denmark, he interpreted the nation's pain at dismemberment, but in his heart he preserved the hope that the day of satisfaction, justice, and happiness would come. Undeserved it has fallen to my lot to see the great day. In deep gratitude to God, remembering the living and the dead who have fought to preserve Danish nationality in Schleswig, and looking with hope to the future, I send from the State Council the first welcome to our returning countrymen, whose long and hard exile has only increased and strengthened their love for the land of their fathers. God preserve Denmark and the Danish people.[12]

All the same, national rejoicing could not mask the unrest below the surface in Denmark. Political dissension with minority governments and coalition ministries, economic instability and industrial antagonism were all coming to a head, in what came to be known as the 'Easter crisis'. Even the crown, and the personal role of King Christian, were to be called into question.

The cabinet of Zahle, who had been prime minister since 1913, had promised a general election after the war. Now that time had come, he declared that he was willing to dissolve the Riksdag, but wanted a newer and fairer electoral bill to be passed first, as well as certain alterations to the constitution. Both houses in the Riksdag failed to agree. At the same time some of the government's supporters in the Folketing, M. Marott, the Socialist leader, and the Radicals, M. Mösgaard and M. Kjöldsen, dissociated themselves from the government on the question of the prospective redrawing of the Schleswig zone. Their defection almost wiped out the government's majority in the Folketing. Opposition groups refrained from moving a vote of no confidence in the Folketing before the Easter recess as some of their supporters would not oppose the government's passive policy in the Schleswig question. However they issued a manifesto declaring that the government had lost its majority in the Folketing and the electorate.

As a result the King asked Zahle to dissolve the Folketing. When he refused the King dismissed him, and asked the lawyer Otto Liebe to lead a caretaker government of officials to supervise immediate elections. This, the Radicals and Socialists maintained, was in effect a royal *coup d'état*. While Radicals inveighed against an 'irresponsible camarilla' around the King, the Socialists, already angered by a threat from employers of a national lock-out in response to strikes for higher wages, called for a republic. It was generally overlooked that their sovereign's action was in accordance with the Danish Constitution, which stated expressly that 'The King appoints and dismisses his ministers'. In this he was supported by the Conservatives and Liberals.

Nevertheless the Executive Committee of Amalgamated Trade Unions in Copenhagen sent King Christian an ultimatum: if the constitutional regime was not re-established by the recall of the Zahle cabinet before 9.30 a.m. on 30 March, all government post offices, postal services and railways would be brought to a standstill after the Easter holiday. Left-wing elements became excited at the prospect of a general strike in Denmark, and an extra edition of *Socialdermokraten* on 29 March rallied its supporters with a call to arms: 'Be ready for a popular rising stronger than that which in 1848 overturned absolutism'.[13]

For a couple of days, the situation looked uncertain. Large crowds gathered in the main thoroughfares of the capital, patrolled by police vehicles, while Amalienborg Square and adjoining streets were closed by police cordons. Some observers detected 'an air of expectancy, resembling that of the first nights of the war'. Later that week, after the police had scaled down security and opened all the streets, there were demonstrations outside the Amalienborg Palace, with a few cries of 'Down with the King!', and 'Long live the republic!' Foreign correspondents were quick to conclude that the crowds did not have a revolutionary character; the only outward sign of unrest was a small amount of window-breaking and 'ruffianism'. The Socialists had expressly called for no acts of violence, and merely advised 'a revolution of folded arms'. They had evidently realized that Denmark was an unlikely breeding-ground for revolution and no longer spoke of a republic, directing their rhetorical fire instead on the 'poisonous Court snakes twisting themselves round the Crown'.

By 4 April the crisis was over. The King agreed to accept a new caretaker ministry agreeable to all parties pending fresh elections. Liebe resigned, the Riksdag was reconvened, electoral law reform measures were passed, and elections took place at the end of April. The trade unions rescinded their threat of strike action, and the industrial situation largely returned to normal.

Once the redrawn border was agreed, King Christian signed the North Schleswig Reunion Act on 9 July. The day was celebrated as a holiday throughout Denmark, and at 11 a.m. salutes from the forts announced that the Act had been signed. Church bells rang for an hour, and thanksgiving services were held in all the main churches, followed by memorial services in the afternoon at the graves of those killed in the Dano-German wars, with wreaths placed on the graves of allies who had died in Copenhagen during repatriation.

That afternoon the King and Queen and their suite left in the royal yacht *Danebrøg* for Kolding, Jutland, to re-enter the reunited districts in state. After mooring early the following morning, the King and rest of the royal party drove off in cars to enter the recovered districts. A few yards north of the old frontiers, the King and his sons left their cars and continued on horseback. As the King crossed the border, resplendent on a white charger, he was greeted by thousands of people from the whole countryside, while the Queen and others followed in cars. A Schleswig Dane welcomed the King, referring to the fact that the last time a Danish sovereign had been in Schleswig was when King Christian VII visited the soldiers' entrenchments on Duppel in 1784. The King rode at the head of the royal procession, passing through eighteen triumphal arches on the first twelve kilometres beyond the frontier. All the way young girls stood at the side of the road throwing flowers in his path. One child was lifted up by the King onto his horse and he entered the town of Christiansfeld with her in front of him. Short services were held in Tyrstrop and Haderslev, where the King arrived at midday. By this time he was in some discomfort, having been bruised by a fall when he mounted his horse shortly before entering the town.

After further festivities and visits to the graves of those killed in the Dano-German war, the King returned to his yacht and they sailed to Apenrade, for a procession through the town and reception by local officials. The royal party returned to the yacht, spending the night on board. On the following day, while the town of Sonderborg was richly festooned with the red and white of Danish flags, a reunion festival was held on the site of the battlefield at Duppel Hill.

With his regular journeys from Norway to England with Queen Maud, or to Denmark with both parents, it was proving difficult to provide Crown Prince Olav with regular schooling. As he talked English at home, some of the ministers voiced concern lest he should be neglecting his education as a Norwegian. King Haakon assured them that there was no risk of his son being unable to manage at a Norwegian school, but he understood their anxiety. In January 1914 he appointed an army lieutenant, Nicolai Ostgaard, to the general development and physical general training of the Crown Prince. Ostgaard was an excellent skier, and the King was delighted when his son took fourth place in a ski-jumping competition at Halling School and won third prize in a rally with more than three hundred other boys taking part.

The Crown Prince inherited his parents' love of music. Attending a court concert in London one evening he was unimpressed by the performance of an opera diva, who was apparently not at her best that evening. He asked his parents if it was true that she sang to people in prisons. 'I believe it is', the King replied gravely, 'so remember that, if you ever feel tempted to do wrong'.[14]

In July 1921 he celebrated his eighteenth birthday, the age at which the Constitution allowed for his admission to the Cabinet council. When he was admitted for the first time, the King presented him with an address warning him to heed the constitutional implications of his position; 'not to take any standpoint in matters which may be of a political nature without having heard your advisers, nor to express yourself to friends or others in ways which may restrict your position and your decision, when the matter in due course comes up for consideration in Cabinet council. Through the press and in other ways you can find guidance in such matters. But never forget that it is your councillors who in all public questions have the responsibility towards the people.'[15]

The Crown Prince also began a three-year course for infantry cadets at the disused naval base of Frederiksvern. The King had told Knudsen, prime minister, that he thought it desirable for the Prince to undergo an officer's training at the Military College, as it was a useful lesson to have to obey orders, and it would be good preparation for regular military service. Knudsen suggested that the Prince could quite well be exempted from military service, but the King insisted that his son should not be granted any undue privilege.

While undertaking his military training, Crown Prince Olav continued to compete successfully in a number of skiing events. By the time he left Military College, he was already one of Norway's most expert amateur skiers, and also renowned for his skill in sailing.

His coming-of-age on 2 July 1924 was celebrated both at Frederiksvern, where he was now a senior sergeant in the third-year class, and at the palace, where he attended a cabinet council and took the oath to the constitution. In September he graduated from the Military College with excellent marks. Thereafter he was sent to Balliol College, Oxford, to take a two-year diploma course in Political Science and Economics. Three weeks after leaving Frederiksvern, he went to England with his mother. The King wrote to the Master of Balliol College to say that he hoped his son would get on well quickly and find his feet, and adding his wish that 'the photographers should not bother him too much'.[16]

King Haakon visited the College in January 1926, and the Prince completed his studies in summer 1927. While in England he undertook various representative duties, including the laying of the foundation stone for the new Norwegian Seamen's Church in London. In July accompanied his father for the first time at the formal dissolution of the Storting. When King Haakon went abroad in December, the Crown Prince's flag was hoisted for the first time over the palace, and a salute was fired at Akershus to mark the fact that he was now acting as Regent.

Queen Maud was happy to remain out of the public eye as much as possible. Fourteen years as a Queen Consort had done nothing to help her overcome her dislike of publicity. Her health had not improved, and with age she suffered increasingly from intense headaches and neuralgia, aggravated by the cold damp Norwegian weather. She preferred their country residence, Bygdöy, to the palace, where she particularly enjoyed tending to her garden.

As ever she kept in touch punctiliously with her relations, writing frequent letters abroad. She still spent several months of each year in England, generally staying at Appleton in the autumn, returning to Norway for Christmas and the New Year, and returning to Appleton early in January. Accompanying her were a lady-in-waiting and sometimes an English secretary, who looked after her finances, including the running of Appleton House. King Haakon generally took the train to Bergen to say goodbye and, on her arrival home again, to welcome her back on her return.

Never really at ease in Norway outside the family circle, she did not succeed in acquiring more than a rudimentary knowledge of national politics, and she always had difficulty with reading the Norwegian press. Yet she supported the King in every way she could, and was the first to react to anything which implied criticism of him. All the same, it never seemed to concern her unduly that with such prolonged absences on her part people might wonder about the state of their marriage. It had not taken her long after their wedding in 1896 to chafe at her husband's lengthy spells of naval service; and while it might be charitable to put the birth of their only child, after seven years of married life, down to ill-health, this continued leading of virtually separate lives, especially after the Great War, suggested that all might not be well between them.

In November 1925 her mother Queen Alexandra died at Sandringham. King Haakon, Queen Maud and Crown Prince Olav, as well as King Christian X, were all present at her funeral and burial in the Albert Memorial Chapel at Windsor. King Haakon's friendly manner endeared himself to the guests at coffee after the service. Noticing a young man of eighteen, his distant cousin Lord Frederick Cambridge, standing forlornly on his own, he strode over with hand outstretched. 'You don't know me', he said genially. 'Let me introduce myself. I'm old Norway.'[17]

Dowager Queen Louise of Denmark, widow of King Frederick VIII, followed her sister-in-law to the grave four months later. Since the death of her husband she had led an increasingly secluded life, devoting herself to her charities and needlework, and living with her unmarried children, Princesses Thyra and Dagmar, and Prince Gustav, until Dagmar married Lieutenant Jörgen de Castenskiold in 1922.* When the Queen Dowager became ill with pneumonia Madame de Castenskiold rushed to her bedside, and Princess Ingeborg was summoned but arrived just too late. She passed away on 20 March 1926, and was laid to rest beside her husband in Roskilde Cathedral.

Regular exchange visits between the cousins in Norway and Sweden continued throughout these years. King Haakon's sister Princess Ingeborg and her husband, Prince Carl, brought their daughters, Princesses Märtha and Astrid, to stay in Oslo in 1925 and 1926, while King Haakon and Crown Prince Olav were among the guests at Princess Astrid's wedding in Stockholm to Prince Leopold, heir to the Belgian throne. If Queen Maud ever wondered lest her husband might be lonely while she was in England, it was some consolation – or at least it set her conscience at rest – to know that his sister and youngest brother paid him annual visits, while every October he went to Copenhagen to meet relations, friends and former shipmates.

The King never had time to be lonely. When not visiting friends and family, he was much preoccupied with the political climate of Norway, where the left-wing government frequently gave the impression of indifference to its royal family, if not downright hostility. The classlessness of Norwegian society did not prevent socialists from venting their anger on 'capitalistic reactionaries' at home, in industry and labour disputes, or on foreign powers. The King was anxious when Britain broke off diplomatic relations with the Soviet Union in 1927, a move which provoked considerable Communist agitation against the British and their allies. When a Soviet diplomat was murdered in Warsaw and blame was laid at the door of 'the reactionaries', a Soviet minister in Norway spoke violently at a reception against the capitalist system in general and that of Britain in particular. Several Norwegian communists made similarly inflammatory remarks, and the King was so alarmed by press reports of the gathering that he asked his foreign minister to tell the Soviet envoy that such an attack on one of Norway's friends could not be tolerated. Yet at the same time, he consistently turned a deaf ear to appeals for him to take a public stand against illegal labour conflicts, on the grounds that it was not for him to express himself on such matters.

* Princess Thyra and Prince Gustav, who died in 1945 and 1944 respectively, never married.

In August 1928 Crown Prince Olav became engaged to Princess Märtha of Sweden. She was staying with her sister in Brussels at the time, which made it easier for her to go over to Amsterdam, where the Prince was sailing with other members of the Norwegian Olympic team, without drawing attention to the impending betrothal. He had told his parents of his intentions before he left home, so he could telegraph the result of his proposal as 'All in order' without making the news public.

In view of old wounds still not fully healed by the dissolution of the union in 1905, King Haakon felt hesitant about the announcement of another marriage alliance between Norway and Sweden, and he was anxious to find a suitable moment for announcing the news. Neither the prime minister, J.L. Mowinckel, nor the president of the Storting, C.J. Hambro, raised any objection to the engagement on political grounds. In their view, it would be a very popular alliance. On 12 January 1929 Prince Olav left Stockholm to spend three weeks with his future parents-in-law, travelling incognito on the night train. Next day, King Haakon announced the engagement at an extraordinary cabinet council at the same time as the news was made public in Stockholm.

As the ministers had foretold, the announcement proved popular in Norway. One of the Oslo papers devoted an inordinate amount of time and space to speculation as to whom would be invited to the wedding ceremony, until King Haakon became mildly irritated. The next time the reporter went to the royal palace he was told that the King wanted to see him. On being shown into the royal presence, the King asked him pointedly: 'Would you be so kind as to ask your editor if I may invite the Duke of York to the wedding?'[18]

The Swedes as a nation expected that the wedding would be in Stockholm, as had that of Princess Astrid. But King Haakon's wish that it should be held in Oslo was deferred to. The wedding was held on 21 March 1929 in Oslo, the Princess arriving two days before the wedding. The bride and groom had a warm reception from the crowd as they drove from the station to the palace, and an even greater one after luncheon, when they drove around the town for several hours in an open landau, which was soon filled with flowers. There was no doubt about national enthusiasm for the match.

The ceremony was celebrated in St Saviour's Church, where the Crown Prince arrived first, accompanied by his best man, the Duke of York (later King George VI of Great Britain), followed by the royal guests and finally by the bride with her father, Prince Carl. After the ceremony, performed by the Bishop of Oslo, the party drove back to the palace amid scenes of tremendous rejoicing.

The couple set off via Malmö for Cannes, Paris, and London, ending up a month later at Appleton House. In May they returned to Norway, and settled at Skaugum, about twelve miles west of Oslo. Unfortunately fire broke out in the building shortly afterwards, and the couple lost everything apart from such furniture as the Prince and a party of volunteers could drag out as the building burned, and some valuables placed in a safe in the cellar. Queen Maud went over to the scene with King Haakon, and described it sadly to Queen Mary; 'It all went so quickly & was the most *dreadful* sight, – they were so *brave* too, and quiet, Olav was wonderful & directed everything.'[19] The first of their three children, Princess Ragnhild, was born at the palace three weeks later, and they moved back into Skaugum in August 1932.

In June 1928 King Gustav of Sweden celebrated his seventieth birthday. Never fond of state ceremonial, he would have been content with just a quiet family celebration. However, Stockholm went *en fête*, with bunting everywhere, various military inspections and processions with addresses of congratulation. Queen Victoria had made a special effort to return from abroad for her husband's birthday, and she too was greeted with enthusiasm. In the evening an unusually ornate state banquet was held at the Palace, attended by over 500 guests. There were more congratulatory messages, and the King responded with a moving address in which he looked back on his life, his reign, and his love for his people.

The next day celebrations continued with army and naval reviews, a service of thanksgiving, and sporting displays, where the King watched some of the eliminating trials of Swedish athletes intending to enter for the Olympic Games. The last item was the presentation to the King of five million kroner (about £20,000 in the day) in twenty-six cheques, one on behalf of each of the provinces, raised for the National Celebration Fund.

These festivities marked the last time that Queen Victoria set foot on Swedish soil. She was living on borrowed time, for two years earlier she was so ill that the doctors had pronounced her condition hopeless, and provisional arrangements were made for her funeral and subsequent rites.

There was another reason for her unhappiness apart from declining health. In his middle sixties King Gustav had taken hormone treatment, which reportedly made him frisky and also homosexual,[20] although comments in the press suggest that such tendencies had manifested themselves in his behaviour earlier in life than this. The King and Queen had been leading separate lives for so long that it made no difference to relations between them, but the knowledge that she was married to a man with such inclinations did not make a loveless marriage any the easier. Yet such male relationships as the King enjoyed were conducted with the utmost discretion, although the moral climate in Sweden was more relaxed and less homophobic than throughout much of Europe. Homosexuality in the country, an American journalist could write some thirty years later, was dealt with as a fact of life, not to be suppressed, but kept in its place; a misfortune, rather than a crime; and for consenting adults, a strictly private matter.[21] Such a liberal attitude was at marked variance with the prevailing view in other countries, summed up by the King's contemporary King George V of Britain, who 'thought chaps like that shot themselves'.

The Queen's physician, Axel Munthe, suggested that as a last resort she should seek a cure in more southerly climes. As soon as she was pronounced fit enough to travel, she was escorted on the royal train to Rome and then to Capri. Life on the Mediterranean island was simple and informal. Attired like the islanders, in plain straw sandals and dresses of white Capri wool, she would often be seen walking with Munthe, his dogs, and her poodle. Her suite and detectives were asked to keep discreetly out of sight. A lady-in-waiting, Countess Taube, despaired of the Queen's passion for climbing up ravines. After yet another pair of shoes was ruined one day, she said to a German guest on a walk on which he had been invited by the Queen, 'Oh, why does Her Majesty insist on climbing up these gutters?'[22]

Despite returning to warmer climates, her strength failed rapidly and she died at the Villa Svezia, Rome, on 4 April 1930. King Gustav and their children reached her side just in time. Her ill health had brought her widespread sympathy in Sweden, and her founding of children's welfare societies had brought her a certain measure of popularity. Nevertheless she had ventured so rarely inside the country in recent years that she was mourned but little.

With the death of Queen Victoria, greater responsibility now devolved on Crown Princess Louise. They had had little in common, for the Queen had grown up in a very sheltered environment, brought up to believe that the monarchy existed by the grace of God; it was part of their position that an invisible wall should separate royalty from subjects. Louise was a democrat at heart. She became the Honorary President of the Sophia Hospital Board, and the work she did for nurses and hospitals was one of her most valuable contributions. She also took over the Queen's Central Committee, begun by Queen Victoria at the outbreak of the Great War, designed to support the work of the Swedish Red Cross.

Such was the mood of the time that a Crown Princess with a genuinely democratic outlook as well as the customary royal dedication to charity work and organization was an immeasurable asset to Sweden. Queen Victoria had been but little known in Sweden, and though ill health had brought her sympathy, she was rarely popular. King Gustav V was respected, but again, hardly liked by his people at large. Crown Prince Gustav Adolf and his vivacious English wife would, to some extent, be the salvation of the Swedish monarchy.

CHAPTER EIGHT

'Things change so quickly'

With a gradual retreat from constitutional and democratic standards throughout many European countries during the 1930s – exemplified on one hand by the rise of Hitler and Mussolini, and on the other by the growth of a totalitarian state in Russia – the democracies of Scandinavia looked askance on events elsewhere in the continent. In turn they were regarded with admiration by many on the moderate left throughout Europe, personifying as they did the virtues of reason, sanity, tolerance and their enlightened attitude to the provision of welfare services at home, and neutrality on an international level. To some it must have seemed as if Scandinavia was the one shining beacon in an otherwise dark and stormy world.

Despite the reputation of his country as one of the exemplary democracies, and though his personal powers and royal prerogative had declined, King Gustav V of Sweden considered that he still had a role to play in his country's foreign policy. When he visited Berlin in the spring of 1933, he spoke to Hitler in an attempt to persuade him to abate his persecution of the Jews. Proudly declaring on his return that he had 'taken Hitler by one ear', he felt that his mediation had been of some effect. As the subsequent history of the Nazi regime would show, he had an absurdly exaggerated view of his own importance and his power to influence events.

Notwithstanding the distaste for pomp and ceremony which had resulted in him foregoing a Coronation, King Gustav was just as eager as his predecessors to demonstrate his sense of regal occasion. The opening of the Swedish Riksdag never lacked splendour where he was concerned. Accompanied by the Crown Prince and other senior princes in uniform or court dress and the princesses in dark velvet gowns, long white gloves and tiaras, 'Mr G' would proceed to the throne in his ermine robes, his crown and regalia nearby, and read his speech with all due solemnity. Dress for the state opening of the Riksdag in Stockholm had changed little from that devised by the first Bernadotte Kings, copied from the court of Napoleon Bonaparte. The contrast between the King and royal family, and those who filled the galleries as spectators, was striking.

Such regal grandeur made no difference to his everyday affability or good humour. Visiting a provincial residence for lunch, he was informed courteously by the lord lieutenant, a teetotaller, that no wine would be served. 'Here in my house', the official said, 'intoxicating liquors are forbidden'. 'Are you so sure it's yours?' the King asked quietly.[1]

The equally affable King Haakon VII of Norway was granted one of the highest accolades possible by an enthusiastic French journalist, who in 1930 praised Norway for having developed the world's most democratic monarchy. The simple lifestyle led by the King, Queen, Crown Prince and Princess, which owed something not only to personal preference but also the reduction in the value of their allowances as a result of inflation during the 1920s, was widely admired. There was a fine line to be trod between royal dignity and approachability, and King Haakon found the balance perfectly.

A wry sense of humour and natural tact helped him to deal with potentially difficult situations. In 1930 he was disconcerted to hear that the foundation stone of Oslo City Hall was to be laid, but the Labour mayor had not invited any of the royal family. He felt that he had every right to be there; moreover, his absence might provoke unfavourable comment from foreign guests. As he and Crown Prince Olav had contributed to the building funds, they were entitled to admission, so he asked his secretary to apply for two tickets. One can only imagine the mayor's embarrassment when he welcomed guests to the ceremony and found himself face to face with the King and his heir seated in the front row.

Modestly aware of his limits as he was, the King was all too aware of the deteriorating international situation, especially after the invasion of Ethiopia by the Italians in 1935, and the outbreak of civil war in Spain the following year. He recognized that he would be failing in his duty if he did not urge his government to maintain adequate defences. The Labour government which had come to power in 1935 was traditionally hostile to the defence services, seeing them as a drain on public finance and the army in particular as an organization which might be used for strike-breaking in the event of industrial unrest. Mobilization of coastal defence personnel, better training for officers and men in all the services, and the development of air defence, he insisted to his prime minister Johan Nygaardsvold, were all vital if Norwegian neutrality was to be defended against potentially belligerent powers to the south and east.

On a personal level King Haakon continued to retain close connections with his relatives throughout Europe, though several of his visits abroad at around this time were for the melancholy purpose of attending funerals. In 1935 Crown Princess Märtha and Queen Maud both lost a sister, with the deaths of the young Queen Astrid of the Belgians in a car accident that August, and the elderly, embittered spinster Princess Victoria of Britain at her Buckinghamshire home, Coppins, in December.

In January 1936, six weeks later, Queen Maud's only surviving brother, King George V died at Sandringham, and King Haakon VII was one of the six heads of state who walked behind the coffin. Also present to pay their last respects were Prince Waldemar of Denmark, Crown Prince Gustav Adolf and Crown Princess Louise of Sweden. 'He was always so kind and friendly to me and so kind to all my family,' Louise wrote to Dolla (11 February 1936), 'and as my King, I admired and respected him so much. Few Kings have been respected so much and his goodness of heart and devotion to his duty made him loved by his people'.[2]

Though she was always glad to return to London, Princess Louise had adapted easily to life in Sweden. She and Crown Prince Gustav Adolf made a happy, unspectacular couple. The enlightened attitude of the Swedish people towards class, the equalizing of the nation's wealth and the emancipation of women, matched her personality and the opinions she had inherited from her forward-looking mother. They lived without grandeur, yet they still kept up a wide range of residences for the various seasons – Ulriksdal Palace just outside Stockholm, their spring and autumn home; a wing of the royal palace in the capital; Drottningholm, the official Swedish royal palace; and Sofiero in the south, where they both gardened with much enthusiasm during the late summer. They enjoyed skiing and skating, and were often seen cycling through the streets of Stockholm.

Crown Princess Louise was an indefatigable sightseer, though her guides' command of English did not always match their enthusiasm. One of King George V of England's favourite after-dinner stories concerned a visit she paid to Uppsala Cathedral. The Archbishop approached a chest of drawers in the sacristy, announcing with pride, 'I will now open these trousers and reveal some even more precious treasures to Your Royal Highness'.[3]

The Princess was devoted to her stepchildren. Soon after her arrival in Sweden there had been talk that she could not be bothered with them, and that she did not seem motherly enough. In appearance she was spinsterish, angular, sharp-witted, and quick-tempered, and cut a much less conventionally motherly figure than the late Crown Princess. Nonetheless in her undemonstrative fashion she was very fond of them.

In 1925 she had given birth to a stillborn girl. Her mother had been apprehensive that because of Louise's indifferent health during childhood and lack of resistance to infections, she might have been a carrier of haemophilia. The stillbirth was one of the greatest tragedies of her life, yet if anything perhaps it only increased the bonds between her and the five children of her husband.

Of these children none was a greater problem than the heir presumptive, Prince Gustav Adolf. In October 1932 he had married Princess Sibylla of Saxe-Coburg Gotha, daughter of Charles, Duke of the German state until he was deposed in 1918. The posthumous son of Queen Victoria of Britain's haemophiliac son Prince Leopold, Duke of Albany, Charles had become a devoted adherent of the Nazi movement and an admirer of Hitler. Distrusting the German Chancellor's views, King George V of Britain had refused to allow the Prince of Wales to attend the wedding, which took place in Coburg. On the evening of the wedding, four thousand Nazis marched in a torchlight procession through the town. On the day itself the wedding route was lined by saluting Brownshirts, and a message from Hitler was read out at the reception. King Gustav had been anxious to attend his grandson's wedding, and was with difficulty dissuaded from doing so, on the grounds that the ceremony would almost certainly be used to stage Nazi demonstrations.

The influence of Charles indeed proved potentially harmful, especially where his son-in-law was concerned in Sweden. Shy by nature, autocratic and irascible, Prince Gustav Adolf was very unlike his father. An annual report for the year 1932 to the British Foreign Office on the Swedish royal family and court commented that the Prince 'is headstrong and often led by his obstinacy into imprudences which expose him to criticism. He does not share in the same measure the popularity with the Swedish people enjoyed by the other members of the family.'[4]

The Social Democrats, the largest party in Sweden, thought he was violently (albeit discreetly) right-wing in his sympathies. The civic dignitaries of Stockholm declined to take part in the festivities held in November 1932 when bride and groom arrived in their capital, on the grounds that during the autumn the Prince had been present at a meeting of the Stahlhelm, a German ex-servicemen's organization committed to upholding and promoting discipline, order and national fellowship. By 1933 Hitler's assumption of power was beginning to create alarm throughout Europe, and although more indulgent to Hitler than most of his fellow-monarchs King Gustav V was becoming apprehensive about his grandson's behaviour and views. Yet he was unable to resist the charm of his granddaughter-in-law, discreet as she was, and they were fast becoming devoted to each other. To the consternation of the government, it was evident that he was taking her unduly into his confidence, and ministers feared that by doing so he was placing the monarchy in danger. It was only twenty years since the Peasants' petition and subsequent republican tendencies in Sweden. Should anything happen to the King and the Crown Prince, as their successor Gustav Adolf could provoke a thoroughly unstable and delicate situation if the new sovereign had no confidence in his advisers, drawn from the largest party, the Socialists.

All too aware of the delicate situation, the King and Crown Prince attempted to reason with the Prince, but to no avail. They accordingly turned to the King's brother, Prince William, renowned as much for his writings on travel and interest in cinema as for his easy-going manner, for help. He had always enjoyed good relations with Prince Gustav Adolf, but his attempts to mediate with the young man failed to make any headway. Finally they turned to the King's nephew, Count Folke Bernadotte, another lifelong friend of the Prince. The Count managed to shepherd him into more popular circles, whereupon the Prince turned over a new leaf and made his peace with the Socialists. A bond was thus forged between the cousins which, together with a mutual interest in furthering the scouting movement in Sweden, united them in almost brotherly affection until the Prince's untimely death.

Thanks to the Count, something of a political transformation in the heir presumptive was brought about, and with it a vital key in strengthening bonds between the working class and the throne. How much the Prince would have remained his own man, and whether he would have seen through the increasingly evil machinations of National Socialism in Germany – as some of his royal contemporaries failed to do – is open to doubt.

Count Folke Bernadotte and King Gustav V were never particularly close. The Count was ill at ease with the artificiality of court life and the King's old-fashioned ways. With the more modern-thinking Crown Prince, whom he called 'Gusty' in private, the Count was much closer, notwithstanding the twelve years' difference in their ages. Both men had a good deal of common ground in their attitudes to religion, charity and public service.

Nevertheless the King was pleased at the Count's success in one delicate family matter, and shortly afterwards asked him to intervene in an equally intractable problem. The Crown Prince's second son, Prince Sigvard, had fallen in love with a German girl of dubious reputation, Erica Patzek, and announced that he intended to marry her. He was fully prepared to resign his royal privileges and titles, but the royal family were anxious to avoid any scandal, especially as he was still third in line of succession to the throne. Count Folke Bernadotte was asked to exercise his powers of persuasion and talk him out of the marriage. The infatuated Prince Sigvard was prevailed on to see reason for a while, and his marriage plans were apparently shelved. No sooner had the Count and family breathed a sigh of relief than Sigvard changed his mind. He married Fraulein Patzek, but within a few years the union was dissolved, and the Prince's ex-wife was being acclaimed as 'the Swedish Princess' in a Berlin night club of dubious reputation during the 1939–45 war.

King Haakon's guarded attitude to Germany and Nazism had been shared by his brother-in-law King George V, although their views were not always echoed by the younger generation. Some of them preferred to see the balance of power in Europe as lying between a degenerate and enfeebled France, and a virile and resurgent Germany. Horror stories which filtered out of the Third Reich were believed to be exaggerated, if not dismissed solely as propaganda based on communist disinformation.

Prince Gustav Adolf had been brought round to see the error of his ways, but others were less easily convinced. As heir to the British throne, and even after his accession in January 1936, King Edward VIII considered that National Socialism offered a solution to the chronic problems of housing for the workers and mass unemployment.

Crown Prince Olav of Norway likewise professed more admiration for Hitler's Germany than inter-war France. He thought the situation in Europe gave cause for great concern, maintaining in a letter (17 December 1935) to the then Prince of Wales that France seemed to have 'double crossed the whole of the League [of Nations], and us all'. The only possible way of improving the stability of the continent would be 'a close relationship between England and Germany'.[5] In view of the fate which would befall Norway within five years, his judgment was somewhat ironic.

In 1935 another marriage alliance was formed between two of the Scandinavian dynasties. Crown Prince Frederick of Denmark, a handsome, well-built man who stood six foot three inches, had joined the Danish navy as a cadet at the age of fourteen, and had worked his way through every rank to that of Rear-Admiral. Widely travelled, in the best naval tradition he had become virtually covered in tattoos. Outside the navy, his chief interests were mechanics and music. An accomplished pianist, he was also a gifted amateur conductor, and one of his great joys was conducting the Royal Danish Symphony Orchestra.

In the spring of 1922 he had briefly become engaged to Olga, eldest daughter of Prince Nicholas of the Hellenes, brother of King Constantine I. This had been a critical time for the embattled Greek dynasty, embroiled in a hopeless war against Turkey. Yet it was not so much the waning fortunes of the Greek royal family as mutual incompatibility and second thoughts on the part of Princess Olga, who caused consternation by announcing flatly that she liked her Danish cousin but did not love him. His father's domestic tyranny had made him (and his brother Prince Knud) a shy young man, lacking in self-confidence and more than ready to find consolation in the bottle. Much as he deserved sympathy in his predicament, she realized that she could obviously do better for a husband. After the wedding had been postponed twice, the betrothal was broken off.

Thirteen years later it was an older, wiser, more sober and more settled Prince Frederick who became engaged to his Bernadotte cousin. Princess Ingrid, daughter of Crown Prince Gustav Adolf of Sweden, had been raised along English lines. In looks, attitudes and interests she was very much like a British Princess, taking after her late mother. Very practical-minded, she could turn her hand to almost all household duties. From her mother she had inherited a love of outdoor life; with her father she had a passion for the arts, in particular opera, books and furniture. As an only girl with four brothers, she was known in the family as an inveterate peacemaker, often called upon as an intermediary between her siblings and their father.

Her mother's death in 1920 – a bereavement which made her a serious child, mature and wise beyond her tender years – had done nothing to weaken Princess Ingrid's ties with her mother's country. She paid long and frequent visits to England to stay with her grandfather, the elderly Duke of Connaught, at his homes at Clarence House and Bagshot Park. Her father's remarriage in 1923 had merely strengthened the association. In 1932 it was rumoured – though with little foundation – that she might become engaged to King George V's youngest son, Prince George, the future Duke of Kent.

In March 1935 Prince Frederick and Princess Ingrid became engaged, and the wedding took place on 24 May 1935 in Stockholm. It was the greatest gathering of inter-war royalty in Europe. Three Kings attended, as did more than sixty Princes and Princesses. For several days the ornate royal barge, all flashing gilt and fluttering fringes, ferried royal guests from the yachts to the Royal Palace. On a day of brilliant sunshine, the ceremony was celebrated in the old Storkyrkan Church beside the Royal Palace. The bridegroom was attired in naval uniform, while the bride wore a slim-fitting, classically severe white satin dress with a lace veil falling from a single wreath of orange blossom.

The general joy at the wedding was overshadowed by anxiety over the health of Queen Alexandrine. She had never been particularly strong, and while she was in Stockholm, after suffering severe pain, an intestinal problem was diagnosed. An emergency operation proved to be effective, but she made a slow recovery. In future years she had to have several further operations for the same complaint.

In his later years King Christian X's attitude towards his family began to soften. Crown Princess Ingrid was a woman of some character in whom, he soon realized, he had met his match. Perhaps because of her readiness to stand up to him, he respected her and became very fond of her, and his relations with his elder son improved correspondingly.

By now he was mellowing into an unpretentious monarch like his predecessors, and he loved to ride on horseback through Copenhagen every morning. At his own wish he would go alone, with no police escort, equerries or grooms, threading his way among cars and cyclists. A few pedestrians would recognize and salute him as he passed, but the majority took no notice, not out of disrespect so much as a desire to accept their citizen King as 'one of us'.

Such a routine was not without its hazards. On one occasion, the mounted King and a motorist were waiting for the lights to change at a crossing. The latter was having trouble with the catch of his door, and slammed it so violently that the King's horse reared. The King politely asked the man to be more careful, and received a fulsome apology. All the same, the penitent motorist evidently had a woefully short memory. He slammed his door again just as hard, and the horse plunged so violently that it slipped and rolled over with the King. They fell so heavily that one of the stirrups was broken in two. Though badly bruised and shaken, the King insisted on remounting and riding back to the palace.[6]

The intervening years brought happiness and sadness to King Haakon VII. On 21 February 1937 Crown Princess Märtha gave birth to a son, who was christened Harald, the name already borne by four medieval Kings of Norway. The baby Prince and his elder sisters were frequent visitors to their grandparents, and the King and Queen often stayed with them at Skaugum. King Haakon found the youngsters' antics thoroughly diverting, and when he was not working at home he was always happy to have them around him, while Queen Maud was in her element giving children's parties at the palace.

However, the Queen's never robust health continued to deteriorate, and from middle age onwards she was increasingly prone to neuralgia and bronchitis. In the autumn of 1938 she travelled to Appleton House with a view to escaping the Norwegian winter. Her journey had already been delayed by a week as King Haakon was anxious at the turn of events elsewhere in Europe, chiefly precipitated by the aggressive behaviour of Hitler. He wanted her to remain in Norway until the result of British prime minister Neville Chamberlain's much-heralded meeting at Munich, supposedly securing 'peace in our time', was known. While King Haakon and King Christian X had made official visits to Stockholm as apparent gestures of solidarity, nobody could take Scandinavian unity for granted. More than his ministers, King Haakon realized that Sweden was economically the strongest country of the three, and thus free to pursue a foreign policy which was fundamentally under German influence if her sovereign or government felt thus inclined.

Queen Maud left for England in October. On a shopping expedition in London the following month, she complained of feeling unwell. She was admitted to a nursing home, and after an X-ray examination the doctors decided to operate. Hearing of her illness, Queen Mary went to stay at Claridge's Hotel so that she could be close, and sat with her for several hours on the day before the operation, 16 November. King Haakon was warned of possible complications, and he went over at once, staying at Buckingham Palace. After the operation she had a disturbed night, but the following day she appeared to be recovering well. However, following a relapse she died in her sleep shortly after midnight on 20 November. Her death was so sudden that only a nurse was present.

The Queen's coffin was brought back to the chapel at Marlborough House, where she had been christened. It was then taken via Victoria station to Portsmouth to be placed aboard a cruiser for Oslo. After lying in state for two days at Akershus Castle, Queen Maud's funeral was held in St Saviour's Church on 8 December.

Returning sadly to Norway, the widowed King spent Christmas at Skaugum with his son and daughter-in-law and family. As he wrote to King George VI in England, 'it was too much for me when I found presents for me from darling Aunt Maud and I realised then how impossible it would have been if I had been alone, and the dear grandchildren helped me a lot to think of them and not only ponder on my sad thoughts'.[7]

Soon after Christmas, another link with the past was broken. King Haakon's uncle Prince Waldemar, the youngest child of King Christian IX, had been a widower for nearly thirty years. Dividing his time between Bernstorff and his childhood home, the Yellow Palace, he was a familiar sight for many years in Copenhagen, either on horseback – it was said that even in his old age 'he was still able to tire two horses a day' – or strolling around the city streets with Prince George of Greece. The latter had married a little late in life, in his thirty-eighth year, and like Waldemar he had taken a French princess, Marie Bonaparte, as his bride. She too was forced to accept sorrowfully the fact that she would never come first in her husband's affections, but found consolation in extra-marital affairs and a passionate interest in psychoanalysis.

By the time of his eightieth birthday in October 1938, Prince Waldemar was ageing fast. A few weeks later he contracted pneumonia, and died peacefully on 14 January 1939. 'A very ordinary creature, neither very handsome, nor very intelligent, nor very generous, and often unpleasant, especially towards his children',[8] had been Princess George of Greece's understandably jaundiced verdict some years earlier. More charitably, the press paid tribute to his modest and cheerful manner which 'made friends for him in all classes'. Like most of the family, he was laid to rest in Roskilde Cathedral.

As the decade entered its last year, the European situation became ever more threatening. During a Norwegian parliamentary debate in February the foreign minister, Halfdan Koht, acknowledged that while the international situation was precarious, people should be warned against panic and the idea that there was an imminent danger of war. Hitler's invasion of Czechoslovakia the following month suggested to all but the most optimistic that that danger was advancing, and in April the Führer repudiated his non-aggression pact with Poland and his naval treaty with Britain. Like many others, King Haakon was convinced that war was impending.

Still he hoped for the best, as he wrote to King George VI of Britain (12 April 1939); 'I do hope the world may get through this crisis without war: Norway wants to keep neutral, my only prayer is that it is Germany who gives us cause to break it, but whatever happens be sure that my personal feelings will always be on England's side'.[9]

He wrote to Queen Mary on the same date, expressing sympathy for Neville Chamberlain as 'all his work and trouble last year all seems to have gone to pieces, but I still hope that he may get his recompense and get proofs that his policy was all right after all. I cannot help feeling pleased that darling Maud has been spared all this anxiety as I am sure she could not have stood the strain of another great war, even if Norway managed to keep out of it'.[10]

Hitler had sought non-aggression pacts earlier that year with all four Scandinavian states, but Denmark was the only one to sign. Like British parliamentarians during the Baldwin-Chamberlain area, Danish politicians from the major parties optimistically believed that the Nazis could be appeased by a general lack of military preparation, and the Danish army was even reduced in strength.

Throughout the summer of 1939, several government conferences in Norway resulted in measures being adopted to improve military and civil preparation, and in order to keep abreast of developments King Haakon and Crown Prince Olav had frequent interviews with the naval and military commanders-in-chief. In August King Leopold of the Belgians invited the heads of the other six 'Oslo states' (Norway, Sweden, Denmark, the Netherlands and Luxembourg, who had signed a low-tariff trade convention in Oslo in 1930, and which Finland signed in 1933) to join him in a last-minute appeal for a peaceful solution to the German-Polish frontier problems. King Haakon had little faith in the exercise. He considered it had been undertaken too late, but he found it difficult to say no, 'as it might look as if I was not interested in the question of peace, but things change so quickly that one cannot tell if some who want to be neutral only make it more difficult for those nations who are standing up for right instead of might'.[11]

The King's forebodings were right. On 28 August he told the defence minister that naval protection should be brought up to full strength, and advised that a test mobilization should be held. On 1 September German forces crossed the Polish frontier. The Second World War had begun.

CHAPTER NINE

'Assume a completely correct and worthy attitude'

With the outbreak of war in Europe in September 1939 the Norwegian government's aim was to keep the country neutral as it had been in 1914–18, but King Haakon knew it would be much more difficult this time. For the first few months, the gravest worry for the Scandinavian kingdoms was the situation in Finland. A delegation was called from Helsinki to Moscow to negotiate with Stalin in October, and the three Scandinavian monarchs met Kyösti Kallio, the Finnish President, in Stockholm to assure him of their sympathy. Nevertheless the Russian threat intensified until November 1939, when Soviet planes bombed Helsinki and other towns on the pretext that the Finns had attacked Russia first. King Haakon agreed wholeheartedly with the appeal of Queen Wilhelmina of Holland and King Leopold III of the Belgians to the combatant nations to stop fighting and accept mediation.

Norway's neutrality was sorely tried, as no other non-aligned European country seemed likely to suffer so badly from German destruction of shipping. During the first few months of conflict several hundred (or possibly several thousand, according to some estimates) Norwegian seamen were drowned in ships which were torpedoed, bombed or mined.

At the opening of the Storting in January 1940, King Haakon spoke at length on Norway's sufferings and her determination to keep the peace as far as possible. His aim was tested to its limits the following month with the *Altmark* incident. The German auxiliary vessel *Altmark* sailed down the Norwegian coast, carrying some three hundred British seamen captured by the *Graf Spee* in the South Atlantic. As a vessel of the German state, the ship was considered diplomatically immune, and allowed free passage through the protected Bergen area. It was stopped twice by the Norwegian navy, but courteous requests to be allowed to make a thorough search were rejected. On 16 February the British destroyer *Cossack* entered territorial waters, ignored the protests of two Norwegian torpedo boats escorting the *Altmark*, boarded it and released all the prisoners despite some resistance from the German crew.

King Haakon and the government were indignant at this infringement of neutral rights. Norwegian naval units could not be expected to repel overwhelmingly superior foreign warships by force of arms, but could only protest. Writing to Queen Mary (16 February), the King admitted that he personally understood it was the only chance Britain had of freeing the prisoners, 'but England's accusing us of not being able to keep our neutrality has provoked a lot of bad feeling against England, which has made it very difficult for me, as I have to be most careful on these occasions not to say too much – so that my ministers can say that I am no more English than Norwegian'.[1]

Franco-British plans were accordingly made for extending the war to Scandinavia by mining Norwegian coastal waters, to hinder shipping movements from and to Narvik, and also transport along the northern route between Germany and the Soviet Union. That minelaying would affect innocent Norwegian shipping as well seemed to have counted for nothing; moreover, it risked provoking strong reactions among neutral countries, especially Norway and Sweden, and forfeiting goodwill. The Supreme War Council met on 28 March 1940, and accepted the French proposal for laying mines at strategic coastal points, primarily to drive iron-ore ships bound for Germany out into the open sea. The Norwegian and Swedish governments were sent explanatory notes beforehand.

Meanwhile it was evident that German forces were preparing for invasion. King Haakon and Crown Prince Olav were warned that naval detachments were being sighted off the Norwegian coast, and shortly after midnight on 9 April, the outer naval defences of Oslo were engaged in combat with German ships. Norway was now at war. The royal family and government ministers arranged for a hasty departure from Oslo to avoid capture. Crown Princess Märtha and the children were escorted by the Crown Prince's adjutant, Major Ostgaard, across the Norwegian/Swedish border for safety. At the same time the King refused a demand by the German Minister to Norway that he should dismiss the incumbent Nygaardsvold ministry and appoint Abraham Vidkun Quisling, a senior government minister well-known for his pro-German sympathies, as prime minister instead. As a constitutional monarch, he said, he could not appoint a politician to the supreme position if he did not have the confidence of his people, a move wholeheartedly endorsed by his government.

As German forces were approaching Hamer, the King, Crown Prince and cabinet went north-east to Nybergsund, where the Luftwaffe bombed the town for over an hour. They moved northwards, intending to establish a safe base on the west coast, but as German attacks escalated the situation became steadily worse.

On 30 May, after the German breakthrough in the Low Countries and France, the Allies decided to evacuate Norway. King Haakon had to recognize that the Norwegians would be standing alone against far superior forces. A severe shortage of ammunition and armaments made the possibility of a prolonged fight untenable, and the only alternatives were to go to Britain and carry on the fight from there as government-in-exile, or surrender to Germany there and then. On 7 June, exactly thirty-five years after Norway had gained her independence, King Haakon, Crown Prince Olav, members of the government and a few officials, sailed for Britain in the British cruiser *Devonshire*. Reaching Gourock, on the Clyde, in the early hours of 10 June, they arrived that evening by train at Euston Station, London. King George VI and Winston Churchill, who had succeeded Neville Chamberlain as prime minister a month previously, were there to meet them. The King and Crown Prince Olav went straight to Buckingham Palace, where they arrived in winter uniform and high boots, and virtually no luggage, to find the royal family still assembled for dinner.

In London the mood was sombre. The British army had just been evacuated from Dunkirk, with considerable loss of equipment. German troops were approaching Paris, and Mussolini had just declared war on France.

Next day King Haakon wrote to Queen Mary, who had been evacuated against her wishes to Badminton, Gloucestershire, for the duration of the war; he expressed his sadness at having to leave his country in the hands of the enemy. He knew that the Germans would do their utmost to make propaganda out his flight. 'Personally I am sure we did right in coming away and not making a separate peace with Germany, as we would have to sooner or later on account of no ammunition after a short stand alone, after the Allies had to recall their forces on account of the war in general.'[2]

When King Haakon arrived at Buckingham Palace, he had followed Queen Wilhelmina and the royal family of the Netherlands, who had likewise come with hardly any of their belongings. Both monarchs were in a position to warn their royal hosts from personal experience about the hazards of air attack and parachute landings.

Once King Haakon asked King George what would happen if a parachute attack was threatened. The latter explained his methods of alerting the guard, and rather sceptically King Haakon asked for a demonstration. Obligingly King George pressed the alarm bell in his study and, together with the Queen, they went into the garden to watch the result. Nothing happened, and an equerry was sent to make enquiries. He returned to report that the officer of the guard had been informed by the police sergeant on duty that no attack was impending as 'he had heard nothing of it'. Police co-operation was speedily obtained, and a contingent of guardsmen entered the gardens quickly. To King Haakon's horror, they proceeded to thrash around the undergrowth more like beaters at a shoot than trained officers engaged in the pursuit of a dangerous enemy. As a result of this incident, precautions were revised and strengthened.

Even before the first major air raid struck London on the evening of

7 September 1940, King Haakon and Crown Prince Olav had been planning to move out of Buckingham Palace to somewhere else within easy reach of London, and the various Norwegian institutions centred there. Later that week they settled at Bowdown House, Berkshire, forty-five miles from London. The house had previously belonged to a brother of Sir Cecil Dormer, the British minister who had accompanied them from Norway. In March 1942 the construction of a military airfield nearby made it unsafe, and they moved to Foliejon Park, near Windsor. This remained their headquarters for the rest of the war. The King had a senior adjutant, Colonel Oswald Nordlie, and a British liaison officer, Eric Smith; the Crown Prince's adjutant, Ostgaard, also lived at Foliejon.

King Haakon's presence in Britain at the head of his government became a rallying-point for all the Norwegians working for the deliverance of their homeland. During his years of exile he devoted his time to helping the organization of 'Free' Norway's war effort, the growth of its Army, Navy, and Air Force, and the welfare of its 25,000 merchant seamen. In his broadcasts he comforted and encouraged his enslaved people and made a point of receiving personally all Norwegians who escaped to Britain. At Foliejon he worked on his speeches and declarations, and with the Crown Prince listened to radio news bulletins. Meetings with his ministers were sometimes held there, but more often the King met them at Kingston House, an eight-storey block of flats in Knightsbridge which had been rented as Norwegian government offices, or in the Norwegian Legation. In his leisure time he had always enjoyed watching films, and from time to time while in England he would relax by slipping, without any fuss, into a local cinema.

At length he became a familiar figure to the BBC staff at Portland Place. The story of one of his first appearances at the building, before he was well known, rapidly passed into legend. A young woman on the reception desk, putting through a call for him on the switchboard, turned to him and asked: 'Where was it you said you were King of?'

Meanwhile, in Norway the resistance movement had adopted the royal monogram as its symbol. To show their support for him and to display defiance of the occupation authorities, people from all walks of life would paint or draw the initials 'H7' on walls, buildings, on the sand on the beaches, in the snow – in fact, anywhere they could. Schoolchildren would even scribble 'H7' on the entrance to their schools, as did political prisoners in their cells.

At the time of the King's and Crown Prince's move to England, Crown Princess Märtha of Norway and their children were in Stockholm. A few days after the arrival of her father-in-law and husband in England, she telegraphed to tell them that efforts were being made to induce her to return to Oslo with the children, so that three-year-old Prince Harald could be proclaimed King in place of his grandfather, with Crown Prince Olav as Regent until the boy came of age.

Meanwhile they had been invited to the United States of America as guests of President Roosevelt, potentially a far safer haven during the hostilities, but her family were advising her that the voyage across the Atlantic would be too dangerous. A cipher telegram from King Gustav to King Haakon* was believed by the recipient and Crown Prince Olav to have advised the King to abdicate in favour of his grandson, as a means of saving the Norwegian people from unnecessary difficulties. The British minister in Stockholm, Victor Mallet, reported that King Gustav was in favour of the regency solution, and King Gustav was supposed to have sent Hitler a telegram making the proposal. King George VI wrote to King Gustav, gravely deploring the idea. Fortunately the letter was not delivered, as it transpired that the minister had found out that the King of Sweden's communication to Hitler merely urged him to show the utmost possible moderation. At no time was the possibility of King Haakon's abdication suggested.

On 1 August 1940, with the worst possible timing – the same day that Hitler ordered intensification of air and sea warfare against Britain – King Gustav of Sweden attempted a personal initiative of his own, secretly offering his services to King George VI and to Hitler to enable contact to be made between the two groups of belligerents in order to examine the possibilities of peace. King George received his letter containing the offer on 2 August, and referred it to his ministers for consideration and for consulation with the Dominions. Privately, however, he was in no mood to talk peace with Germany at this stage, 'after they have overrun & demoralized the peoples of so many countries in Europe'. Until the Third Reich was 'prepared to live peaceably with her neighbours in Europe, she will always be a menace. We have got to get rid of her aggressive spirit, her engines of war & the people who have been taught to use them'.[3]

This view concurred with those of his governments at home and in the Commonwealth. He replied to King Gustav (12 August), declining the offer and reiterating that 'the intention of My peoples to prosecute the war until their purposes have been achieved has been strengthened'.[4]

Meanwhile Crown Princess Märtha and her children accepted Roosevelt's offer; they left Stockholm for Petsamo on 12 August, and sailed to the United States. For a few weeks they lived at Hyde Park, the President's country home, then accepted an invitation to stay at the Cape Cod property of a Norwegian-American, Frederick Schaefer. Later in the autumn they

---

* The telegram could not be traced during Tim Greve's researches for his biography of the King, published in 1983.

moved to Pook's Hill, a house in Maryland within half an hour's journey from Washington DC.

The Crown Prince came to visit them in mid-December, travelling under the alias of 'Alexander Carlsen' to conceal his identity from enemy agents, and the news media. He stayed in North America until April 1941, on the first of several wartime visits to see his family and work for the Norwegian cause in the Americas. He and the Crown Princess involved themselves to the full in propaganda activities, speaking on various occasions on the American and Canadian broadcasting systems, holding press conferences, and in general helping to publicize the Norwegian war effort.

Crown Princess Märtha and her son Prince Harald came in for no little praise from William Hassett, Roosevelt's aide. She was 'very gracious to all the servants', while the little Prince, he noted, 'shook my hand and bowed from the waist in best Continental style, all with a grand flourish – very bright youngster. One wonders, in a world of change and transition, whether he will ever occupy a throne'.[5]

The President's wife, Eleanor, was interested to see something at first hand of the upbringing of royal children. Expecting them to be excessively pampered and cosseted, she too was impressed by Prince Harald, whom she initially thought rather frail. Not only did she find him apparently devoid of fear, but also very tough to swim when the water was very cold – until it was gently pointed out to her that he was used to swimming off the coast of Norway, where it was much colder.

Although Eleanor Roosevelt's memoirs refrained from uncharitable comment, others were less charitable about the future King's wife. According to the White House maid, Lillian Rogers Parks, 'Princess Märtha was the most flirtatious of the royal crowd', forever making eyes at the President, and 'Eleanor did not take kindly to it'. He had always been ready to make passes at pretty women, and this had threatened his marriage at least once in the past. Parks thought that he was infatuated with the Crown Princess, whom he told to address him as 'the Godfather', and considered that Eleanor was more disturbed by her husband's flirtations with royalty than with pretty secretaries or American society matrons. The egalitarian in her 'hated phoniness and was annoyed that he was so impressed with royalty.' Thereafter any woman who made a fuss of the President, Eleanor would remark with scorn, was 'just another Martha'.[6]

Although Sweden was also officially neutral, she was traditionally more well-disposed to Germany than her fellow Scandinavian monarchies. Throughout Europe, particularly in the British Foreign Office, King Gustav V was regarded with suspicion as being more neutral than most of his pro-allied family, 'rather liked by the Führer' as the first monarch to visit him some years previously, and 'most careful never to commit himself to any word or deed which could provoke German criticism'.[7] The Swedish ministers believed that the allies were primarily interested in getting a foothold in Sweden in order to seal off the northern iron mines and cut the flow of iron ore to Germany. As Swedish ore provided almost half of Germany's imports of twenty million tons annually, the government was concerned at the economic implications of any such move.

In June 1941 the Third Reich attacked the Soviet Union. As a nation Sweden dreaded sharing the fate of Denmark and Norway, and finding herself under German occupation. Military reprisals were threatened if the Swedish government refused to cooperate with German demands for transit facilities across her territory from Norway to Finland. After consultation between the King and his senior ministers, a communiqué was published in the morning papers of 26 June stating that, while Sweden would 'resolutely pursue her endeavours to maintain her integrity and independence', in view of representations made by Germany and Finland requesting permission to transport on the Swedish railways from Norway to Finland a force of troops limited to one division, 'after consulting the Riksdag, the Government has agreed that this shall take place in a manner safeguarding Swedish sovereignty'.[8]

It was alleged that King Gustav threatened to abdicate if thwarted, and insisted that his heir would do likewise. Post-war opinion maintains that the 'German transit' measure saved the country from invasion, if not from world condemnation owing to the ineptitude of Swedish foreign policy and diplomacy.[9] If it was another exercise in brinkmanship and playing for high stakes to preserve his throne and his country, it succeeded, though it angered the British Foreign Secretary, Anthony Eden, and his parliamentary under-secretary, R.A. Butler, who said that the King had 'exercised his usual Pétain-like influence for Peace at all costs'.[10] From London, King Haakon was furious with the brother-monarch whom he had never really trusted, and vowed that once he returned to Norway he would never set foot on Swedish soil while 'that old scoundrel' was alive.

Whether the abdication threats were more than rumour is open to doubt. Victor Mallet at Stockholm thought they were 'entirely fictitious'. From various sources, he gathered the impression that 'His Majesty is personally determined that Sweden shall not be drawn into the war and that he wishes to go down to posterity as the man who succeeded in steering his country clear of two catastrophes. It is possible that he considers no price too high to pay for this honour.' The only other explanation for the abdication stories, he continued, was possibly that the Social Democratic leaders, 'having agreed against their better judgment to make concessions to Germany, sought to justify themselves to their more resolute supporters and voters by claiming that their hand had been forced by the King'.

A powerful Swedish industrialist, who was a fervent supporter of Britain and fiercely critical of the decision to allow troop transits, discussed the King's attitude with Mallet: 'he knows the King well and sees him often. I was somewhat surprised to hear him assert that King Gustav still had the strength of mind to say "No" when necessary and that he would never sell Sweden "down the river" to Germany but in the last resort would fight as public opinion would demand.' The King, he maintained, 'is regarded as the real leader of the country and will not fail it. His death would be a disaster because the Crown Prince, though fundamentally pro-British, has not the same strength of character as his father.'[11]

In another despatch, Mallet reported on the effect of the outbreak of war between Germany and Russia and the likelihood that it would cause a dangerous split in Swedish public opinion. On one hand lay the age-long antagonism to Russia, exacerbated by the Soviet Government's assault on Finland in 1939 and her swift, practically bloodless absorption of the three Baltic States in 1940. On the other hand lay the fairly recent but no less intense hatred of the Nazi regime, which rapidly turned the pro-German Sweden of 1914 into the fervently anti-Nazi Sweden of 1941, 'a hatred vastly stimulated by the brutal and clumsy behaviour of the Nazis in Norway.' The Social Democratic party in Sweden, he maintained, was 'the most steadfast in its faith in Britain's cause', but was by no means pro-Soviet, and hesitated to incur responsibility for breaking up the coalition government as this would play into the hands of German propagandists and fifth columnists who were particularly active in Sweden. King Gustav's instinct was therefore right in favouring acceptance of German demands. Nevertheless his motives were suspect. Not only was he anxious to keep Sweden out of the war at any cost, but 'he detests and fears bolshevism much more than he dislikes what he considers the parvenu and rather crazy posturing of Hitler'.[12]

Ministers continued to support the principle of a free press, immune to the attacks of German newspapers and broadcasters condemning the Swedes for 'their lack of comprehension in the face of the new forces in Europe.' The Swedish press expressed a multitude of opinions on the King's actions. A pro-Nazi newspaper, *Aftonbladet*, praised his 'purposeful will with which he has performed his task of leadership' during the crisis. The Swedish Communist paper *Ny Dag* attacked the journal's 'bowings', calling its sentiments 'approval from the swine', and declaring the policy 'not beneficial for the King's prestige; it can one day make the Throne totter'.[13] Swedish opinion against Germany steadily mounted, and in September 1944 the Swedish government announced that all Swedish Baltic ports and waters would be closed to foreign shipping, owing to the new situation in the Baltic produced by the Russo-Finnish armistice of that year. This meant the virtual stoppage of Swedish-German trade for the duration of the war.

The Crown Prince and Princess of Sweden felt the division of wartime loyalties keenly. Mallet called the Crown Prince 'a charming man to meet, and has easy and democratic manners, but those who know him well say that he is unable to make his mind up in an emergency, and that the fact that the King will devolve none of his duties or authority upon his son has produced a listlessness regarding political matters which will make him a weak King when his time comes. Be that as it may, his whole instinct and environment and his successive marriages to two British princesses make him intensely pro-British, even though he has to exercise great care in showing where his sympathies lie'.[14]

Although technically German-born – the onetime Princess Louise of Battenberg had entered the world at her family's ancestral home, Heligenberg – the Crown Princess was British through and through by upbringing. She and her husband were horrified by the behaviour of Hitler and Mussolini, and they were among the first members of European royalty to know the evil truth about German concentration camps. However, they agreed with Sweden's neutrality, as long as Germany did not threaten to invade the country.

One friend in England to whom the Crown Prince could speak his mind was Lady Astor. Apologizing for his apparent tardiness in answering her letter of 9 January 1941, he explained that it had only just reached them (7 April):

That is only *one* of the many things to remind us of how fundamentally upset Europe is at the present time. It is all too horrible. A brilliant and outstanding thing is the wonderful way in which the British people have stood the immense moral and physical strain. I have always had a very high opinion of the good nerve of that race, but my admiration *now* is unlimited. . . . We are all quite well here. Three of my boys are working hard, each on their particular job in the army or navy. Louise is as plucky and cheerful as can be. It is of course very hard on her being separated from her people for so long. But she has a very well balanced mind and excellent self control, like most English people. Ingrid I have not seen for a year now. But we are able to correspond by letter and I am also able to call her up on the 'phone, which I do about once a week. Of course you are then only able to talk about trivial matters as I feel certain that the "guests", as they call them in Denmark, listen to every word that is said. It is just possible I may be able to see her for a few hours when we visit our country place for a few days towards the end of this month. She may be able to hop across from Denmark. It is not that she would not be allowed to, but she – quite rightly – thinks that she ought to remain there under present circumstances. I am told that she is very much liked in her new country, especially on account of her dignified behaviour and present circumstances. Naturally they have to live under a good deal of strain. She is wrapped up in her baby,* which must be very sweet and it is just going to be a year old in 9 days time. And I am very glad to say, that she is intensely happy! That is a great comfort to me.

For obvious reasons I cannot write about those things I should best like to discuss with you. But let me say that I keep optimistic and cheerful and that I feel sure we shall meet again to discuss freely all that has happened and still will happen during this unhappy war. There *must* be some meaning in it all, though *we* cannot grasp it. I firmly believe everything will come right in the end.

Of course we feel very cut off here. But you must not think that we feel oppressed for all that. The people are working stubbornly to make up for those things which we cannot import any longer. All our motor cars are being altered for charcoal fuel or for wood. Tens of thousands are already running in that way and more will follow. A great deal, in fact unbelievably much has been done to strengthen and to build up national defence. Many of our industries have been occupied for a year or more in manufacturing war material of every description. Of course there are large arrears to make up. Also the reservists have been called up for periods of training, thus giving much increased efficiency to the fighting forces. I have given up a good part of my time for this, inspecting troops, going to manoeuvres etc. The spirit of the people is good.[15]

Relatives in Germany, England and other countries who could not write to each other during the war used the Crown Princess of Sweden to clear their correspondence. She acted as a go-between in much the same way as Queen Alexandrine of Denmark had done for other relatives during the Great War. Louise's task was not simply restricted to forwarding letters. For security reasons she also had to copy out every letter and re-address it as if from herself.

Throughout her adult life she had been involved in humanitarian work of some kind. At the outbreak of the Great War she had trained as a Red Cross nurse, serving in military hospitals in France between 1915 and 1917. Soon after her marriage she had taken over the chairmanships of various charitable institutions in Sweden, which entailed attending a large number of committee meetings, offering advice and opinions.

As part of the war effort she came to the aid of some 40,000 Finnish children who sought refuge in Sweden, setting up a home for them at Radan, near Ulriksdal. The expenses and keep of the children were paid for by various members of the royal family, although she was responsible for the day-to-day running. Accommodation for eighteen children was provided, a

---

* Princess Margrethe. See below, p. 117.

superintendent was appointed, and children's nurses were engaged; in February 1942 they were ready to receive the first eighteen. She spent much time with them, and they were devoted to her. The home was closed in 1943, but she continued to take an interest in the children's progress and kept in touch with many of them after their return home.

In addition Louise established a fund, *Vinterljus* (Winter Light). Many rural areas of Sweden lacked electricity, and when petrol and paraffin were requisitioned for the war effort, people in many parts of the countryside were left without any source of light, and money was needed to supply them with carbide lamps and candles. She also broadcast on the radio for *Kronprinsessans gåvokommitté för Neutralitetsvakten* (the Crown Princess's Committee for Gifts to the Defenders of Neutrality), which she set up to provide warm clothing for the troops. The forces claimed they were inundated with stockings, jerseys, scarves and protectors. Encouraged by parcels of clothes, the men were emboldened to ask for other things. One asked for an accordion and added his thanks in advance at the end of his letter. As he had already thanked them, she said, they might as well send him one.

The Red Cross in Sweden collected pillows and mattresses for schoolchildren who were being evacuated, and asked Princess Louise if the bedding could be stored in the palace at Stockholm. An apartment was therefore opened up and she organized sewing groups at the palace. With help from the Singer Sewing Machine Company, machines were quickly installed, and soon about forty women helped to make clothes, sent wherever they were needed, especially to children at home and abroad.

Although eighty years old and increasingly deaf the King's brother Carl, Duke of Västergötland, still actively presided over the Red Cross in Sweden. Like their youngest brother Eugen, Duke of Närke, he was strongly anti-German. Ingeborg, Duchess of Västergötland, remarked Mallet, 'is a sister of the Kings of Denmark and Norway, so that the feelings of the family can well be imagined; nor does the Princess attempt to conceal her detestation of everything German, though she has to be discreet'.[16]

Despite a non-aggression pact which Hitler had signed with Denmark on 31 May 1939, the country had every reason to fear invasion. At around 4 a.m. on 9 April 1940, German troops began pouring across the Jutland border, parachute troops were dropped at key points around the country, and soldiers stepped ashore in Copenhagen from innocent-looking German merchant ships. Surprise air attacks wiped out most of the grounded small Danish air force, and such was the swiftness of the operation that the Danish army, numbering around 14,000, had no chance to emerge from barracks. A few detachments put up a spirited resistance in Jutland, while the Royal Life Guards at Amalienborg Palace were issued with live ammunition and managed to hold off a German detachment which had been instructed to capture King Christian.

The Prime Minister, Thorvald Stauning, and his cabinet urged the King to capitulate; while the Danish Commander-in-Chief argued for resistance, but was outvoted and had no choice but to give the order to surrender. The German forces, insisting that they had merely stepped in to save Denmark from being invaded by the British, promised to respect Danish integrity and political independence. King Christian broadcast an appeal on the wireless to his subjects 'to assume a completely correct and worthy attitude, since every thoughtless action or statement can have the most serious consequences'.[17] A core of resistance hardened under the lead of J. Christmas Møller, the Conservative leader and minister of commerce, but he was soon ousted by the Germans. Effective power passed from Stauning to the collaborationist foreign minister Eric Scavenius.

Despite German assurances to the contrary, inestimable havoc was soon wrought on the country as a result of interference in the government and economy. Leading politicians were forced out of office and replaced with Nazi sympathizers; writers were arrested; and fierce censorship was established. The only Danish naval assets, her eight torpedo boats, were commandeered by the Germans, while the army was reduced to the size and function of a mere police force. Danish agriculture and industry were pressed into German service.

Yet their presence did not dissuade King Christian X from enjoying his customary morning ride, unescorted, through Copenhagen. 'Who guards him?' asked the incredulous Germans. 'We all do', was the Danes' reply. In his own way, King Christian X became as much a national symbol to the Danes as Churchill did in Britain; his character and attitudes discouraged collaboration and inspired the spirit that manifested itself in the Danish resistance. By his daily ride through the city, he 'became the symbol of resistance by the Danish people to a fate which they had been powerless to prevent but to which they were determined not to be resigned'.[18] Queen Alexandrine accompanied him to the stables when he went out to his horse every morning, and always waited at the front door to welcome him on his return.

Ill health soon put an end to this routine. During the summer of 1942 he was admitted to hospital briefly for treatment for jaundice. He had recovered and been discharged by the time of his seventy-second birthday on 26 September, an event marked by celebrations in Copenhagen and at a reception for seven hundred guests at the Danish Legation in London. At the latter the Danish Minister, Count Eduard Reventlow spoke of his joy in seeing so many of his countrymen together in what he called 'this little piece of Denmark' in England. It testified to the deep bond of fellowship between the King and the Danish people, never more than since the

Germans had broken in and enchained 'our proud and beloved Fatherland, whose people for a thousand years have maintained Denmark's liberty'.[19]

As usual Hitler sent King Christian X a congratulatory telegram on his birthday, to which the King replied with a laconic 'Cordial thanks'. Early in October 1942 it was announced that the German minister in Copenhagen and the Danish minister in Berlin had been recalled to their respective capitals as a result, it was maintained, of the Führer's displeasure at King Christian's acknowledgement of the birthday greeting. Quite why the Nazi leader should have taken offence was never satisfactorily explained. Even though the King wrote a friendly letter reiterating his telegram of thanks, the Danish Nazi newspaper *Faedrelandet* predicted that the King's ruling days were over, and that his 'autumn is giving place to a long winter'.

In one respect the prophecy was about to be fulfilled, although not in the way the paper had suggested. During the King's ride on 19 October his horse shied and threw him. He was taken to hospital suffering from shock, with injuries to his head and left knee. At first bulletins made light of his condition, but gangrene developed in his left foot, pneumonia soon set in, and for some time his life was almost despaired of. On 28 October he signed a decree appointing the Crown Prince as Regent. Through sheer will-power he pulled through; he was determined to live long enough to see the end of the occupation. He left hospital on 22 November, but he never walked again, and spent his remaining years in a wheelchair. From then on, his appearances in public were few and far between.

One exception was at a memorial service on 3 June 1943 at Roskilde Cathedral, held to commemorate the centenary of the birth of King Frederick VIII. All the late King's surviving children, as well as various ministers and former court officials and functionaries attended. It was an emotional experience for all. Two former court officials, Gotthold Krag, former Lord of the Bedchamber, and the former Lord Chamberlain Count Moltke, were both aged eighty-six. As small boys, their memories could perhaps just reach back as far as the death of King Frederick VII and the accession, in similarly troubled times, of King Christian IX. Once again neighbouring Germany was the aggressor. From Bismarck to Hitler, history had repeated itself, and the wheel had come full circle.

The ceremony began with an address in which a review was given of the short reign of King Frederick VIII. A hymn was sung, and the Archbishop presented his congratulations to King Christian for having been able to attend the ceremony in spite of ill health.

As a Mecklenburg by birth, Queen Alexandrine suffered from a conflict of loyalties, but she identified herself totally with the Danish cause, and her patriotism was never in doubt. In her granddaughter's words, 'the Occupation clearly put a strain on her, being of German descent. It represented a Germany she could not identify with, not in any respect whatsoever'.[20]

Shortly after the start of the occupation, two of her nephews came to Denmark from Mecklenburg. One telephoned Crown Prince Frederick, now Regent, and asked if it was satisfactory to visit, as they had always been on good terms. Yes, replied the Crown Prince – provided he was not in uniform. His brother tactlessly turned up in uniform, and was given the cold shoulder. After the war the Crown Prince and Princess never received him in their home again, and they avoided him at family gatherings. The 'civilian' cousin, however, was rewarded for his commonsense by staying friends with the Danish royal family for the rest of his life.

Only one German-born member of the royal family had no qualms about her partisanship of the Nazis. Princess Helena, daughter of Frederick Ferdinand, Duke of Holstein-Sonderburg-Glucksburg, was married to Prince Harald, younger brother of King Christian and King Haakon. Her behaviour during the Nazi occupation of Copenhagen utterly appalled her embarrassed husband and children. Watching a Luftwaffe squadron overhead from the terrace one day, she gazed fondly at them, saying to a nearby officer, 'Aren't our planes wonderful?' With commendable restraint, the officer asked her brusquely to remember that she was a Danish princess, and stalked away. In her rooms she regularly entertained the notorious General von Pancke, head of the Gestapo in Copenhagen, and his mistress Baroness von Busche.

Prince Harald and their sons Gorm and Oluf, both in their twenties, would avoid the dining room when she was entertaining them. Gorm, an officer in the Guard Hussars, was so distressed by his mother's behaviour that he spent most of the time in barracks. When the Germans disarmed Danish soldiers in August 1940, Oluf remained in Denmark as a member of the Resistance Movement, while Gorm fled with many others to Sweden, remaining there until the country was liberated. On his first night, he dined with his parents and Prince Oluf. All went amicably until a bottle of brandy was brought to the table after the meal. It was two-thirds full, and Gorm asked lightheartedly who had drunk the rest. Oluf leaned over to him and whispered, 'General von Pancke'. Flushing with anger, Gorm grabbed the bottle, threw it against the fireplace, and stalked out.

Princess Helena was shameless about flaunting her friendship with Pancke. Her car was often parked in front of his headquarters at Dagmar Hous, or the Tourist Hotel, where Baroness von Busche entertained guests prodigally with looted champagne. Sometimes the infuriated Danes shattered the windows of her limousine, but it made no difference to her behaviour.

In the summer of 1943 the Nazis delivered an ultimatum to the government to declare martial law, ban all strikes, and impose the death penalty on saboteurs. Though Scavenius was now prime minister, the government refused. In August the German military forces took over executive power and the Danish government and monarch effectively ceased to function. The following month, the Danes organized a secret Freedom Council to lead the Resistance movement. During the autumn they also helped around 7,000 Danish Jews – almost the entire Jewish population of Denmark – to escape to safety in Sweden. The Germans arrested thousands of Danes, including about two hundred Jews, policemen, leading citizens and Resistance fighters. Most of these were shot, tortured, or sent to prison camps in Germany. The Danish navy scuttled its ships before the Germans could get to them. The Resistance was particularly successful in Jutland and Funen, where German troop transports from Norway to the Normandy front were cut to about a quarter of their schedules.

The invalid King was virtually a prisoner in his palace – initially at Sorgenfri, then Amalienborg – and leading citizens were arrested and sent to concentration camps. For many years, the story persisted that King Christian X wore the yellow star of David to demonstrate solidarity with the Jews. According to his granddaughter Margrethe, he never did, as the Germans knew better than to insist that Danish Jews did wear the star. The story, she maintained, originated from a remark by a Copenhagen errand boy who said that 'if they try to enforce the yellow star here, the King will be the first to wear it!'[21]

Overseas, King Christian's acceptance of a difficult role was widely appreciated. At a luncheon of the Anglo-Danish Society at the Dorchester Hotel, London, in January 1944, Anthony Eden praised Danish devotion to the allied cause in the face of German aggression, particularly the King, as 'very few constitutional monarchs have had a more difficult role to play. We understand the ordeal through which he, with his people, has had to go in Denmark, and through which he is still going. It has won for him the increased admiration and affection of his people and his friends everywhere'.[22]

The admiration and affection was even greater among the select few who knew what dangers the King and Queen faced. Visitors who were received at the royal summer palace of Sorgenfri would notice two bullet holes in a window just behind the King's desk, while from a German hostel overlooking the Amalienborg, they could see Germans throwing hand grenades into the gardens. The King and Queen refused to leave for safer quarters, but the strain took its toll of the already weakened King's declining health.

Another cross the King had to bear in his last years was the independence of Iceland. In June 1944 the government of the island decided to cut their ties with Denmark and proclaim a republic. Putting his personal feelings aside, he sent a generous message in which he conveyed his best wishes for the future of the Icelandic nation.

Yet during the war years there was occasion for rejoicing as well. Princess Margrethe had been born on 16 April 1940, exactly a week after the invasion. Her arrival was good news for the dynasty, especially as the Crown Prince and Princess had been married for nearly five years. Their lack of children had given rise to speculation about the state of their marriage, with rumours of mutual incompatibility and threats by the Crown Princess to return home to Sweden if her husband did not curb his drinking. In April 1944 a second daughter was born to the Crown Prince and Princess. She was named Benedikte, and among her godparents was Queen Elizabeth of Great Britain. Because of the occupation of Denmark she was unable to attend the ceremony, though she attended her goddaughter's wedding some twenty-seven years later.

By summer 1944 the war was turning against Germany. The Danish Resistance was now being actively supported by the allies and stimulated by Free Danish broadcasters in London. Railways and factories were sabotaged, and strikes broke out across the country. The Germans employed ex-convicts who had originally been recruited to fight on the eastern front to help crush the saboteurs, and this led to more revolts. A German officer was trampled to death when he fired on demonstrators at an Odense shipyard. Sabotage became more commonplace, with strikes and demonstrations over much of the country. The biggest was the Copenhagen uprising in June 1944, during which eighty-eight Danes were killed. For five days the city was a battleground, with Danes erecting barricades in the streets, while the Nazis cut off gas, electricity, water and food supplies.

Within a few months it was clear that the conflict in Europe would soon be over. Broadcasts from London were eagerly anticipated and listened to, until on 4 May the long-awaited BBC announcement informed them that German troops in northern Germany, Holland and Denmark had surrendered unconditionally. There was singing and dancing in the streets, and from one end of the country to the other, Danes put lighted candles in their windows.

On 5 May Queen Alexandrine visited her son, daughter-in-law and grandchildren in their quarters at Frederick VIII's Palace in the Amalienborg. She wanted to be at the window where she could see the royal standard rise above King Christian VIII's palace once again. For Princess Margrethe, an abiding memory was and always would remain the first changing of the guard on the square, with the police replaced by the guards, and standing on the balcony watching the huge crowds, overwhelmed with joy at the promise of a return to peace and normal life.

That same day King Christian broadcast to his people for the first time since the German seizure of power in 1943. He paid tribute to the

Resistance movement, and asked all Danes to give their confidence to the new cabinet he had just appointed.

Four days later King Christian and Queen Alexandrine were given an enthusiastic welcome by thousands of Copenhageners as they drove in an open car along the ranks of the Freedom Fighters from Amalienborg to Christiansborg, where they opened the first Free Parliament after the German occupation. After the opening ceremony the King greeted the Allied representatives to thank them for all the help they had given Denmark during the war. An enthusiastic welcome also awaited Field-Marshal Montgomery as he entered Copenhagen on 12 May ostensibly to meet military and naval personnel, and dine with the King and Queen at Amalienborg; but also to reassure Winston Churchill that there was no truth in the rumour that the Russians were 'trying to forestall us in Denmark' by contacting the Resistance movement with the object of putting a Communist government in power.

Although King, military leaders and ministers were weary after the years of occupation, there were ample celebrations, and while there was still much work to be done, there was time to rest as well. Among the posters and signboards seen in the streets of the capital that month was one reading '*Lukket paa Grund af Glaede*' ('Closed on account of joy').

CHAPTER TEN

'Absolutely without any feeling of class or rank'

King Haakon and Crown Prince Olav witnessed the VE celebrations in London on the night of 8–9 May 1945, after which the Crown Prince and two ministers crossed in a British destroyer from Edinburgh to Oslo. The remaining members of the Norwegian government, including the President of the Storting, C.J. Hambro, and nearly 800 other Norwegians, left London on 27 May to sail from Liverpool to Oslo. King Haakon, who had been joined in the meantime by Princess Märtha and her three children at Foliejon, left London on the evening of 4 June, after visiting both Buckingham Palace and the BBC, where he recorded a farewell message of thanks to the British people. Next day the five of them sailed from Rosyth in HMS *Norfolk*, the flagship of the 1st Cruiser Squadron, escorted by the *Devonshire*, which had brought him to Britain five years earlier.

On 7 June, the date which was proving of such great significance to the King, they arrived back at Oslo. They stepped ashore in front of the city hall at 12.00 midday, to be received formally by the Crown Prince, as cheering crowds drowned the salutes from ships' guns and sirens. A series of speeches followed, but what moved the King much more was the procession of 130,000 people that evening, filing past the royal family assembled on the palace balcony. It was the climax of triumphant celebrations which demonstrated that the sacrifices made by King, royal family and nation during the bitter war years had been triumphantly vindicated.

Shortly after this return, the King had to find someone to undertake the formation of a caretaker ministry in Norway until elections could be held in the autumn. 'In politics, things don't go so easy as I had hoped', he wrote rather despondently to King George VI. Though he had no desire to exceed his limits as a constitutional monarch, some of his subjects felt that as he had achieved such a unique position in the public mind, he should surely be entitled to choose his own council and government. One anonymous correspondent wrote to him that 'the jubilation directed in these days towards the throne must surely have led Your Majesty to understand that it was a *ruling* King we wished to welcome home'.[1]

In his late eighties when the war ended, King Gustav V was still comparatively sprightly. Playing tennis regularly with the vigour of a man half his age, he continued to wield a racquet well into his ninth decade. During a game with the highly seeded player Kalle Schröder, he chided the latter for not being on form. 'I'm just warming up, Your Majesty!' was Schröder's reply. 'Oh, I thought you were cooling off!'[2] the King answered with a chuckle. On 1 April 1945 his reign became the longest in Swedish history. Having worn the crown for 37 years, 3 months and 24 days, he had surpassed by one day the reign of the founder of Swedish national unity, King Gustav Vasa, who had died in 1560. Although aged eighty-six, *The Times* correspondent noted solemnly, His Majesty 'celebrated his tie by playing lawn tennis'.

With the passing of the years came inevitable absent-mindedness. Inaugurating a new football stadium at Råsunda, he caused a moment's consternation by proudly declaring 'this new tennis court' open.

In old age his loneliness was assuaged particularly by the company of Axel Munthe, the late Queen's physician-in-ordinary. Munthe had stayed with the King in Stockholm every summer since the thirties, and finding life increasingly irksome in Capri during the war, he left in June 1943 to spend his remaining years as the King's personal guest at the palace. Memories of the past bound the two contemporaries together.

Rumour suggested that there was a closer family connection as well. The two men, who were almost exactly the same age – Munthe was eight months older – were similar in appearance, and it was assumed by some that the physician was the illegitimate child of either the King's father, King Oscar II, or of his uncle, King Carl XV. If either assertion is true, then they were half-brothers or cousins. A basic sense of insecurity throughout Munthe's long life was ascribed in part to his knowledge that he was apparently a royal bastard.[3]

Though after all these years they had little to say to each other, the King still insisted that Munthe should have lunch with him at least once a week. Putting his best coat on as he was getting ready one day, Munthe complained to his valet Vittorio that he found it an awful business lunching with the King, as it was so dull. Vittorio asked him what the King thought about it. 'He also thinks it is dull.' 'Then why do you go on meeting for lunch?' Munthe paused before muttering, half to himself, 'Well, you see it's more fun being dull together'.[4]

Both men remained friends to the end, though they frequently agreed to differ. In particular, with his affection for animals, Munthe was often roused to anger at autumn during the height of the elk-hunting season. Asked one day by his staff what was troubling him, he expostulated that the royal family 'talk of nothing else but killing animals'.

At least one of the King's friendships was handled with extraordinary discretion. In his eighties he fell in love with one of his tennis partners, a businessman named Haiby. This affair came to a sudden end when Haiby was lured into exile and jailed abroad. Even the tolerance of the Swedes towards their sovereign's proclivities, it seems, had its limits, and this would evidently have been one scandal too far if it became public knowledge. In fact it was successfully suppressed for over twenty years, until well after the King's death.[5]

Two unexpected family deaths saddened King Gustav V's last years. On 26 January 1947 his grandson Prince Gustav Adolf, second in succession to the throne, was due to return home after spending a few days hunting wild boar in the Netherlands as the guest of Prince Bernhard. He caught a flight on a Dutch airliner running a daily service from Amsterdam to Stockholm, stopping en route at Kastrup airport, near Copenhagen. Immediately after taking off at Kastrup the plane crashed, and all twenty-two on board – sixteen passengers, including the Prince and another celebrity, the American opera singer Grace Moore, plus six crew – were killed instantly.

Princess Louise and her niece Dolla were having tea with the King at Drottningholm, when Louise was told by a footman that she was wanted on the telephone. 'It was a completely different person who returned', recalled Dolla, 'walking with heavy steps and despair in her eyes'.[6]

The Prince's troubled years were long since forgotten. A devoted husband and father, he left four daughters and a baby son, Prince Carl Gustav, the latter only nine months old. As President of the Swedish Boy Scout Movement, he had helped to make a valuable contribution to the community and welfare of the people over whom he had hoped to reign. A keen sportsman, he had become one of the country's best fencers and horsemen, as well as chairman of the Swedish Olympics Committee. During the war, Victor Mallet had thought him less popular and accessible than his younger brothers, 'and is said to have a violent temper, but he is active and keen on military and Boy Scout questions, and many people think that he would make a better King than his father, because he is a stronger character'.[7]

Messages of condolence and sympathy came from friends far and wide. In reply to a letter from Mrs Constance Spier, governing director of a firm in London specializing in Chinese works of art, the Crown Prince wrote (8 February 1947) of the 'terrible blow . . . (which) came down on all of us without the slightest warning. And the loss to our country is most severe – as you so rightly say'.[8]

To his old friend Lady Astor he unburdened himself at greater length (21 February 1947):

It is hard to realize yet, that my dear Edmund has passed on. He was so full of life and so keen on everything he did. And, oh, I had pinned my faith on his being able in due time to take over from me. I honestly believe, though I may be biassed because of being his father, that he would have done extraordinarily well as a king.

That was not to be. You know, Lady Astor, I have made up my mind for once and for all I did it when Daisy was taken away out of my sight in 1920 – never to put the question: *why*. For I firmly believe there is a meaning in everything that happens. Only we are not given always to see the reason. Besides, it is no use. It only wastes and saps your strength.

Therefore, though it may be difficult at times, and the flesh is weak, I am looking *forward*, not looking back unduly. We are meant to face the future with as stout a heart as may be humanly possible, and to make the best of a new situation. In this case the situation is of course quite unforeseen. It may be full of difficulties and complications. Yet they must all be faced – and overcome. There always is a way out of every difficulty. Every problem, however complicated, has a solution.

I grieve for my poor daughter-in-law and for the 5 children. She is wonderful. I am full of admiration. May she be granted strength to continue, I fear as time goes on it may be more difficult even than at the present moment. She never lost her moral balance, though it was a devastating blow. I can only repeat: she is an example to all of us.[9]

To Lady Astor, Crown Princess Louise wrote (19 February 1947):

You can understand how my heart aches for my Gustaf. So like you to offer to do any thing to help him, I know you would want to do any thing for him. I can reassure you that he is bearing his deep great sorrow in a wonderful & typically selfless way. Now that he has got over the first shock & overwhelming despair he really is alright. He has things to do which take up his thoughts quite a lot & has taken up playing tennis 5 (?) afternoons a week again which is so good for him. Ingrid has been here for just over a fortnight & on Sunday evening he is going to Copenhagen to stay with her for 6 days, it is such a comfort to Gustaf to be with her & he is looking forward to seeing his grandchildren there, & Sigvard & his dear wife. It will do him so much good to get away for a little now as later on he won't be able to leave the country as his father hopes to be able to go to the Riviera next month for a change & some sunshine & warmth. My poor old father i(n) l(aw) has not been out of the country for 8 years & he feels his favourite grandson's death most terribly.

I need hardly tell you that Gustaf's great feeling of responsibility & high sense of duty though they were alas to have to weigh so heavily upon him are at the same time a support and help. His great wish & thought is to be a help to poor Sibylla,* he really means so much to her & they are such

* The widowed Princess.

good friends that though Gustaf is so diffident & modest I know he is of the greatest help to her. She is a help to him through the quite wonderful way she bears her loss & sorrow, a spiritual courage & calmness & balance which is truly quite marvellous. The one thing one must be grateful for is that Edmund's life was such a full & happy one & that one need have no regrets that his life might have been different. His life was what he wished & what one could wish for him. It does one good to feel that he passed on from a content happy & full life. That makes Gustaf's sorrow not a bitter one which is just every thing. . .[10]

Equally unexpected, and even more shocking, was the violent death of King Gustav V's nephew, Count Folke Bernadotte. Despite ill health as a young man which necessitated his retiring from the Swedish army at the age of thirty-eight, he had been a loyal servant of the dynasty. In 1935 he was appointed adjutant to Prince Gustav Adolf, the eldest son of the Crown Prince, as the Count was seen as likely to prove a moderating influence on the sometimes wayward young man. Appointed Vice-Chairman of the Swedish Red Cross shortly after the outbreak of World War II, he took a leading role in the welfare of interned foreign personnel and the release of political prisoners from concentration camps. It said much for his diplomatic skills that Himmler and other senior Nazis had confidence in him, and that he was regarded as a natural mediator between enemy powers. In April 1945 he had helped to negotiate the German surrender in Denmark, and later that year he went to Norway to help negotiate the German capitulation there. When his uncle Prince Carl retired from the Chairmanship of the Red Cross in 1946, Count Folke devoted all his efforts to the well-being and repatriation of prisoners of war.

He was therefore an obvious choice in 1948 when the United Nations required someone of authority and a proven record of negotiating, to mediate in Palestine; to supervise a truce between the warring Jews and Arabs; to demilitarize Jerusalem and resettle refugees. Through meetings with the Arabs he was soon in a position to submit peace proposals, but he was distrusted by the Jews. In September 1948 he was driving in a convoy, when men in Israeli army uniforms approached his car and calmly fired on him. The assassins, who were never caught, justified his 'execution' by claiming that he was acting as a spy for Britain and America, and was responsible for Jewish deaths by his negotiations with the Arabs.

By the end of the war, King Christian X was in poor health. The injuries sustained as a result of his riding accident in October 1942, coupled with the strain of living with constant anxiety and danger during the occupation, had severely undermined his constitution. His ministers were obliging enough to spare him one disagreeable task. In Denmark the death penalty had fallen into abeyance, but after the conflict was over, demands for retrospective legislation providing for the execution of war criminals and Danish Nazis became overwhelming. As the King objected to signing death warrants, a bill was introduced exempting him from doing so, while allowing him to retain the right of reprieve. During the post-war period seventy-eight Danes were condemned to death, and of these forty-six were executed.

Early in January 1947 King Christian fell ill with pneumonia. On 6 April he had a heart attack, followed by inflammation of a lung. Gangrene developed in his right foot, though unconnected with the gangrene contracted when his left foot had been injured. Crown Prince Frederick was designated Regent and summoned home urgently from Stockholm, where he had been taking an Easter holiday with his wife and daughters. They followed him back a few days later, and the King's surviving sister, Princess Ingeborg, came to help nurse him. By the middle of the month his condition gave increasing cause for concern.

'My task on this earth is over', the weary King told the family assembled around his bedside at Amalienborg Palace, shortly before he lapsed into unconsciousness on the afternoon of 20 April. 'I am at peace with my God and myself – I am so tired.'[11] Outside, thousands of people flocked into Amalienborg Square as the news spread. At 11.04 p.m., the monarch who had personified the defiant stand of his people against German occupation was indeed at peace. He was aged seventy-six.

Generous tributes were paid, ironically, by the press of the formerly republican Social Democratic Party and the Communists, the only newspapers appearing in their regular form at that time owing to a compositors' strike. They remarked that 'His Majesty had maintained his promise never to act in disagreement with the democratic and parliamentary principles of the country, and that, in a changing world, he had caused all dispute about the form of government in Denmark to become superfluous'.[12] The controversy surrounding his role in the Easter crisis was evidently long forgiven.

His elder son was proclaimed King Frederick IX from the balcony of the Christiansborg Palace the following day. At the end of his speech to the crowds, Queen Ingrid joined him. Alec Randall, the ambassador, noted that he kissed her publicly in front of the crowd, 'with a touch which augurs well for the popularity of his reign'.[13] In 1947 such openly warm-hearted gestures from royalty were virtually unknown in public.

Like his father, he was more than content to remain strictly above party politics. As a constitutional King, his role in government was limited to presiding over the weekly meetings of the Council of State comprising the ministers from the ruling government. Here he affixed his signature to all new legislation, which was drawn up in his name. He also formally appointed civil servants and military officers.

At six foot six inches the King was a giant of a man, as befitting the King of a race descended from the Vikings. Having joined the Royal Danish Navy as a cadet and worked his way up through every rank to Rear-Admiral in 1945, he had a lifelong love of all things nautical. From the palace windows he enjoyed watching steamers leaving the city, and sometimes, with the aid of a flashlight, he would signal greetings in Morse code to the captain of the vessel. Though he had officially left the Danish navy on his marriage, he retained honorary command of the royal yacht *Danebrøg*. On this vessel he spent some of the happiest hours of his life, cruising in and out of the Danish islands, sailing her to Greenland and across the North Sea on visits to Britain, when the yacht would anchor in the Thames above Tower Bridge. It was a second home for King and family, and he and Queen Ingrid would sometimes stay on board overnight when they paid official visits to coastal towns in Denmark, in order to avoid giving their hosts the additional trouble and expense of accommodating them. On occasion, when at home he would even slip out of the palace at night and walk to the mooring, a few hundred yards away, in order to sleep on board. In true naval tradition he boasted a tattoo on his chest of an elaborate Chinese dragon, and he was highly amused when an English Sunday newspaper printed a photograph of it on the eve of his visit to King George VI and Queen Elizabeth in 1951.

Underneath this bluff, jolly exterior, his eldest daughter Margrethe maintained that he was at heart a very shy, modest person. She would recall with admiration his lively imagination, and an ability to tell wonderful stories. As a child he had often made up extraordinary tales about himself, which suggests a lonely child seeking sanctuary in the refuge of a fantasy world. The good-natured cartoons of the royal family which regularly appeared in the press amused him, and he kept a comprehensive collection of them. In the same way he enjoyed hearing jokes about himself, which he would often retell to the family, sometimes adding one or two he had made up himself.

Like his forebears he was no intellectual, and was not in the habit of writing things down. Nevertheless he had inherited the passion for music shared by his mother and his great-grandmother, and had taken piano lessons during boyhood. He had an extraordinary skill for learning by heart, and loved memorizing quotations, which he would often introduce into conversation wherever suitable. With his passion for opera he could quote reams from favourite librettos at will. Musical soirées at Amalienborg were regularly arranged by him, and his mother was always there. With her he had often played four-handed at the piano until, as he once put it in a moment of irritation, 'the gramophone ruined everything'.

In fact the advent of recorded sound did not 'ruin everything', least of all for him. At the age of sixteen he had conducted the Royal Life Guards Band, and until advancing age and rheumatism made it too painful for him to raise his arm above his shoulder, he loved to conduct the Danish Royal Symphony and the Royal Theatre Orchestras. When Hovkapellet, the Swedish house orchestra, issued a record with excerpts from important performances over the years, included was a concert which he had conducted in 1952 in honour of King Gustav VI Adolf's seventieth birthday. One of the achievements which gave him most pleasure was conducting a performance in Copenhagen of the overture to Wagner's *Tannhaüser*, and Isolde's *Liebestod* with Britta Harzberg as the soloist. Almost overcome by emotion at the end, he impulsively embraced the diva on stage afterwards. Some elder members of the family could not but shake their heads in disapproval of such a spontaneous display in full public view.

Although two of them had been born during the years of war and German occupation, the three Princesses – Margrethe, Benedikte, and Anne-Marie – had had a much happier upbringing than the previous generation. As one of only two brothers, King Frederick had had a rather remote childhood. As a boy, he was devoted to his gentle, self-effacing mother, but very much in awe of his father. Even in maturity, notwithstanding mutual respect, there were definite differences of outlook and disagreements between father and son.

Most of the Danish family had been afraid of the stern, unbending King Christian X. The then Crown Princess, now Queen Ingrid, was an exception. She was used to dealing with elderly, rather stiff gentlemen in the Swedish royal family. Tactful beyond her years, she had soon found a ready rapport with her father-in-law, their relationship had made a perceptible difference in enabling Crown Prince Frederick to lead the government as Regent in the place of his incapacitated father during the war.

With the accession of the King, his wife and three attractive young daughters, the Danish monarchy took on a new image. Each year on his birthday, the citizens of Copenhagen would gather in the square of the Amalienborg Palace to greet him. 'King, King, come out or we'll never go home', the schoolchildren would chant. His Majesty duly appeared. 'Has anyone else a birthday today?' was his first question. Several eager hands were raised and he gave them his greetings.

Modern Danish monarchy was not entirely shorn of regal splendour. On New Year's Day King Frederick and Queen Ingrid maintained the tradition of riding in a glass coach through the streets of Copenhagen, the King in full dress uniform and the insignia of the Order of the Elephant, fetched from the security of its display cabinet at Rosenborg Museum. Yet on the day before or the day after, or indeed at almost any time of the year, the citizens of Copenhagen were just as likely to encounter their King and Queen dressed smartly yet inconspicuously in gabardine coats, visiting bookshops, art exhibitions and auctions, or attending the theatre.

In the new reign, Fredensborg came to life again. Although it had been King Christian IX's favourite residence, it had been hardly used since. King Christian X had merely visited it as a child, and as an adult admitted to his family that he still felt a visitor there. He only stayed between its walls for three or four weeks during the shooting season in October and November. During the Occupation it had stood empty and deserted. However King Frederick IX had always loved it, and he and his family moved inside in September 1947. Making it habitable again was a challenge to which Queen Ingrid rose with enthusiasm as she rearranged the furniture and chose new material for the interior decoration. On their return from school each day, the daughters would run indoors eagerly to see the latest changes and improvements that were transforming an imposing, stately building into a home once more.

Although Amalienborg Palace remained their official residence, they also made use of a summer home, Grasten Palace in South Jutland; and a hunting lodge, Trend, 'an unpretentious cabin', was where the family celebrated Christmas while the princesses were still unmarried and at home.

One of King Christian X's first acts as soon as his authority was restored in 1945 had been to issue a private order banishing his aunt, Princess Helena, for her reckless partisanship of Nazis during the occupation. In order to avoid imprisonment or forcible ejection from the country, she was exiled and went back to her castle at Glucksburg. However some members of the family were critical of this decision. King Frederick IX magnanimously pardoned her on his accession and allowed her home. Prince Harald was in declining health and she was allowed back to care for him. He died in 1949, and she spent her widowhood quietly in a villa in suburban Copenhagen until her death thirteen years later.

On 16 June 1948 King Gustav V of Sweden entered his tenth decade. Although he grumbled at the idea of 'any fuss' in the way of celebrations for his birthday, his people were determined to pay their homage to the King who had reigned over them for over forty years and, despite his faults, had won the respect of most. A church service, a procession of four thousand schoolchildren paying homage, and representatives of parliament, the church and armed forces offering their congratulations, were all part of the programme. From Denmark King Frederick, Queen Ingrid and Princess Margrethe, from Norway Crown Prince Olav, Crown Princess Märtha and their son Prince Harald, and most surviving members of his own family, rode with the King in state coaches through the streets of Stockholm to acknowledge the hundreds of thousands who lined their way to wave and cheer. The day ended with a great state dinner at the palace and a grand display of fireworks.

It marked the last series of festivities the King would see during his long life. On 29 October 1950 he passed away. Aged ninety-two, he was Europe's oldest reigning monarch, and at sixty-eight his son had been Europe's oldest heir.

King Gustav VI Adolf, as he now became, had long been known affectionately as 'Sweden's number one professional man'. With his devotion to archaeology, Etruscan art and gardening, he had for long lived the life of a country squire and had little taste for racehorses, vintage cars or other playthings of princes. The American journalist Cy Sulzberger, who had met him shortly after the end of the war, found him 'a tall, plain, genial-looking man with spectacles, pale face and colourless brown hair, who might be president of an American insurance company and looks something like a Grant Wood painting. He was very friendly but not interesting'.[14] Such judgment was somewhat jaundiced; but others with whom he came into close personal contact tended to be more generous.

A popular anecdote of the day told of the King driving around Stockholm in an open car, being greeted by friendly crowds, when a voice called out, 'I, Alf Eriksson, am as good as anyone else. I'm a republican and I don't give a damn for the King!' As a policeman grabbed him for disturbing the peace and angry crowds closed in on him, the King restored the good humour by calling out, 'And the King doesn't give a damn for Mr Eriksson!'[15]

Another remarked on the Swedish royal family's readiness to dine openly in their capital, and on the King's being asked if he had a bodyguard when he did so. Echoing King Christian X's retort to the Nazis in occupied Copenhagen, he chuckled, 'Yes, seven million of them!'

Unlike his father King Gustav VI Adolf made no effort, and indeed had no desire, to exceed his brief as a model constitutional monarch. Admittedly he was fortunate in that his reign spanned two decades of peace, instead of the preceding turbulent half-century which witnessed two world wars and the rise of the dictators in Europe. Even so, 'Sweden's number one professional man' was content to go with the flow of a more egalitarian society, enjoying his numerous hobbies. He presided at weekly meetings, generally lasting between fifteen and thirty minutes, of the cabinet at the royal palace in Stockholm. Here they made the formal, final decisions on up to eight hundred different matters, with the King and minister concerned signing and countersigning the relevant papers. The results were announced as the work of the 'King-in-Council', although in fact the King was merely informed what had already been decided. According to one government official, he was the perfect constitutional monarch, as 'he doesn't interfere, although he may ask a few questions if something strikes his interest'.[16]

In conversation the art historian, Bernard Berenson, once told the King that he did not envy him: 'Kingship is a hereditary form of slavery.' 'Don't say that,' the King replied. 'You have no idea how interesting this post, such as it is, can be; and how much it enables me to do about things I think are essential, right and interesting.'[17] The friendship between both men went back a long way. After the King's accession, Berenson sometimes addressed him when he was a guest in his house with old-fashioned courtesy as 'Sire', only to earn a gentle reproof that he wished to be treated merely as another guest.

The King of Sweden, Berenson noted in his diary (10 October 1952), was

the most completely humanized person of my acquaintance. He seems to be absolutely without any feeling of class or rank, of anybody being below him. Also in politics he is the most complete liberal, opposing no measure that promises improvement of conditions for 'working' classes, is even a believer in universal suffrage – at all costs. Speaks of his kingship in the most impersonal way as a job he at present has to do, without the faintest perceptible trace of pride. . .[18]

Berenson was roused to the 'utmost envy' of his friend, 'not because he is a King on a throne, nor that he has all the advantages of his position. . . I envy him for boyishly enjoying as a 'lark' everything he has to do, all the inspections, all the receptions, all the speechifying, all the listening, all the deciding . . . and all the ceremonial of a King on the throne'.[19]

His granddaughter, Princess Margrethe of Denmark, found that as a discerning collector of contemporary drawings and prints, the King's opinion of her work was invaluable. 'His criticism always gave me grounds for thought', she wrote, 'and his praise was sweet music'.[20] It was a boost to her self-confidence, she recalled, when Queen Ingrid told her that he had included a couple of her paintings in his collection.

Although nearly seventy at the time of his accession, the King's zest for active archaeology had not diminished. He continued to spend much of his leisure time on archaeological digs in Italy and Greece. His status as an authority on Chinese antiquities was such that collectors throughout Europe would often consult him for a final opinion on the date and origin of pieces which were difficult to place. Queen Louise was said to have remarked that she thought she had married a Crown Prince: 'it turned out that I married a professor.'

His mental energy and a positive outlook on life undoubtedly helped to keep him young for his years. Writing to Lady Astor from Stockholm a week after his seventieth birthday (18 November 1952), he noted:

We returned about 2 weeks ago from a month's stay in Italy and Malta. It was a real and a lovely holiday for both of us and we thoroughly enjoyed it, all the more, as we had warm, even hot summer weather throughout. Now we have settled here in Stockholm for the winter and gone back to our duties of varying kind. Even if some things one has to do naturally are less interesting or less amusing than others, I find that one can always get some interest or some fun out of everything one does or has to do. Life really is absorbingly interesting after all. There is much to be done, to be improved, to be renewed or to be freshly created. . . .[21]

King Gustav VI Adolf and Queen Louise both regularly visited the opera, theatre and ballet. He did his own landscape gardening, designed the layout of flower beds, and on their annual visits to London took the Queen to Chelsea Flower Show from which he never came away empty-handed. With enthusiasm worthy of his green-fingered late wife he planned and directed the restoration of great gardens and grounds at the Palace of Drottningholm. For exercise he enjoyed playing tennis, like his father, and golf, until well into his eighties.

Queen Louise found the adjustment to being a Queen difficult at first. Relatives maintained that 'she found the promotion grossly exaggerated', and was irritated when people crowded so closely round the royal palace that her car could hardly get out of the gates. Sweden had not had a Queen for twenty years, and the curiosity was perhaps only to be expected – but not for her. 'People look at me as if I was something remarkable', she complained in a letter to Dolla. 'I don't look any different from what I did yesterday, do I?'[22]

Queen Louise did not share her husband's robust health. After a heart attack at the comparatively early age of sixty-one in May 1951 her strength gradually diminished, and she tired easily. Nevertheless, she undertook her role as a Queen Consort conscientiously. When appearing in public, she was 'the personification of queenliness'. She took great care with her clothes and the jewels she wore with them on state occasions, and she enjoyed entertaining and going out. The King and Queen were always keen to meet people from different walks of life, and at dinners they tended to discourage formality, determined to make the most of the opportunity to get to know their people. At 'representation dinners', they invited guests from a much wider circle than before, including people from commerce and industry, the cultural world, the civil service and diplomatic corps.

They still relished their regular visits to family and friends in England. The King's love of the country which had given him both his wives remained strong in his affections, as the author Maurice Collis saw at first hand when he spent a weekend at Cliveden in November 1953 as a guest of Lady Astor. Collis was impressed to notice that this most unpretentious of monarchs had arrived without even a valet, and that their hostess's manner to the King was 'a mixture of license and respect. This sort of open friendliness with a trace of deference was what he liked about English society, for the knack of it was rare on the continent.'[23]

In May 1955 the King and Queen were entertained to dinner by the Board of the Admiralty at the Royal Naval College, Greenwich. Queen Louise's surviving brother, Earl Mountbatten of Burma, was First Sea Lord, the post which had been held by their father with such outstanding distinction and resigned with great unhappiness.* In his speech the First Lord of the Admiralty said that HRH 'has probably seen more of the famous warships of those days [before World War I] than any naval officer in this room tonight.'[24]

According to her nieces, Queen Louise was 'a great family person'. She was always fascinated by weddings and engagements in the family. Generous to others, she was wary of spending money on herself. She frowned on unnecessary expense, especially where the royal palaces were concerned. She often complained about the high prices in shops. The lean years between 1917 and 1923 had had a lasting effect on her. With her lively temper, she could be hasty and occasionally get angry. She disliked gossip, and if anyone came to her with spiteful remarks about others she would break off the conversation abruptly with an unmistakable gesture of disapproval. If anyone had come to her asking to write her biography, she would have given an emphatic no. 'I don't like things written about royalty while they are still alive', she would say. 'Wait until I'm dead. Then you may with pleasure write about me. Not until then can you tell the truth.'[25]

Books about deceased royalty, however, held endless fascination for her with their family connections, even if the subject was not particularly inspiring to start with. One she devoured eagerly was about Queen Sophia Magdalen, wife of King Gustav III: 'she was not a very interesting person and had when young a sad and miserable life on the whole with Gustav III', she wrote (31 January 1960) to Miss Eardley Willmott, a friend since their nursing days together during the Great War. 'His clever, & dominating mother, Frederick the Great's sister, was jealous of his wife and really was beastly to her. The book gives a very good picture of the life and times.'[26]

Much more fascinating was a biography of her aunt Grand Duchess Serge of Russia, *An Unbroken Unity*, by E.M. Almedingen, published four years later. The Grand Duchess, born a princess of Hesse and the Rhine, had become a nun after the assassination of her husband in 1905, and was herself murdered by the Bolsheviks in 1918; thrown down a mineshaft shortly after her younger sister the Tsarina had been shot with her husband and children at Ekaterinburg. 'I have told my bookseller to send you a book about my aunt, my mother's nearest sister, who I deeply revered & loved', she wrote to Miss Willmott (13 September 1964). 'A Russian born lady Miss

---

* Shortly after the outbreak of the Great War, when his German birth made him one of the prime targets of anti-German hysteria.

Almedingen wrote it, I asked her to. . . . I felt it was a pity that no body in the future should [know] that all Russian Grand Dukes & Duchesses were not just rotten, worthless people. I think it is well written, may be some things of her child & girlhood not quite right but that is not of great consequences.'[27]

On a state visit to Paris in May 1963 the French President, General de Gaulle, was charmed by the Queen. At a state banquet she made excuses for her linguistic shortcomings. 'I hope you will excuse me not speaking very good French', she said. 'But, after all, it was the French spoken by your soldiers in 1914.'[28]

Her personality harboured no sentimentality for its own sake. In England, to help clear up her mother's home in Kensington Palace after her death in September 1950, her niece, Lady Pamela Hicks, found her tearing out fly-leaves of books with ruthless energy as the pages fluttered forlornly around the floor. They were books which had been given to her mother by Queen Victoria, mostly inscribed 'To dearest Victoria from her affectionate Grandmother V.R.I.' Queen Louise had weeded out the books she wanted to give away, but decided it would not be fitting to leave Queen Victoria's signature inside. When Lady Pamela pointed out tactfully that anybody would be thrilled to have a book inscribed by Queen Victoria, Louise retorted, 'Do you think I'd want to have a book in my personal library just because it had Queen Victoria's signature on the fly-leaf? That wouldn't make it any more interesting, would it?'[29] Out came several more pages. Many a collector and book dealer would surely have sided with Lady Pamela that day.

Queen Louise took great pleasure in modernizing royal routines in Sweden. This included abolishing some of the more antiquated formalities at court, making changes in court posts, cutting staff, reorganizing palace officials, and bringing court etiquette more up to date. She went through every one of the 550 rooms in the palace at Stockholm and decided which needed renovation. She refurnished some with Savonnerie carpets, Oriental rugs, groups of sofas and chairs in matching colours. Guest apartments were redecorated, staff amenities were brought up to date, radios and electric heating were fitted. Drottningholm Castle, a seventeenth-century castle created by Queen Hedvig Eleanora, widow of King Carl X Gustav, became the palace where the royal family lived in winter. Queen Louise devoted considerable time to making it more comfortable.

She fretted constantly about the number of engagements her husband was undertaking as King, and urged the Grand Marshal of the Court to reduce them. She insisted that at his time of life he should follow his doctor's advice and relax more. He had only read two novels since their marriage, she claimed with asperity, and even then he asked her whether he had to read every page. Unlike archeological treatises, she told him, novels were read for pleasure and so one could 'skip the dull bits'.

Crown Prince and Princess Christian of Denmark and their sons, Princes Frederick and Knud, 1907

King Edward VII and Queen Alexandra's state visit to Stockholm, April 1908

Souvenir postcard commemorating the state visit of King Gustav V and Queen Victoria of Sweden to England, November 1908

Crown Princess Gustav Adolf of Sweden and her daughter, Princess Ingrid

Prince Gustav Adolf of Sweden

The children of the Crown Prince and Princess of Sweden shortly after their mother's death. Left to right: Princess Ingrid; Princes Sigvard, Carl Johan, Bertil, Gustav Adolf

Princess William of Sweden, formerly Grand Duchess Marie of Russia

Prince Eric of Sweden

Prince and Princess William, Duke and Duchess of Södermanland, and their son Prince Lennart

The Swedish royal family, c. 1923. Standing: Princes Sigvard, William, Lennart, Gustav Adolf; Princess Märtha; Prince Eugen; Princess Astrid; Crown Prince Gustav Adolf. Seated: Queen Victoria; Princes Bertil, Carl (in front); Princess Ingrid; King Gustav V; Prince Carl Johan

King Christian X of Denmark

Queen Alexandrine of Denmark

Princess Ingeborg, Duchess of Västergötland,
and her children. Left to right: Prince Carl;
Princesses Margretha, Astrid, and Märtha

King Christian X and Queen Alexandrine's state visit to Paris, May 1914

Queen Maud of Norway and her sister Princess Victoria at Sandringham

Wedding of the Crown Prince of Sweden and Lady Louise Mountbatten, November 1923. Prince William, Duke of Södermanland (standing right) was best man; Princesses Theodora, Margaret, Cecilia and Sophie (seated and standing, centre and back), daughters of the bride's sister, Princess Andrew of Greece and Denmark, were bridesmaids; the Earl of Medina and Lady Tatiana Mountbatten (front), were train bearers

Prince Carl of Sweden, Duke of Västergötland (seated right) and his family on his seventieth birthday, 27 February 1931. Rest of group, standing, left to right: Crown Prince Leopold of Belgium; Prince Carl, Duke of Östergötland; Crown Prince Olav of Norway; seated, left to right: Princess Ingeborg, Duchess of Västergötland; Astrid, Crown Princess of Belgium; Märtha, Crown Princess of Norway; Princess Margretha

King Haakon VII, Queen Maud, Crown Prince Olav and Princess Märtha

Prince Gustav Adolf and Princess Sibylla of Saxe-Coburg Gotha on their wedding day, October 1932

Crown Prince Frederick and Crown Princess of Denmark, shortly after their wedding in May 1935

Prince and Princess Gustav Adolf and their eldest child, Princess Margaret

Crown Prince Olav of Norway and his family, c. 1940. Left to right: Princess Astrid; Prince Harald; Princess Ragnhild; Crown Princess Märtha

King Gustav V of Sweden; Crown Prince
Gustav Adolf; and his granddaughter,
Princess Margretha, c. 1937

Princess Helena of Glucksborg

King Christian X of Denmark, Queen Alexandrine and Field-Marshal Montgomery at Amalienborg, 12 May 1945

King Christian X of Denmark (centre) with his surviving brothers and sisters, 1946. On his left: Princess Ingeborg, Duchess of Västergötland; King Haakon VII of Norway; on his right: Prince Harald; Princess Dagmar, Mme Castenskiold

Prince Gustav Adolf of Sweden

Princess Sibylla of Sweden

Crown Princess Louise of Sweden

Funeral procession of King Christian X of Denmark, Copenhagen, 30 April 1947. Left to right: King Haakon VII of Norway; King Frederick IX of Denmark; Prince George of Greece; Prince Knud of Denmark

King Frederick IX and Queen Ingrid on board Danebrøg, *September 1966. With them are, left to right: Princess Benedikte; Princess Margrethe; and her fiancé Count Henri de Laborde de Monpezat*

King Olav V of Norway at the Norwegian Seamen's Church, Rotherhithe, London, July 1968

The contented state of her husband's kingdom gave her great satisfaction, not to say pride. 'Look at Sweden', she would say nonchalantly to others – 'no slums, no unemployment'. But still her position took some getting used to. In February 1952, less than sixteen months into the new reign, she went to England to attend the funeral of King George VI, and a sumptuous Daimler appeared for her. 'For me!' she exclaimed. 'No, it must have come for a Queen.'[30] When in London she usually stayed at the Hyde Park Hotel, and had a card in her handbag saying I AM THE QUEEN OF SWEDEN. 'I like going out shopping by myself', she explained, perhaps remembering the confusion that King Frederick VIII of Denmark had inadvertently caused on his demise, 'and it would be so inconvenient if I got run over and they couldn't find out who I was!'[31]

Like many people of her generation, the pace of twentieth-century life and the changes it wrought on old haunts were not something she welcomed. To Miss Eardley Willmott, she commented (23 June 1961) on her dread of seeing new alterations at Hyde Park Corner on a forthcoming visit to London: 'Alas with the constant increase in traffic, everybody seems to have a car, something had to be done. Every country seems to build the same kind of skyscrapers or high buildings, nothing to tell one in which country one is in if one only looks at the modern architecture, mostly all glass & a little concrete.'[32]

Queen Alexandrine, the widow of King Christian X of Denmark, survived her husband by five years. For the rest of her life, she generally spent Christmas with her son and his family. Always the most modest and self-effacing of women, and increasingly a martyr to ill-health, she had borne the strain of nursing her husband by day and night during his last few years. In widowhood she withdrew even further from the public eye, though she continued to take a keen interest in her nursing and children's charities.

Queen Margrethe recalled the last years of her grandmother with affection: 'I was very fond of her. She was very sweet and she read aloud to me. Her voice was slightly "different", because her Danish had an accent. She often spoke English with my mother, also with a slight accent.'[33]

Shortly before Christmas 1952 she fell ill with a recurrence of her intestinal complaint, and was admitted to hospital. Despite an operation her condition gave increasing cause for concern, and on 27 December, three days after her seventy-third birthday, a bulletin announced that she had been unconscious since the previous evening. She passed away on the next day. Replying to a letter of condolence from Lady Astor, Queen Ingrid wrote (18 January 1953) that she had been 'a very kind understanding mother-in-law & never mixed up in our affairs. She adored my husband & admired him tremendously, perhaps that was not a good thing always in his young days, but he certainly deserved it now'.[34]

Queen Alexandrine was laid to rest on 4 January 1953. Determined to pay their last respects, ten thousand Danes defied a heavy snowstorm outside the palace courtyard at Amalienborg, where a short ceremony was held in the Copenhagen Great Hall. When the palace gates were opened and the coffin appeared, everyone spontaneously joined in singing a simple old hymn. It was the people's farewell to a much-loved Queen, whose patriotism and courage – notwithstanding her German birth – had never been in doubt during the German occupation. The coffin was transferred to the church at Christiansborg Castle for another short ceremony at which no sermon was preached, only texts from the Bible. The bier was then taken through crowded streets to the railway terminus, and thence to Roskilde Cathedral to join the resting place of the other Danish Kings and Queens.

In 1953 the right of succession to the Danish throne was still restricted to male heirs, but then Denmark realized that it had no Crown Prince, only three little princesses. Prince Knud, the younger brother of King Frederick, was heir to the throne. On his brother's accession he should have inherited the title of Crown Prince, but was given the perhaps ominous title of *Arveprins* (heir presumptive) instead. Like his brother he had joined the Danish navy as a boy, and rose to the rank of Rear-Admiral. Married in 1933 to his cousin Princess Caroline Matilda, daughter of King Christian X's son Prince Harald and the notoriously pro-Nazi Princess Helena, he had two sons, Ingolf and Christian, both of whom were granted the title Count of Rosenborg, and a daughter, Elizabeth.

As one despatch after another to the British Foreign Office from ministers in Copenhagen put it discreetly, Prince Knud did 'not enjoy the same popularity as his brother'. His apparent unfitness for the throne was the subject of much comment, some of a distinctly uncharitable nature. What his detractors were not always quick to realize, or point out, was that his sensitive personality had suffered as a result of his father's tyranny at home, and he was even more shy and lacking in confidence than his brother.

Shortly after the accession of King Frederick IX, leading politicians of all parties had drawn up plans for a change in the Danish Constitution, and alterations in the succession at the same time. They recommended that the succession to the throne should be altered in favour of the King's eldest daughter in place of his brother Prince Knud. Equal rights for women – not least the brotherless daughters of King Frederick IX – and doubts about the personal shortcomings of Prince Knud were foremost in the political mind. Gallup polls held in Denmark since the King's accession showed a steady increase in respondents favouring the succession to the throne of Princess Margrethe, rather than her uncle. A poll in October 1952 showed 69% agreeing with such a change. The succession of Queen Elizabeth II to the British throne earlier that year, it was remarked, was 'a further stimulus to reform'.[35] Had the line of succession passed only through male heirs in

Britain as it did in Denmark, King George VI would have been followed on the throne by his only surviving younger brother Henry, Duke of Gloucester.

At the same time proposals were drafted for the abolition of the upper house or Landsting, the lowering of the franchise from twenty-five to twenty-three, and a change in the status of Greenland which now became part of Denmark, all of which were accepted by the King under pressure from Hans Hedtoft, the Social Democratic prime minister. They were however to be placed before the people in a referendum; and, perhaps, out of deference to the feelings of Queen Alexandrine regarding her younger son, they were held in abeyance during her lifetime.

According to Princess Margrethe, talk about an amendment to the constitution only became an issue in the winter of 1952–3, after her grandmother's death. Her parents, she commented, 'had done what they could to leave me in peace for as long as possible. The actual Law was entirely the work of the politicians, my parents had not had anything to do with it, but acceded to the wishes of the public and the government.'[36]

The proposals were submitted to the Folketing, on 4 February 1953, by the prime minister, Eric Ericksen, who had succeeded Hedtoft in October 1950. Both houses passed the bill on 30 March, subject to its acceptance in a plebiscite which would obtain the assent of at least 45% of the whole electorate. In the vote on 28 May 1953, the new constitution was approved by an overwhelming majority, with 1,181,173 in favour, and only 318,075 against.

King Frederick IX signed the new Constitution at a Council-of-State at Christiansborg Castle on Constitution Day, 5 June. The day was declared a public holiday, twenty-five criminals were released from prison in an amnesty, and a sum of 200m Kroner (in sterling, equivalent to about £10 million) was given to charities supporting the poor. It was said that when she heard that she was her father's heir to the throne, Princess Margrethe exclaimed, 'I wish I were an ordinary girl who could grow up like everybody else and marry a man named Olsen'.[37] She was granted a few days off school, 'because my father thought I should be at home and away from all the hullabaloo'.[38]

Prince Knud and his family 'were granted certain economic advantages' by way of compensation for their reduced positions in the order of succession, as a result of negotiations with Ericksen. Although he was careful not to express in public his feelings, privately the Prince was always bitter about the change that deprived him of the throne.* He claimed that

* At the time of his death on 14 June 1976 Prince Knud was seventh in the line of succession behind Queen Margrethe and her sons, and behind her sister Princess Benedikte and her three children. His youngest niece Anne-Marie, consort of King Constantine II of the Hellenes, was excluded from the Danish line of succession.

it had been achieved by a trick, combining the succession question with another related issue in the plebiscite. According to one modern Danish historian he appealed to Joseph Stalin, on the grounds that a clause at the Congress of Vienna in 1814 gave Russia responsibility for the Danish succession, but Stalin took no notice. This is disputed by another historian, who suggested that this was unlikely on the grounds that such an appeal would have been high treason; and doubts that in any case Prince Knud would have been capable of writing such a letter.*

Amendment of the law covering the succession, it was initially thought, would require the consent of the major European powers, who had guaranteed the succession of the present Royal House by the Treaty of London in 1852. Under this Treaty the Powers reserved their right to be consulted should the male line of the Royal House come to an end. But constitutional experts advised that the amendment now proposed did not necessitate an approach to the Treaty of London Powers; and the Danish government were relieved by this advice, since Russia was one of the original signatories.[39]

---

* Stalin had died in March 1953, three months before the new Constitution took effect. Though several of Prince Knud's obituaries refer to his appeal to the Russian leader, it has been impossible to ascertain the precise date of his doing so.

CHAPTER ELEVEN

'Oh – I'm the King'

Meanwhile King Haakon VII of Norway, as the longest-reigning Scandinavian monarch, was feeling the weight of his years. Princess Thyra, his sister, had been a regular visitor to him in Norway until shortly before her death soon after the end of the war. When King Christian X followed her to the grave less than two years later, he felt increasingly isolated. Yet he was devoted to his nephew who now reigned as King Frederick IX of Denmark, and in February 1948 he paid a state visit to Copenhagen. His appearance in the city was a salutary reminder to the people that he had shared in the hardships and sacrifices during the years of occupation, and the press saluted the monarch who, for them as well as for his own people, 'was a leading figure in the evil years; if one names individuals who influenced Danish youth in wartime by word and deed, his name will be among the very first'.[1]

With the death of King Gustav V in October 1950, at seventy-eight he was the oldest reigning monarch in Europe. True to his vow never to set foot inside Sweden while 'that old scoundrel' was still alive, he attended the funeral in Stockholm in November.

King Haakon was happy to delegate some of the representative duties of his position to the Crown Prince, among them the royal New Year's Eve radio broadcast. In 1946 he proposed that the Crown Prince and Princess should join in, so that he only needed to do so every third year and he had fewer ways of varying his greetings. Due to illness Crown Princess Märtha was only able to undertake the function twice, and it devolved increasingly on her husband. In deference to his age the King decided to give up skiing, admitting ruefully that the winter ice made him very cautious as he was afraid of falling and breaking something.

During his seventy-fifth birthday celebrations in 1947 he had had the Crown Princess at his side to discharge the duties of a royal hostess, but she left immediately afterwards for America to have an operation on her back. From that time onwards her health gave cause for unceasing anxiety. In February 1951 she was admitted to hospital in Oslo with suspected jaundice. Discharged a few weeks later, she returned to Skaugum in time for her fiftieth birthday at the end of March, but she was in hospital again from midsummer to late November, too ill even to accompany the King and

Crown Prince to the funeral of her father, Prince Carl, at the beginning of that month.

Meanwhile the royal family were concerned over the future of Princess Ragnhild, who wanted to marry a shipowner, Erling Lorentzen, whom she had met six years previously. King Haakon was alarmed lest marriage between a member of the royal family and a commoner with 'an un-aristocratic profession' might be damaging to the dynasty, even in the more liberal modern world. At length he consulted the prime minister, Oscar Torp, who suggested that any public reaction would probably prove favourable. When the engagement was announced in February 1953, and the marriage took place three months later, there was no serious debate.

The following year, Crown Princess Märtha was again admitted to hospital. Her condition worsened, and she died on 5 April 1954. 'The sunbeam of the home', King Haakon wrote sadly to a friend, 'is now extinguished'. It was ironic that both the sovereign and his son and heir, the latter only in his early fifties, should both be widowers. When the author James Pope-Hennessy was talking to various members of royalty in the course of his research for the official biography of Queen Mary, he found Crown Prince Olav 'gave an impression of a capable as well as most amiable man, lonely perhaps, somewhat jovial'.[2]

King Haakon still maintained the closest of personal relations with the British royal family. In June 1951 he had sailed on the royal yacht *Norge* to England to pay an official visit to his nephew King George VI, whom he did not realize was seriously ill and had merely eight months to live. In June 1955 he was host to his great-niece Queen Elizabeth II and Prince Philip, on the Queen's first visit of her reign to any country outside the Commonwealth, when they arrived at Oslo on board the royal yacht *Britannia*. The King and Crown Prince, accompanied by Prince Harald and Princess Astrid, welcomed them at Oslo, where considerable crowds had come to see the royal family and their British royal guests. At a gala dinner for over two hundred guests at the palace that night the King spoke of his memories of his wartime sojourn in England, and the Queen paid tribute to 'the unshakable courage and resolution shown by Your Majesty'.

After the dinner he invited Hambro to come and have a quiet chat. 'Let's sit a bit and talk', he suggested. 'The younger ones can go on standing.'[3] Hambro expressed concern. On enquiring after His Majesty's health, the King said he was not exactly tired, but he looked forward very much to his summer holiday and a peaceful time on the royal yacht. It would be a good rest, he maintained, before the inevitable strain of his Jubilee celebrations in November.

Unhappily it was not to be. Early the following month the King had a fall in his bathroom at Bygdöy, and was in such pain that he could not get up unsupported. A servant found him completely helpless the following morning. He was admitted to the Rigshospital in Oslo, where a broken thighbone was diagnosed.

There were some Jubilee celebrations in November, but on a very modest scale. While the King received bedside visits from Crown Prince Olav, Prince Harald and Princess Astrid, and later the prime minister, gifts poured into the palace and diplomatic representatives came to write their names in a book of homage. Radio stations broadcast special programmes dedicated to his fifty years of service, and in the evening a gala dinner was held at the Rigshospital, with chicken and apricot jelly provided for the 2,500 patients and staff.

After several months in hospital the King was discharged, but once he was back in the palace, his family and ministers found him very depressed by his general helplessness and dependence on a wheelchair. He took less interest in current affairs and the newspapers, and seemed to be resigning himself to the onset of extreme old age. On a couple of occasions he remarked privately to senior ministers that perhaps there should be an age limit for monarchs. The prime minister, Einar Gerhardsen, tried to obtain an opinion from an expert in constitutional law as to the legal practicalities on abdication, and on new year's day 1957 one of the newspapers published an article speculating on the possibility that King Haakon might choose to abdicate before his eighty-fifth birthday that August. Deeply wounded, the King complained at his grave disappointment that there should be people who thought him too old for his job. Gerhardsen thus felt unable to say anything more to the King on the subject.

The mood of gloom rarely left him. 'When I am gone', he remarked sadly to his physiotherapist, Aadel Bülow-Hansen, 'Norway will get its first Norwegian King'. Hastily the man assured him that 'I do not believe we can get a more Norwegian King than we have had in Your Majesty'.[4]

Gerhardsen and Prince Harald took part in a special radio programme to pay the King tribute on his eighty-fifth birthday, 3 August, but it was almost an epitaph. Within a few days the King was virtually bedridden, and his bronchial condition gave the doctors cause for concern. The Crown Prince visited his father on the evening of 20 September and sent a message to the Prime Minister that the end was near.

On the following day a statement was issued to announce that His Majesty King Haakon VII had passed away at 4.35 a.m. 'His condition during the night had not been especially disquieting, and the King slept peacefully until symptoms of heart failure appeared and this led to death in the course of a few minutes.'[5]

With the death of the octogenarian King Haakon VII of Norway, King Gustav VI Adolf of Sweden, like his father before him, became the oldest of the Scandinavian monarchs. Like his father, too, he had the misfortune in that his consort plainly did not enjoy the same robust health.

By the time she was seventy Queen Louise, who had already survived one heart attack, was ageing fast. Even the simple pleasures of her garden at Sofiero could not be enjoyed to the full, as she wrote with some sadness (13 June 1959) to Miss Eardley Willmott:

> The early spring has resulted in most things are earlier this year. The rhod[odendro]ns & azaleas going over. We ate our first strawberries 11th June which is quite exceptionally early for here. Alas I cannot enjoy more than an occasional single one as most raw fruit especially berries do not suit me. We are all getting old! I find with my bad back I can do little bending, such as picking flowers any length of time, weeding does not really go. Well, well in a few years time I shall just stately walk around the garden & look the other way if a weed should be pulled up or other things should be done![6]

Her public appearances were gradually cut down, the last being at the Nobel Prize celebrations and ceremonies in December 1964. Soon afterwards she had a second, more severe heart attack, and was admitted to hospital. In the first week of February 1965 she was well enough to return to Drottningholm, but she was plainly losing strength and weight.

'It was pathetic to see how the Queen struggled to force herself to eat', recalled her Mistress of the Robes, Astrid Rudebeck. 'I had the impression that she would have preferred to give up out of sheer exhaustion, but for the King's sake she mustered all her strength to live.'[7] Yet he was under no illusions. For several weeks he had felt that she was sinking, and knew that she was too weak to withstand a second attack. On 3 March she was back in hospital. A blood clot had formed in the lower part of the main artery leading to her heart, and a six-hour operation was undertaken, but she only lived for another three days, fell into a coma, and passed away just before midnight on 7 March.

After her death King Gustav VI Adolf turned increasingly for companionship to his brother-in-law, Earl Mountbatten of Burma, who had been a widower himself for five years. When they were apart, relatives noticed how the King loved having the rest of the family around him. In May 1966 Mountbatten and his daughters accompanied him on a walking tour of Stockholm. After ninety minutes on foot, the Earl noted, they were 'more than usually exhausted, but 83-year-old Gustav remained fresh and gay'.[8] Too fresh and gay, perhaps. On a subsequent visit to Sweden three years later, Mountbatten was warned by the King that his family were worried about his overdoing things. He must remember that he was an old man of nearly seventy and could no longer continue at the same pace. 'I thought it was a case of the pot calling the kettle black', the younger man noted in his diary, 'because I was only 68 and he was 86 and still doing too much'.[9] At length they agreed with each other and 'promised we would both see if we could do less'.

Since the death of Prince Gustav Adolf in 1947, the heir to the throne had been his son, Prince Carl Gustav, born the previous year. In 1965 the Riksdag passed a law which prevented the heir from becoming King before the age of twenty-five. The following year, thirty-four members of the Social Democratic Party sponsored a motion for a parliamentary inquiry on the advisability of instituting a republican form of government. At the start of the King's reign, republicanism had not been seen as a threat. As he pointed out, all forms of government had their advantages and disadvantages, but one was not likely to get one that cost less than a monarchy. All the same, within a few years there were those in public life who felt otherwise – and were prepared to say so. While leading Swedish republicans readily paid tribute to the personal qualities of King Gustav VI Adolf, they still claimed that the monarchy was an anachronism.

By the late sixties the young Prince was understandably anxious for his future, and he wrote to Lord Mountbatten that most of his friends were republicans. Mountbatten replied soothingly that, as the Prince 'developed and became better known, agitation for a republic would die down'. In fact the elder man was more pessimistic at heart than he was prepared to admit. Even after Prince Carl Gustav had first taken the chair at a cabinet committee two years later, Mountbatten was impressed at the progress the young man had made, but even so thought there seemed little hope of his being able to retain the crown after his grandfather's death. The question continually vexed him, and in July 1972 he wrote to King Gustav Adolf asking whether he had considered retiring in favour of his grandson on his ninetieth birthday, which would fall on 11 November.

The King did not want any spectacular celebrations for his birthday, particularly as his widowed daughter-in-law Princess Sibylla was seriously ill. She had been admitted to hospital in September; an examination confirmed that she was suffering from cancer, and she died on 28 November, aged sixty-four. Out of respect for the bereaved sovereign's feelings, Mountbatten forbore to pursue the retirement issue again too soon. However, early the following year he had a premonition that if he did not come over to Sweden soon he would never see his brother-in-law again. When he visited him in Stockholm in July he found the King looking very frail and feared he would not last the year out. Yet he had the vigour, as well as the rashness to refer to his late father, who had also lived into his nineties, as old and obstinate. 'You are a very old King and have become just as obstinate', the younger man told him bluntly. The King insisted that the constitution did not permit him to abdicate unless mentally incapacitated.

Privately Mountbatten was saddened at the effects of old age on the venerable monarch. King Gustav VI Adolf seemed 'very cheerful but getting terribly deaf', and was obviously depressed at having lost the sight of his left eye and the prospect of going blind in the right as well. He admitted that he would be unable to come to England and pay his annual visit to Mountbatten's home at Broadlands that year. On their departure, 'we embraced each other emotionally, almost tearfully', doubtless realizing that they would never meet again.

A few weeks later the King took to his bed for the last time. Large numbers of well-wishers kept vigil as he lay gravely ill in Helsingborg hospital, and the whole country anxiously followed bulletins on his health. He died on 15 September 1973, two months short of his ninety-first birthday. Mountbatten, who had been closer to him than anybody else during the last years, represented Queen Elizabeth II at the funeral. Perhaps he realized that the pessimism of his darkest moments had been unfounded. The young King Carl Gustav, he remarked in his diary, had 'done magnificently. It is all very exciting if the young man has suddenly developed to the point at which he can make the Monarchy live and able to continue'.[10]

To the citizens of Copenhagen, it would come as no surprise to the people to see King Frederick IX and Queen Ingrid eating in the Tivoli restaurants while the Princesses stood patiently in line waiting for their turn on the Ferris wheel or roundabouts. An Australian couple in the 1960s, however, enjoying their meal, were greatly astonished by the family's free and easy ways. 'That woman at the next table – I'm sure I've seen her photograph', said the wife to the waiter, 'Who is she?' 'The Queen, madam',[11] replied the waiter.

Cycling through the Tivoli Gardens one morning, King Frederick stopped to chat with an American tourist. 'I'm a storekeeper from Chicago', the latter announced, 'Who are you?' 'Oh – I'm the King',[12] was the reply.

He also held frequent audiences open to any of his subjects with a reasonable petition or matter to discuss. With a regular programme of foreign tours and royal visits, he and Queen Ingrid soon became as popular abroad as at home. Refreshing moments of family informality, if not always intentional, displayed the human touch. At a public function Princess Margrethe, then aged seventeen, accidentally trod on her mother's dress. 'Good heavens, child! Watch where you are going!' Queen Ingrid reprimanded her briskly, in full hearing of the public. Such gestures, the journalist Geoffrey Bocca commented, were 'calculated to endear a sovereign to her subjects more than any number of speeches from the throne'.[13]

In 1966, at the age of twenty-six, Princess Margrethe became engaged to Count Henri de Laborde de Monpezat, Third Secretary at the French Embassy in London. They were married the following summer, although the happy occasion was marred for the family by one shadow – the absence of her youngest sister Anne-Marie, Queen of the Hellenes. King Constantine had only been on the throne for three years, and his Danish consort (whom he had married in September 1964, six months after his accession) just over two, when the military junta came to power in Athens. Princess Margrethe and her fiancé had celebrated her twenty-seventh birthday in Greece and returned home fortuitously a day before the coup. Though they knew that Queen Anne-Marie and the family were out of danger, parallels with the Bolshevik revolution of 1917 and the tragic end of the Romanov dynasty were perhaps not far from their minds. King Frederick and Queen Ingrid were extremely hurt when told by the prime minister that their youngest daughter and her husband, the King and Queen of the Hellenes, would not be welcome in Denmark for the festivities.

Nevertheless the wedding at Fredensborg on 10 June was celebrated in style. To the bride, her friends and relations who were present, it was 'an especially lovely feast', with a church ceremony in the evening, dinner at home 'and dancing afterwards for as many guests as the house [Fredensborg] may hold, and ours is a large house'.

On 11 March 1969 King Frederick IX celebrated his seventieth birthday. As usual, he was cheered enthusiastically by his subjects who followed tradition and gathered in the Amalienborg Square, where the Household Guards marched in their red gala uniforms. At a dinner that evening, he said in a very personal speech, transmitted by radio and television, just how much his family had meant to him over the years. 'I have never found a four-leaf clover', he said, in a voice close to breaking with emotion, 'but with the years one has grown in my own house – you, my friend, the Queen, and our three children. You became the four-leaf clover that brought happiness in my life, and sunshine into my heart. I thank you for the support to me that you have been, and for everything you have meant to me through the many years'.[14]

There were almost three years of this happy family existence left. Princess Margrethe and her husband, in her own words, 'were a happy couple with two healthy sons, ready to meet whatever the future would bring.' Prince Frederick had been born in May 1968, and Joachim thirteen months later. 'The anxiety I had felt as a young girl, about how I would manage when my father was no longer here, had eased.'[15] It was as well, for she realized that her father 'was not a type who lives to a very old age'. For an energetic man such as he was, the prospect of spending his last years as an invalid, like his wheelchair-bound father had done, would have been an intolerable indignity. Yet a couple of years after his seventieth birthday, it was evident that his physical powers were declining, and he appeared less strong and robust than usual.

Thankfully, for all of them the end came quite suddenly. King Frederick and Queen Ingrid spent Christmas of 1971 with their eldest daughter and son-in-law at Marselisborg, as they had done every year since 1968, and returned to Copenhagen together for New Year's Eve.

Although the King had a cold, he made his usual New Year appearance on television, but viewers were shocked to notice how frail he looked. The next day, Queen Ingrid telephoned her daughter to say that he had been taken ill during the night and could not attend the New Year levee.

Instinctively she knew it was the beginning of the end. Influenza and pneumonia were followed by a massive heart attack, and he was admitted to hospital in Copenhagen. For a few days he and his daughter could talk, but at times he was rather vague, and his mind was evidently wandering. She did not believe that he was going to put up a fight. 'I think he was one of those people who know when to let go – it is a great gift.'[16] Perhaps the words of her great-great-grandfather on her mother's side, Albert, Prince Consort, came to mind – 'I do not cling to life'. Day by day King Frederick grew weaker, lost consciousness, and passed away on 14 January, aged seventy-two.

Many were the tributes paid to the sovereign who 'through his wisdom, tact and love of simplicity . . . proved a successful and popular King of a country where "few have too much, and fewer still too little". Though the Danes have little use for the outward show of monarchy and adopt a cynical attitude towards what remains of their aristocracy, they took the good-humoured King Frederik to their hearts.'[17]

Although under the Norwegian constitution there was no coronation for King Olav to follow his accession in September 1957, a modified service of dedication and blessing took place. When the Labour government, in a rather small-minded moment, ordered that no Labour members of the Storting should attend, the ruling was widely defied by representatives. It was ample demonstration to the cabinet that it had seriously misjudged opinion as regards the monarchy among its own supporters. King Haakon had overcome a deep-seated resistance to monarchy by his devotion to duty, and above all his performance during the war; and there was every reason to suppose that King Olav would be just as successful a constitutional monarch as his father. History would prove the case.

King Olav had scrupulously observed his father's stipulation that the Norwegian monarchy should have only a small court and observe a simple lifestyle, a tradition which his son followed to an extent which startled foreigners. Genial and approachable, he appeared on the balcony of the royal palace every year on 17 May, Norway's National Day, to greet the long parade of schoolchildren, each school headed by its own brass band. He was often described as having the appearance of an old sea-dog, and was known among his subjects as 'the sporting sovereign'. In 1958 he was elected honorary President of the International Yacht Racing Union. In 1976 he was second in the World Yachting Championship at the tiller of *Bing IX*. He spent his eighty-sixth birthday in July 1989 sailing in an Oslo regatta aboard his eighteen-foot craft. To a similar age, he continued to take to the ski slopes at his mountain retreat Kongsseteren ('the King's mountain farm').

Throughout his reign, appropriately in view of his birth in Norfolk, he maintained his parents' close links with Britain. In 1962 he paid a three-day state visit to Edinburgh, where he was guest of Queen Elizabeth II at the Palace of Holyrood House, on what was the first state visit to Scotland's capital for more than 150 years. He received the freedom of the city of Edinburgh, and an honorary LLD from Edinburgh University. He was admitted to the Order of the Thistle as an extra knight. In June 1963 he attended the celebration of the 700th anniversary of the founding of Balliol College, Oxford, and the occasion was marked by a Norwegian subscription of £20,000 for the reconstruction of the junior common room, which was reopened in 1964 as the Norway Room.

King Olav was the only head of state in modern times to pay two state visits to Britain. On the second of these, in 1988, his last state visit abroad, he was made an Honorary Admiral of the Fleet by Queen Elizabeth II. He was already Honorary Colonel of the Green Howards, a position which he cherished, and he was meticulous in performing his regimental duties. As he had always spoken English with his mother, so Norwegians would say with a smile that this was his first language. Like his mother, he always visited England in the autumn, two or three weeks incognito, when he would attend meetings of the International Yachting Association and meet old friends. With his devotion to the bowler hat, it was said, he cut a figure that was more British than the British themselves.

Yet since Crown Princess Märtha's death, it had been a lonely existence for him. Most evenings he spent alone in his private drawing room at the palace, reading or watching television. Gossips in Norway and Britain suggested that he had been courting Queen Elizabeth the Queen Mother – widowed, like him, in her early fifties – only to meet with the firm answer, 'I must put my country first'. In 1983 she flew to Oslo to act as a 'temporary consort' at his eightieth birthday celebrations. When they entered the city concert hall royal box together, the audience rose as one while the choir sang *God Save the Queen* in English. King Olav kissed her hand, saying gently, 'You see, my dear Elizabeth, how much my people love you. What a wonderful Queen you would have made for them'.[18] If the story is true, however, it was meant lightly. Both were committed to serving their respective countries; both cherished the memory of their late spouses; and the idea that either would have considered remarriage is surely laughable.

During the oil crisis in the winter of 1973–4 the Norwegian government urged people to travel by public transport on Sundays rather than by private car. One Sunday King Olav was photographed seated on a suburban tram on his way to a day's skiing on the slopes above Oslo, and he made a point of paying his fare personally. The presence of a photographer, it must be admitted, was hardly an accident. Nonetheless it said a good deal about the sort of image that he wished to present – a public-spirited, democratic monarch who was happy to mingle with his people. Sir Frederick Ponsonby might have turned in his grave, but in the 1970s monarchs could come down from their pedestals without compromising their dignity in a way which would have been inconceivable at the turn of the century.

He enjoyed the same good relationship with his son and heir, Crown Prince Harald, as he had enjoyed with his father. There was some controversy when the Crown Prince wanted to marry Sonja Haraldsen, the daughter of an Oslo textile merchant. For nine years King Olav withheld his consent, but eventually the marriage took place in Oslo Cathedral on 29 August 1968. As a wedding present the King gave them the home where Harald had been born, at Skaugum, just outside Oslo. They had two children, Märtha Louise, born in 1971, and Crown Prince Haakon Magnus, born in 1973.

Like his father, King Olav V lived to a great age. In June 1990, shortly before his eighty-seventh birthday, he suffered a stroke which left him partly paralysed on his left side. Crown Prince Harald was appointed Regent. Seven months later, on 17 January 1991 in Oslo, King Olav passed away.

'King Olav summed up in himself all our recent history', recalled Gro Harlem Bruntland, the prime minister, in an address which recalled royal resistance to the Nazi occupation during the war. 'Smiles and human warmth were his personal characteristics. Above all, he was a living human being who actively took part in all the joys and sorrows of life.'[19]

Not only in Norway, but throughout Europe, generous tributes were paid to the 'Peoples' King'. Not the least of the achievements left by him and his father before him was to make the Norwegian crown secure in the hearts of the people – a nation who had accepted a monarchy with no great enthusiasm in 1905. As the London press was quick to emphasize shortly after his death, 'Perhaps surprisingly for what was until recently a staunchly Socialist country, Norway's monarchy is still supported by some 90 per cent of its populace'.[20]

Shortly after the fall of Communism in Eastern Europe at the end of the 1980s Noel Malcolm, Foreign Editor of *The Spectator*, argued on behalf of the restoration of Balkan monarchies, partly on the grounds that it would 'mark in a psychologically important way their final break with Communism'; and that there could 'be no more fitting symbol of belonging to the "family" of European nations than to have rulers who (like other European monarchs) belong literally to the family of Queen Victoria.'[21]

He might have added that the odds were that any potential rulers – or, in the era of constitutional monarchy, royal heads of state – would also probably belong to the family of King Christian IX. The prince born in 1818 with scarcely a hint of a glittering future before him had indeed become the father of Europe, and given his name to European dynasties in two countries as well as his own. Through marriages with the Bernadottes from Sweden, who had given Denmark two Queens consort in the twentieth century, the Scandinavian monarchs had genuinely become a family in their own right. It could be observed at the same time that King Carl XVI Gustav of Sweden is a great-great-grandson of Queen Victoria on his mother's and his father's side, while Queen Margrethe of Denmark is a great-great granddaughter of the same monarch through her mother. Both are grandchildren of the former Princess Margaret of Connaught. King Harald is likewise another great-great-grandson of Queen Victoria, on his father's side.

At the same time, this family of monarchs has become increasingly popular in an ever more egalitarian world. The almost invisible transition to a 'bicycling monarchy', a less regal way of life, tells part of the story; while the role played by the Kings of Denmark and Norway – again, literally, the family, being brothers – symbolized the courage and endurance that their nations needed to see them through five years of resistance in the face of German occupation. In Sweden, the affable personality of King Gustav VI Adolf was enough to melt the heart of all but the most dyed-in-the-wool republican, proving that – as during the long reign of his father – socialism and republicanism need not be natural bedfellows. The deprivation of potentially controversial functions by his successor and grandson, such as initiating the search for a new government after an indecisive general election result, means that politically the King can literally do no wrong. The monarchy is thus not merely perpetuated, but often strengthened in popularity. A Swedish opinion poll conducted in the first years of his reign showed King Carl XVI Gustav enjoying far more public confidence than any elected politician.

At the end of the twentieth century, the Scandinavian monarchies have the same love-hate relationships with their subjects, their politicians and their media as their counterparts elsewhere in Europe. In 1975, as rumours began to circulate regarding his forthcoming engagement to Silvia Sommerlath, King Carl XVI Gustav appealed to the Swedish press to stop its persistent and ruthless probing into his private life. 'I accept gratefully that the Press and the public want to follow my work, and I respect the journalists' ambitions', he was quoted as saying, 'but I am distressed to see that news competition has created a situation that makes both the newspapers and myself seem ridiculous'.[22]

His words had little effect, but for the most part the probing was borne out of affectionate interest, albeit motivated to a certain degree by the quest for greater sales. Eight years later, a spokesman for the Swedish gossip magazine *Svenska Dantidning* confirmed that circulation always showed a fall if the royal family was omitted from their pages.[23] The monarchy still remained a source of fascination for the average Swede, notwithstanding the egalitarianism of Sweden and a prime minister, Olaf Palme, whose Social Democratic Party remained officially committed to the abolition of the monarchy.

In November 1995 when Prince Joachim of Denmark, the second son of Queen Margrethe, married Miss Alexandra Manley, a British correspondent reported soberly that television portrayed deserted city streets 'as most people sat glued to their sets to follow the denouement of a rare royal romance in a country where the monarchy is fairly down-to-earth, untainted by controversy, and seemingly at its most popular'.[24] Scandinavian monarchies may be an anachronism at the end of the twentieth century, but they are none the less popular for all that.

Scandinavian Monarchs, 19th and 20th Centuries

KINGS AND QUEENS REGNANT OF DENMARK

	BORN	REIGNED
Frederick VI	1768	1808–39
Christian VIII	1786	1839–48
Frederick VII	1808	1848–63
CHRISTIAN IX	1818	1863–1906
FREDERICK VIII	1843	1906–12
CHRISTIAN X	1870	1912–47
FREDERICK IX	1899	1947–72
Margrethe	1940	1972–

KINGS OF SWEDEN

	BORN	REIGNED
Gustav IV Adolf	1778	1792–1809 (abdicated, died 1837)
Carl XIII	1748	1809–18
Carl XIV Johan	1763	1818–44
Oscar I	1799	1844–59
Carl XV	1826	1859–72
Oscar II	1829	1872–1907
GUSTAV V	1858	1907–50
GUSTAV VI ADOLF	1882	1950–73
Carl XVI Gustav	1946	1973–

KINGS OF NORWAY

	BORN	REIGNED
HAAKON VII	1872	1905–57
OLAV V	1903	1957–91
Harald	1937	1991–

Only the lives and reigns of those in capitals are examined in detail in this book. The remainder, mentioned in passing, are listed merely for reference

Kings of Denmark

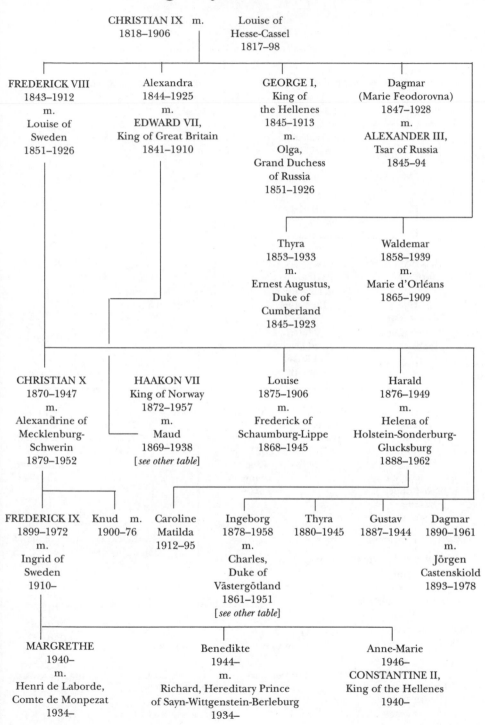

CHRISTIAN IX m. Louise of
1818–1906   Hesse-Cassel
                1817–98

FREDERICK VIII   Alexandra   GEORGE I,   Dagmar
1843–1912   1844–1925   King of   (Marie Feodorovna)
m.   m.   the Hellenes   1847–1928
Louise of   EDWARD VII,   1845–1913   m.
Sweden   King of Great Britain   m.   ALEXANDER III,
1851–1926   1841–1910   Olga,   Tsar of Russia
                                         Grand Duchess   1845–94
                                         of Russia
                                         1851–1926

                                 Thyra   Waldemar
                                 1853–1933   1858–1939
                                 m.   m.
                                 Ernest Augustus,   Marie d'Orléans
                                 Duke of   1865–1909
                                 Cumberland
                                 1845–1923

CHRISTIAN X   HAAKON VII   Louise   Harald
1870–1947   King of Norway   1875–1906   1876–1949
m.   1872–1957   m.   m.
Alexandrine of   m.   Frederick of   Helena of
Mecklenburg-   Maud   Schaumburg-Lippe   Holstein-Sonderburg-
Schwerin   1869–1938   1868–1945   Glucksburg
1879–1952   [see other table]   1888–1962

FREDERICK IX Knud m. Caroline   Ingeborg   Thyra   Gustav   Dagmar
1899–1972   1900–76 Matilda   1878–1958   1880–1945   1887–1944   1890–1961
m.   1912–95   m.   m.
Ingrid of   Charles,   Jörgen
Sweden   Duke of   Castenskiold
1910–   Västergötland   1893–1978
                                     1861–1951
                                     [see other table]

MARGRETHE   Benedikte   Anne-Marie
1940–   1944–   1946–
m.   m.   CONSTANTINE II,
Henri de Laborde,   Richard, Hereditary Prince   King of the Hellenes
Comte de Monpezat   of Sayn-Wittgenstein-Berleburg 1940–
1934–   1934–

Kings of Sweden and Norway

All Kings are of Sweden unless stated otherwise

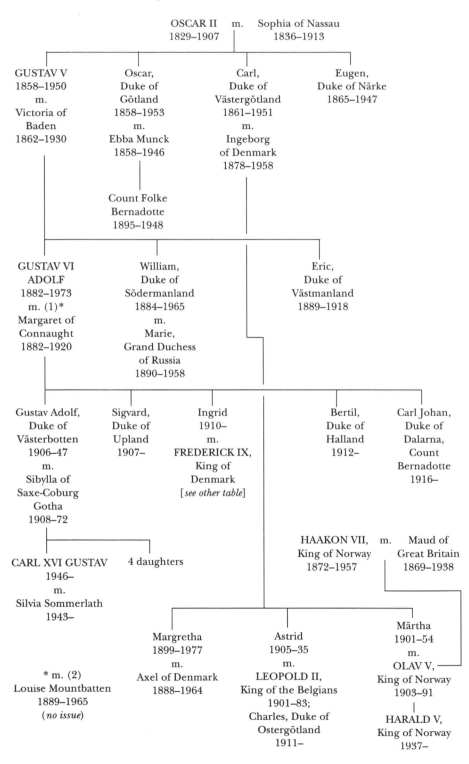

OSCAR II m. Sophia of Nassau
1829–1907 | 1836–1913

GUSTAV V
1858–1950
m.
Victoria of
Baden
1862–1930

Oscar,
Duke of
Götland
1858–1953
m.
Ebba Munck
1858–1946

Carl,
Duke of
Västergötland
1861–1951
m.
Ingeborg
of Denmark
1878–1958

Eugen,
Duke of Närke
1865–1947

Count Folke
Bernadotte
1895–1948

GUSTAV VI
ADOLF
1882–1973
m. (1)*
Margaret of
Connaught
1882–1920

William,
Duke of
Södermanland
1884–1965
m.
Marie,
Grand Duchess
of Russia
1890–1958

Eric,
Duke of
Västmanland
1889–1918

Gustav Adolf,
Duke of
Västerbotten
1906–47
m.
Sibylla of
Saxe-Coburg
Gotha
1908–72

Sigvard,
Duke of
Upland
1907–

Ingrid
1910–
m.
FREDERICK IX,
King of
Denmark
[see other table]

Bertil,
Duke of
Halland
1912–

Carl Johan,
Duke of
Dalarna,
Count
Bernadotte
1916–

CARL XVI GUSTAV
1946–
m.
Silvia Sommerlath
1943–

4 daughters

HAAKON VII, m. Maud of
King of Norway   Great Britain
1872–1957   1869–1938

Mårtha
1901–54
m.
OLAV V,
King of Norway
1903–91

* m. (2)
Louise Mountbatten
1889–1965
(no issue)

Margretha
1899–1977
m.
Axel of Denmark
1888–1964

Astrid
1905–35
m.
LEOPOLD II,
King of the Belgians
1901–83;
Charles, Duke of
Ostergötland
1911–

HARALD V,
King of Norway
1937–

Reference Notes

* denotes author of a periodical article cited in Bibliography section IV

Abbreviations:
RA   Royal Archives, Windsor
PRO FO   Public Record Office, Foreign Office (Papers), London

CHAPTER ONE (pp. 1–9)

1   Battiscombe 2
2   Madol 25–6
3   ibid. 32
4   ibid. 33
5   ibid. 35
6   Birch 360
7   Madol 156
8   ibid. 157
9   ibid. 159
10,11 ibid. 164
12   *Letters QV* II i 234

CHAPTER TWO (pp. 10–18)

1   Wake 101
2   Madol 175–6
3   *Letters QV* II i 416
4   Madol 185
5   ibid. 186
6   Victoria, Queen, *Your dear letter* 106
7   Aronson, *Family of Kings* 33
8   Bramsen 270 [trans]
9   Madol 205–6

CHAPTER THREE (pp. 19–32)

1   Victoria, Queen, *Darling Child* 200
2   Pope-Hennessy, *Queen Mary* 153
3   Vorres 52
4   Pope-Hennessy, *Lonely Business* 259
5   Madol 228
6   Vorres 51
7   Victoria, Queen, *Your Dear Letter* 102

8   *Letters EF* 392
9   Madol 233
10   Hein 16
11   Battiscombe 5
12   Victoria, Queen, *Darling Child* 129
13   Madol 245
14   Battiscombe 200
15   Medrano*
16   Madol 258

CHAPTER FOUR (pp. 33–43)

1   Ponsonby 186
2   Madol 260
3   *The Bernadottes* 33
4   Madol 282
5   Bülow 150–1
6   Lee ii 318
7   ibid. 319
8   ibid. 321
9   Magnus 346
10   Pope-Hennessy, *Queen Mary* 408
11   Greve 38–9
12   Madol 285
13   Jusserand 190
14   Hein 18
15   Jusserand 217
16   ibid. 182
17   PRO FO 372/7
18   Lee ii 526

CHAPTER FIVE (pp. 44–60)

1   Ponsonby 188
2   Pope-Hennessy, *Queen Mary* 328
3   Hardinge 152

4   *Illustrated London News* 10.2.1906
5   *The Times* 13.9.1906
6   Bülow 294
7   *The Times* 3.5.1907
8   ibid. 11.6.1907
9   ibid. 5.7.1907
10 ibid. 1.8.1907
11 Herbert 191
12 ibid. 181
13 ibid. 167
14 Marie 135
15 *The Bernadottes* 102
16 Van der Kiste, *Edward VII's Children* 112
17 Greve 50
18 Michael 117
19 Sanderson & Melville VI 109
20 Ponsonby 193–4
21 Roosevelt*
22 Bertin 95
23 Van der Kiste, *Crowns in a Changing World* 73
24 PRO FO 372/348
25 Pope-Hennessy, *Queen Mary* 466
26 RA GV AA43/181
27 *The Times* 16.5.1912

CHAPTER SIX (pp. 61–74)

1   Ponsonby 188
2   *The Times* 7.2.1914
3   Van der Kiste, *Crowns. . .* 111
4   RA GV Q1550/XVIII/197
5   Van der Kiste, *Crowns. . .* 112
6   RA GV Q1550/XVIII/212
7   Van der Kiste, *Crowns. . .* 125
8   Greve 78
9   Van der Kiste, *Crowns. . .* 131
10 ibid. 134–6
11 Van der Kiste, *Edward VII's Children* 144
12 ibid. 145

CHAPTER SEVEN (pp. 75–91)

1   RA GV AA43/290
2   RA Add A15/8979
3   RA Add A15/8405
4   Aston 253
5   Eulalia 206
6   *The Bernadottes* 69
7   ibid. 67
8   Aston 324
9   Fjellman 98
10 ibid. 99

11 Wolden-Raethinge 29
12 *The Times* 12.2.1920
13 ibid. 31.3.1920
14 Michael 205
15 Greve 105
16 ibid. 106
17 Bolitho 128
18 Michael 200
19 Greve 109
20 Money 185
21 Connery 34
22 Munthe & Uexküll 147

CHAPTER EIGHT (pp. 92–101)

1   *The Bernadottes* 108
2   Fjellman 119
3   Rose 344
4   PRO FO 371/17279
5   Ziegler, *King Edward VIII* 206
6   Christopher of Greece 272–3
7   Greve 113
8   Bertin 105
9   Greve 119
10 ibid. 120
11 ibid. 120–1

CHAPTER NINE (pp. 102–118)

1   Greve 128
2   ibid. 147
3,4 Wheeler-Bennett 465
5   Hassett 84
6   Parks 96
7   PRO FO 371/29677
8   PRO FO 371/29664
9   Hewins 18
10   PRO FO 371/29665
11,12,13   PRO FO 371/29664
14   PRO FO 371/29677
15   Astor Papers MS 1416/1/4/10
16   PRO FO 371/29677
17   *The Times* 10.4.1940
18   Wheeler-Bennett 452
19   *The Times* 28.9.1942
20   Wolden-Raethinge 27
21   ibid. 14
22   *The Times* 13.1.1944

CHAPTER TEN (pp. 119–136)

1   Greve 173
2   *The Bernadottes* 108

3   Money 230–1
4   Munthe & Uexküll 58
5   Brown*
6   Fjellman 123
7   PRO FO 371/29677
8   Argyll Etkin Letters
9,10 Astor Papers MS 1416/1/4/10
11   *Daily Express* 21.4.1947
12,13 PRO FO 371/65878
14   Sulzberger 265
15,16 Connery 326
17   *The Times* 17.9.1973
18   Berenson 278
19   Samuels 563
20   Wolden-Raethinge 147
21   Astor Papers
22   Fjellman 149
23   Collis 213
24   Fjellman 156–7
25   ibid. 204–5
26,27 Eardley Willmott Letters
28   Fjellman 155–6
29   ibid. 208
30   ibid. 205
31   ibid. 208
32   Eardley Willmott Letters
33   Wolden-Raethinge 27
34   Astor Papers
35   PRO FO 371/106190
36   Wolden-Raethinge 41
37   Connery 102

38   Wolden-Raethinge 42
39   PRO FO 371/106190

CHAPTER ELEVEN (pp. 137–148)

1   *Information*, 17 February 1948; Greve 179
2   Pope-Hennessy, *Lonely Business* 253
3   Michael 191
4   Greve 186
5   Michael 192
6   Eardley Willmott Letters
7   Fjellman 218
8   Mountbatten 142
9   ibid. 172
10   Ziegler, *Mountbatten* 675–6
11   Simpson 9
12   *Time* 24.1.1972
13   Bocca 201
14   Dwinger 5
15   Wolden-Raethinge 81
16   ibid. 82
17   *The Times* 15.1.1972
18   *Sunday Express* 20.1.1991
19   *Independent* 19.1.1991
20   *Daily Telegraph* 19.1.1991
21   Malcolm*
22   *To The Point* 7.2.1975
23   Mosey*
24   *The Times* 20.11.1995

Bibliography

I MANUSCRIPTS

Royal Archives, Windsor
Argyll Etkin Letters, privately owned
Astor Papers, Reading University
Foreign Office Papers, Public Record Office, London
Montgomery Papers, Imperial War Museum, London
Miss M. Eardley Willmott Letters, privately owned

II BOOKS

Aronson, Theo, *A Family of Kings: the Descendants of Christian IX of Denmark.* Cassell, 1976
— *Grandmama of Europe: the Crowned Descendants of Queen Victoria.* Cassell, 1974
Aston, Sir George, *His Royal Highness the Duke of Connaught and Strathearn: a Life and Intimate Study.* Harrap, 1929
Baily, Leslie, *The Gilbert & Sullivan Book.* Cassell, 1952
Battiscombe, Georgina, *Queen Alexandra.* Constable, 1969
Berenson, Bernard, *Sunset and Twilight: from the Diaries of 1947–1958*; (ed.) Nicky Mariano. Hamish Hamilton, 1964
The Bernadottes: their Political and Cultural Achievements; (trans.) Paul Britten Austin. Läckö Castle Foundation, 1991 [exhibition catalogue]
Bertin, Celia, *Marie Bonaparte: a Life.* Quartet, 1983
Birch, J.H.S., *Denmark in History.* John Murray, 1938
Bocca, Geoffrey, *The Uneasy Heads: a Report on European Monarchy.* Weidenfeld & Nicolson, 1959
Bolitho, Hector, *My Restless Years.* Max Parrish, 1962
Bramsen, Bo, *Huset Glucksborg i. 150 ar.* Forum-Kobenhavn, 1978
Bülow, Prince von, *Memoirs 1903–1909.* Putnam, 1931
Christopher of Greece, Prince, *Memoirs.* Right Book Club, 1938
Collis, Maurice, *Nancy Astor: an Informal Biography.* Faber, 1960
Connery, Donald, *The Scandinavians.* Eyre & Spottiswoode, 1966
Dwinger, Joanna, *Portrait of the Queen of Denmark: Queen Ingrid, 60 years.* Danish Ministry of Foreign Affairs, 1970
Eulalia, Infanta of Spain, *Court Life from Within.* Cassell, 1915
Fjellman, Margit, *Louise Mountbatten, Queen of Sweden.* Allen & Unwin, 1968
Gore, John, *King George V: a Personal Memoir.* John Murray, 1941
Greve, Tim, *Haakon VII of Norway: Founder of a New Monarchy*; (trans. and ed.) T.K. Derry. Hurst, 1983
Hardinge, Charles, Baron, *Old Diplomacy: the Reminiscences of Lord Hardinge of Penshurst.* John Murray, 1947
Hassett, William D., *Off the Record with F.D.R. 1942–1945.* Allen & Unwin, 1960
Hein, Jørgen, *The Royal Danish Collections: Amalienborg, Christian VIII's Palace.* De Danske Kongers Kronologiske Samling, 1994

Bibliography

Herbert, Basil, *King Gustave of Sweden*. Stanley Paul, 1938
Hewins, Ralph, *Count Folke Bernadotte: his Life and Work*. Hutchinson, 1949
Hough, Richard, *Louis and Victoria: the First Mountbattens*. Hutchinson, 1974
Jones, W. Glyn, *Denmark*. Benn, 1970
Jusserand, J.J., *What me Befell*. Constable, 1930
King, Stella, *Princess Marina, her Life and Times*. Cassell, 1969
Lee, Sir Sidney, *King Edward VII*, 2 vols. Macmillan, 1925–27
Louda, Jiri, & MacLagan, Michael, *Lines of Succession: Heraldry of the Royal Families of Europe*. Macdonald, 1991
Madol, Hans Roger, *Christian IX*. Collins, 1939
Marie, Grand Duchess of Russia, *Things I Remember*. Cassell, 1930
Mentze, Ernst, *5 Years: the Occupation of Denmark in Pictures*. A–B Allhems Förlag, 1946
Michael, Maurice, *Haakon, King of Norway*. Allen & Unwin, 1958
Money, James, *Capri: Island of Pleasure*. Hamish Hamilton, 1986
Mountbatten of Burma, Earl, *From Shore to Shore: the Tour Diaries of Earl Mountbatten of Burma 1953–1979*; (ed.) Philip Ziegler. Collins, 1989
Munthe, Gustav, & Uexküll, Gudrun, *The Story of Axel Munthe*. John Murray, 1953
Oakley, Stewart, *The Story of Denmark*. Faber, 1972
Parks, Lillian Rogers, *The Roosevelts: a Family in Turmoil*. Prentice-Hall, 1981
Ponsonby, Sir Frederick, *Recollections of Three Reigns*. Eyre & Spottiswoode, 1951
Pope-Hennessy, James, *A Lonely Business: a Self-portrait of James Pope-Hennessy*; (ed.) Peter Quennell. Weidenfeld & Nicolson, 1981
— *Queen Mary 1867–1953*. Allen & Unwin, 1959
Radziwill, Princess Catherine, *The Disillusions of a Crown Princess, being the Story of the Courtship and Married Life of Cecile, ex-Crown Princess of Germany*. John Lane, 1919
Roosevelt, Eleanor, *The Autobiography of Eleanor Roosevelt*. Hutchinson, 1962
Rose, Kenneth, *King George V*. Weidenfeld & Nicolson, 1983
Samuels, Ernest, *Bernard Berenson: the Making of a Legend*. Harvard University Press, 1987
Sanderson, Edgar, & Melville, Louis, *King Edward VII: his Life & Reign*, 6 vols. Gresham, 1910
Simpson, Colin, *The Viking Circle*. Hodder & Stoughton, 1967
Sulzberger, C.L., *A Long Row of Candles: Memoirs and Diaries 1934–1954*. Macdonald, 1969
Thornit, Per, *The Royal Commemorative and Coronation Medals of Scandinavia 1892–1982*. Ordenshistorisk Selskab, 1984
Van der Kiste, John, *Crowns in a Changing World: the British and European Monarchies, 1901–36*. Alan Sutton, 1993
— *Edward VII's Children*. Alan Sutton, 1989
Victoria, Queen, *Letters of Queen Victoria, second series: a selection from Her Majesty's Correspondence and Journals between the Years 1862 and 1885*; (ed.) G.E. Buckle, 3 vols. John Murray, 1926–8
— *Letters of Queen Victoria, third series: a Selection from Her Majesty's Correspondence and Journals between the Years 1886 and 1901*; (ed.) G.E. Buckle, 3 vols. John Murray, 1930–2
Victoria, Queen, and Victoria, Consort of Frederick III, *Your Dear Letter: Private Correspondence between Queen Victoria and the Crown Princess of Prussia, 1865–71*; (ed.) Roger Fulford. Evans Bros, 1971
— *Darling Child: Private Correspondence between Queen Victoria and the Crown Princess of Prussia, 1871–78*; (ed.) Roger Fulford. Evans Bros, 1976
Victoria, Consort of Frederick III, *Letters of the Empress Frederick*; (ed.) Sir Frederick Ponsonby. Macmillan, 1928
Vorres, Ian, *The Last Grand-Duchess: Her Imperial Highness Grand-Duchess Olga Alexandrovna, 1 June 1882 – 24 November 1960*. Hutchinson, 1964
Wake, Jehanne, *Princess Louise: Queen Victoria's Unconventional Daughter*. Collins, 1988
Wolden-Raethinge, Anne, *Queen in Denmark: Margrethe II Talks about her Life*. Gylendal, 1990
Ziegler, Philip, *King Edward VIII: the Official Biography*. Collins, 1990
— *Mountbatten: the Official Biography*. Collins, 1985

III PERIODICAL ARTICLES

Anon, 'Exile for the Princess' [Princess Helena of Holstein-Sonderburg-Glucksburg]. In *New York Journal*, 1945, repr. in *Royalty Digest*, September 1994

Brown, Andrew, 'Sweden's cycling royals do it better'. In *The Independent*, 18 October 1994

Galloway, Peter, 'In the twinkling of an eye: The war-born monarchical "might-have-beens". Part 1: Finland and Ukraine'. In *Royalty Digest*, April 1995

Hall, Coryne, '"Our lovely place here": Hvidøre – the forgotten royal house'. In *Royalty Digest*, February 1996

Horbury, David, 'Poor dear Charlie' [Charles, Duke of Saxe-Coburg Gotha]. In *Royalty Digest*, November/December 1995

Malcolm, Noel, 'Time to reconvene the royal families of Europe?' In *Daily Telegraph*, 30 April 1992

Medrano, Ricardo Mateos Sainz de, 'A child of the Caucasus' [Grand Duchess Anastasia of Russia, later Grand Duchess of Mecklenburg-Schwerin]. In *Royalty Digest*, July 1993

Mosey, Chris, 'The sights that Sweden will not show the Queen'. In *Observer*, 22 May 1983

Roosevelt, Theodore, 'Exactly what was needed'. In *Royalty Digest*, September 1994

Zeepvat, Charlotte, 'The father-in-law of Europe: Christian IX of Denmark'. In *Royalty Digest*, March 1992

IV PERIODICALS

Daily Express
Daily Telegraph
Illustrated London News
The Independent
Royalty Digest
Sunday Express
Time
The Times
To The Point

Index

Index

Margarita of Hohenlohe-Langenburg, Princess (1905–81) 79

Marie, Duchess of Edinburgh, later Duchess of Saxe-Coburg Gotha (1853–1920) 20, 69

Marie, Queen of Roumania (1875–1938) 69

Marie, Princess of Greece (1876–1940) 22

Marie of D, Princess, formerly Marie d'Orléans (1865–1909) 26–7, 29, 35, 37, 57–8

Marie, Grand Duchess of R, later Duchess of Södermanland (1890–1958) 52, 53

Marie of Mecklenburg-Schwerin, later Grand Duchess Vladimir of R (1854–1920) 69

Marie Feodorovna, Empress of R, formerly Princess Dagmar of D ('Minnie') (1847–1928) 17, 19, 24, 25, 33; birth 3; engagement and marriage 10–3; and Alexander III's accession 22; and family reunions in Denmark 23; and Christian IX's death 42; and Hvidøre 45; and Christian X 80–1; and 'Anastasia' 82

Marott, M. 83

Märtha, Crown Princess of N (1901–54) 52–3, 93, 99, 119, 127; engagement and marriage 88–9; during World War II 103, 105–7; ill-health and death 137–8

Märtha Louise of N, Princess (b. 1971) 146

Mary, Queen of GB, formerly Duchess of York (1867–1953) 26, 33, 44, 48, 59, 67, 74, 81, 99; Haakon VII's letters to 71, 101, 103, 104

Mary, Duchess of Gloucester (1776–1857) 2

Maud, Queen of Norway (1869–1938) 26, 66, 90, 93, 101; engagement and marriage 30; and husband's election to Norwegian throne 38, 40; early years in Norway 54–6; and Great War 70–3; visits to England 85, 87, 88; death and funeral 99–100

Melba, Nellie 48

Michael, Grand Duke of R (1878–1918) 22

Michelsen, Christian (1857–1925) 41

Møller, Johan Christmas (1894–1948) 113

Moltke, Count 114

Monet, Claude (1840–1926) 77

Montgomery of Alamein, Field-Marshal Bernard 1st Viscount (1887–1976) 118

Moore, Grace 121

Mösgaard, M. 83

Mowinckel, J.L. 89

Munthe, Axel (1857–1949) 90, 120

Mussolini, Benito (1883–1945) 92, 104, 110

Nansen, Fridtjof (1861–1930) 38, 54–5

Napoleon III, Emperor of the French (1808–73) 17

Napoleon Bonaparte (1769–1821) 1, 36, 41, 92

Nicholas II, Tsar of R (1868–1918) 29, 37, 42, 58, 68, 70

Nicholas, Tsarevich of R (1843–65) 10–1

Nicholas of Greece, Prince (1872–1938) 32, 37, 97

Nordlie, Oswald 105

Nygaardsvold, Johan (1879–1952) 93

Olav V, King of N (1903–91) 38, 40, 53, 55, 70, 87, 93, 101, 127, 139; education 85–6; engagement and marriage 89; admiration of G 97; and World War II 103–6; return to N after World War II 119; reign and death 144–6

Olga, Queen of the Hellenes (1851–1926) 13

Olga, Grand Duchess of R (1882–1960) 22, 23, 25, 80, 82

Olga, of Greece, Princess, later Princess Alexander of Yugoslavia (b. 1903) 97

Oluf, Count of Rosenborg (b. 1923) 115

Oscar I, King of S (1799–1859) 36

Oscar II, King of S (1829–1907) 16, 22–3, 36, 40–1, 47, 51, 56, 78, 120; death 50

Oscar of Prussia, Prince (1888–1958) 73

Ostgaard, Nicholas (1885–1958) 85, 103, 105

Otho, King of Greece (1826–67) 4

Paget, Sir Augustus (1823–96) 6, 12

Palme, Olaf 148

Palmerston, Henry John Temple, Viscount (1784–1865) 6

Pancke, General von 115

Parks, Lillian Rogers 107

Patzek, Erica 96

Petersen, Professor 4

Philip, Duke of Edinburgh (b. 1921) 79, 138

Poincaré, Raymond (1860–1934) 66

Ponsonby, Sir Frederick (1867–1935) 33–4, 44, 56, 61, 146

Pope-Hennessy, James (1916–74) 138

Quisling, Abraham Vidkun (1887–1945) 103

Ragnhild of N, Princess (b. 1932) 89, 138

Randall, Alec 124

Reutersvärd, Oscar 77

Reventlow, Eduard 113

Rinman, Louise 52

Rodd, Sir Rennell 50

Roosevelt, Franklin Delano (1882–1945) 106

Roosevelt, Eleanor (1884–1962) 107

Roosevelt, Theodore (1858–1919) 57

Rørdam, C.H. 27, 32, 45

Rudebeck, Astrid 140